For years they were so secretive most people thought they were a myth. For decades their actions in the fight for freedom were unknown and unhearalded. Even today the governement officially denies their existence. But anyone who follows the United States military knows the truth: DELTA FORCE *is America's deadliest weapon.*

WANTED: VOLUNTEERS FOR PROJECT DELTA. WILL GUARANTEE YOU A MEDAL, A BODY BAG, OR BOTH.

When Charlie Beckwith issued this call to arms in Vietnam in 1965, he revolutionized American armed combat. This is the story of what would eventually come to be known as **Delta Force,** as only its maverick creator could tell it—from the bloody baptism of Vietnam to the top-secret training grounds of North Carolina to the political battles in the upper levels of the Pentagon itself. This is the heart-pounding, first-person, insider's view of the missions that made **Delta Force** legendary, including a brutally honest account of their most infamous defeat: the failed rescue of the Iranian hostages.

"IF THERE'S ONE LESSON IN THE STORY OF CHARLIE BECKWITH AND HIS DELTA FORCE, IT'S THAT IT DOES MATTER TO BE AN AMERICAN CITIZEN AFTER ALL."

USA Today

(more praise on the following pages)

"BLUNT AND UNFLINCHING . . .
straightforward and suspenseful."
Houston Chronicle

"FASCINATING DETAIL . . . [IT] JOLTS THE READER . . . Beckwith writes in the hard-charging vernacular of the elite soldier . . .
I enjoyed it immensely."
St. Louis Post-Dispatch

"THIS IS THE TALE OF A MILITARY MAN JOHN WAYNE MIGHT HAVE ADMIRED.
[Beckwith's] language is earthy; his opinions, unreserved; his determination, boundless."
Library Journal

"EYE-OPENING ACCOUNTS
of methods and techniques in planning and operations."
Richmond Times-Dispatch

"MORE EXCITING THAN DERRING-DO FICTION."
Los Angeles Times

"MARVELOUSLY READABLE . . .
[Beckwith] is a fine storyteller, and this book is a fine tale . . . The concept and maneuvering which made [Delta Force's] formation possible are fascinating."

San Diego Union

"ENGROSSING AND EYE-OPENING . . .
There's flavor, color, drama, and conviction here."

Kirkus Reviews

"BEHIND-THE-SCENES . . .
Beckwith has some hard things to say about military planning and high level planners."

Fayetteville Observer-Times

"EXTRAORDINARY . . .
packed with drama, facts, and straight talk."

Armed Forces Journal

"BECKWITH IS A MAN WHO KNOWS THE INTIMATE DETAILS OF THE DIRTY BUSINESS OF TERRORISM."

Chicago Tribune

DELTA FORCE

THE ARMY'S ELITE COUNTERTERRORIST UNIT

COL. CHARLIE A. BECKWITH (Ret.)
Founder and First Commanding Officer of DELTA FORCE

AND DONALD KNOX

WITH AN EPILOGUE BY C.A. MOBLEY

AVON BOOKS
An Imprint of HarperCollins*Publishers*

AVON BOOKS
An Imprint of HarperCollins*Publishers*
10 East 53rd Street
New York, New York 10022-5299

ISBN: 0-380-80939-7
www.avonbooks.com

First Avon Books Printing: June 2000

Printed in the U.S.A.

OPM 11 10 9 8 7 6 5 4

Colonel Beckwith dedicates this book
to his wife Katherine
and their three daughters.

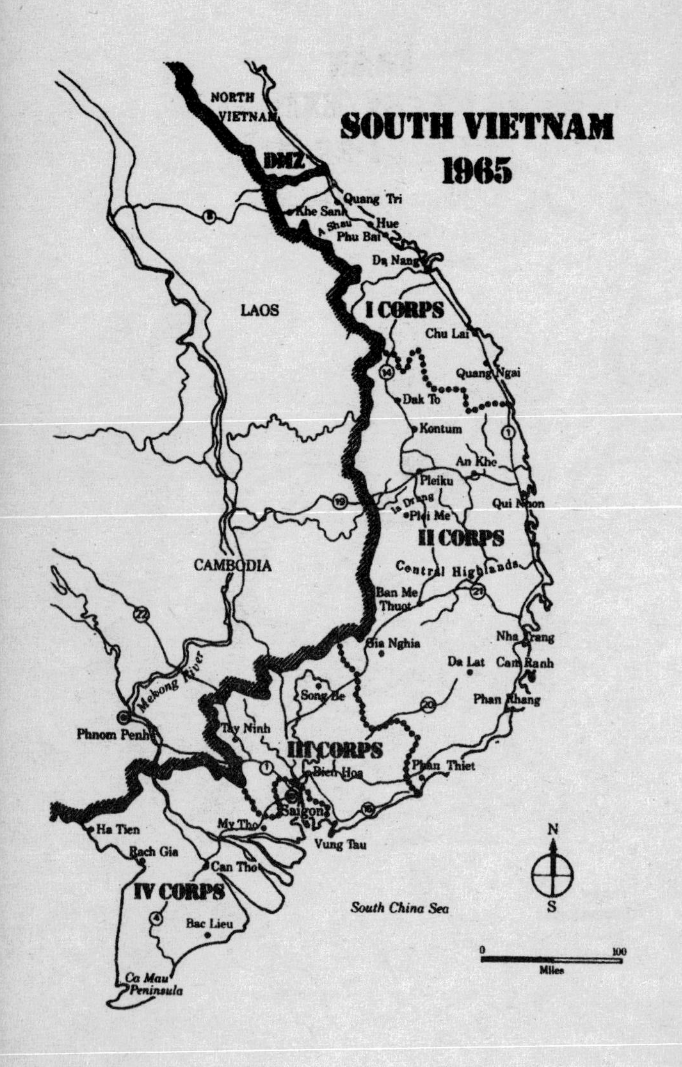
SOUTH VIETNAM
1965
NORTH VIETNAM
DMZ
Quang Tri
Khe Sanh
A Shau
Hue
Phu Bai
Da Nang
LAOS
I CORPS
Chu Lai
Quang Ngai
Dak To
Kontum
An Khe
Pleiku
Ia Drang
Plei Me
Qui Nhon
II CORPS
Central Highlands
CAMBODIA
Ban Me Thuot
Gia Nghia
Nha Trang
Da Lat
Cam Ranh
Mekong River
Song Be
Phan Rhang
Tay Ninh
Phnom Penh
III CORPS
Phan Thiet
Bien Hoa
Saigon
Ha Tien
My Tho
Vung Tau
Rach Gia
Can Tho
IV CORPS
South China Sea
Bac Lieu
Ca Mau Peninsula
N
S
0
100
Miles

IRAN
DELTA ENTRY/EXIT PLAN, APRIL 24-26, 1980

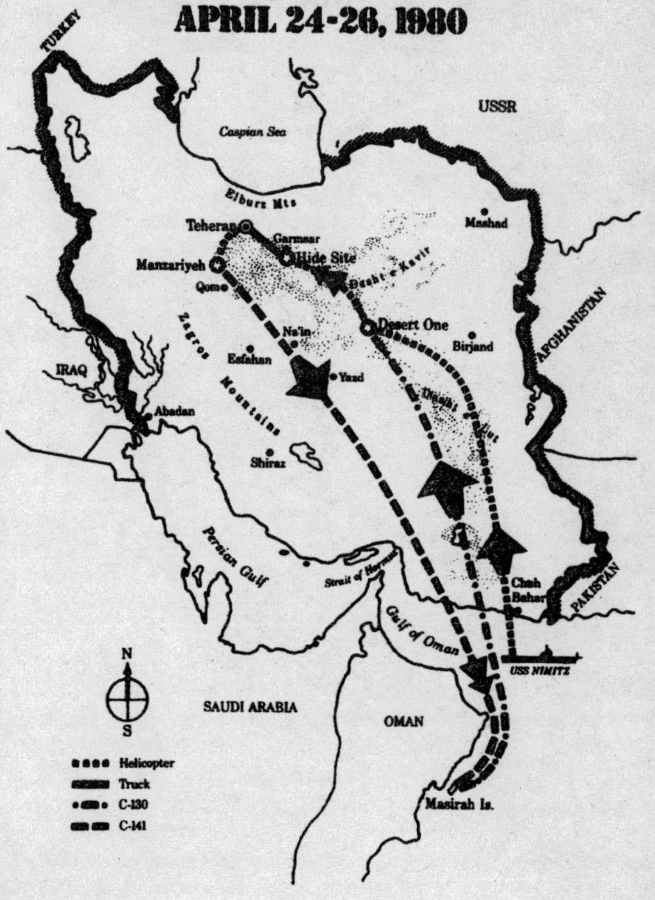

GLOSSARY

Special Military Terms and Acronyms

ADC	Assistant division commander.
APU	Auxiliary power unit.
ARVN	Army of the Republic of Vietnam.
ATT	Army Training Test.
Bérets Rouges	*See* BPC.
Bergen	Rucksack (British).
BPC	Bataillon de Parachutistes de Choc; crack French paratroop unit (*Bérets Rouges*).
C-130	Lockheed Hercules 4-engine multipurpose transport aircraft.
C-141	Lockheed StarLifter is larger than C-130 and lacks that aircraft's versatility.
CIB	Combat Infantryman's Badge.
CIDG	Civilian Irregular Defense Group (Vietnam).
CINCPAC	Commander in Chief, Pacific.
CJCS	Chairman of the Joint Chiefs of Staff.
CJTF	Commander Joint Task Force.
CSA	Army Chief of Staff.
CT	Communist Terrorist.
DCM	Deputy Chief of Mission.
DCSOPS	Deputy Chief of Staff for Operations and Plans.

Delta Force 1st Special Forces Operational Detachment—Delta (*SFOD-D*).
DELTA Project, Detachment B52 Special Forces recon unit Beckwith commanded in Vietnam; also *Project DELTA*.
DOD Department of Defense.
DZ Drop Zone.
Eagle Claw Code name of mission to free hostages in Iran.
E and E Evade and Escape.
EEI Essential elements of information.
EOC Emergency Operations Center.
FAC Forward air controller.
FM Field Manual.
FORSCOM Forces Command.
GIGN Groupe d'Intervention de la Gendarmerie Nationale; French counterterrorist unit.
GSG-9 Grenzschutzgruppe 9 (Border Patrol Unit 9); West German counterterrorist unit.
IAD Immediate Action Drill; aspect of counter-insurgency and counterterrorist training, stressing readiness for any eventuality.
IR Intelligence report.
IRG Iranian Revolutionary Guards; also known as *Pasdaran*.
JCRC Joint Casualty Resolution Center, assigned to search for bodies of men killed in Southeast Asia.
JCS Joint Chiefs of Staff.
JFK Center United States Army John F. Kennedy Center for Military Assistance (formerly Special Warfare Center).
JTF Joint Task Force.
LLBD Luc Luong Dac Biet; South Vietnamese Special Forces.
LZ Landing Zone.
MAC Military Air Command.
MACV Military Assistance Command, Vietnam.

MACV-SOG	Military Assistance Command, Vietnam Studies and Observation Group.
MILPERCEN	*See* USAMILPERCEN.
MOS	Military occupation specialty.
MRLA	Malayan Races Liberation Party (Communist).
NVA	North Vietnamese Army.
OPSEC	Operations Security.
ORs	Other Ranks (British).
Pasdaran	Iranian Revolutionary Guards (*IRG*).
PINS	Palletized Inertial Navigation System.
Project DELTA	*See* DELTA Project.
RDF	Rapid Deployment Force.
REDCOM	Readiness Command.
RH-53D	Twin turbine heavy lift helicopter; called Sea Stallions.
Rice Bowl	Code name of planning phase of Iran rescue mission.
RV	Rendezvous.
S&T	Selection and Training.
SAS	Special Air Service; elite British military special operations unit.
SATCOM	Satellite Communications.
SAVAK	Iranian National Intelligence and Security Operation (under the Shah).
SAVAMA	Iranian (revolutionary) secret police.
SCIF	Secure Compartmented Information Facility.
Sea Lions	*See* RH-53D.
SEALS	Navy Sea, Air, and Land Teams—equivalent to the U.S. Army Green Berets.
SFOD-D	*or* SFOD-Delta *See* Delta Force.
Sit rep	Situation report.
SOTFE	Special Operations Task Force Europe.
STOL	Short Takeoff and Landing type of aircraft.
TDY	Temporary duty.
TO&E	Table of Organization and Equipment.
TRADOC	Training and Doctrine Command.
UW	Unconventional Warfare.

USAMILPERCEN United States Army Military Personnel Center; also *MILPERCEN*.

ZSU-23-4 ZSU is a Soviet designation for self-propelled anti-aircraft gun, 23 is for caliber of gun (23 mm), 4 for number of guns.

★ PROLOGUE ★

I COULDN'T SEE any reason for hanging around the pentagon. I wasn't accomplishing anything.

It was April of 1980. After several months I was nearly certain Delta would now deploy to Egypt. That's where we'd stage. General Jones, before leaving the Stockade with General Vaught the day before, had asked me to a briefing of the Joint Chiefs of Staff (JCS) this day. It would be another meeting, I was sure, like all the others I'd attended in the past five months. I was wrong. The meetings on Wednesday, April 16, 1980, were to be different.

I'd been in the JCS tank before, when I worked for Admiral McCain of the Pacific Command. On those occasions the room was packed. This day, however, there wasn't anyone there except the Chiefs of each service and some of us "Rice Bowl" people. Admiral Thomas Hayward, Chief of Naval Operations, was there; so was the Commandant of the Marine Corps, General Robert H. Barrow. So, too, was the Air Force Vice Chief of Staff, General Robert Mathis. Of course, the Army's Chief of Staff, General E. C. Meyer, was in attendance, as were Generals Vaught and Gast. I chose a seat behind "Moses." He turned and slapped my knee. He was grinning.

General Jones began the brief. "As you all know, we have been working hard to develop a means to rescue the hostages from Teheran. We have been working the problem since November. Now I believe we have a sound plan. I want you to hear the plan and then to ask questions. It's not a simple plan;

however, we have tried to make it as straightforward as possible. Jim," he turned to General Vaught, "how about starting off?"

The Task Force Commander discussed the mission's background. He was nervous at this meeting and didn't articulate the various aspects of the overall plan as well as we'd come to expect from him.

Next, I covered the ground tactical plan, the actual operation—how we were going go get from Desert One to Teheran, free the hostages, and escape. After I'd finished, General Barrow asked tactical questions: "What weapons will you carry? Can you interdict Roosevelt Avenue with covering fire, and from what location? How long will you be in the compound?"

Then it was General Meyer's turn. "Charlie, from the time you leave Egypt to the time you go over the wall you will be under stress—for thirty-six hours. I want you to tell me how you're going to handle that. I'm concerned with what kind of condition you and the operators will be in when you go over the wall."

I explained I was going to discipline myself and catch sleep where I could—probably some in Egypt, and on the following day in the hideout. I talked about how Delta Force was going to rotate during that period—50 percent on alert, 50 percent standing down.

General Meyer had another worry. "I'm apprehensive. How will the operation be controlled here in the Pentagon? I'm concerned that it be carefully controlled by only those who need to be involved—and by no one else." He went on to talk about when the JCS regulated the chopping of the tree in the Korean DMZ, which was being used for observation purposes by the North Koreans, and the controls that had been placed on General Dick Stilwell. He spoke against the large number of both military and civilian people who had access to the JCS Control Center during that earlier crisis. He hoped it would be different this time. His admonition hit home. It was apparent General Jones, too, was anxious about this management problem. The briefing adjourned around 3:30 P.M.

Because things seemed to be heating up some, I wanted to

get back to Bragg to look into some last minute details. General Vaught thought I should hang around a while, but wouldn't tell me why. Something was up. General Gast, while we walked down to the Special Ops Division of the JCS, enlightened me.

"We want you to stay in Washington, because we're going to go over tonight to the White House and brief the President and the National Security Council." I nearly fell over! The meeting I just left had been, certainly, a rehearsal for showtime that evening with President Carter and his foreign policy advisors.

During the next three hours, I drank a lot of coffee with some of the guys in the ops office. I worried whether what I was wearing—a sport coat and tie—was right. Maybe I should be wearing a three-piece suit.

In one of the offices I ran into Buckshot, who was in the Pentagon on another matter. I confided in him where I was going in a few hours. He became as excited as I. He was wearing his SAS regimental tie and he gave it to me to wear that evening. I wanted it for good luck.

At 6:30, General Vaught, General Gast, and I, all in civilian clothes, were driven to General Jones's residence in Fort Myer, Virginia. The General wore a smart-looking Harris tweed sport jacket, gray slacks, and tie. I figured my dress was appropriate. We climbed back into the car and were taken to the White House. During the drive, all jammed together, there was little talk but there was a tangible sense of purpose. We would never be more prepared.

The Secret Service uniformed officer was shown some identification and waved us through the gate. I'd never been on the grounds of the White House before. We were led through the corridors and up and down the staircases that led to the Situation Room. I tried to memorize everything in sight. I was a long way from my pea patch.

"The Room" is small, maybe 15 × 20 feet, and windowless. Comfortable office chairs were placed around a central conference table. Another row of chairs was situated in front of the paneled wood walls. There were some people waiting for us. Among them, Jody Powell impressed me by the way he talked and asked questions. As for the chief of staff of the White House, I expected he'd have a little age on him. But Hamilton Jordan looked awfully young. He wore Levi's.

I was introduced to the Agency's man and to Warren Christopher, the Deputy Secretary of State. Cyrus Vance was talking to someone in the corner. Dr. Brown came in right behind us and had with him his Deputy Secretary of Defense, Mr. Claytor. Dr. Brzezinski appeared suddenly. Finally, Vice-President Mondale arrived, wearing a sweat suit and fancy sneakers—which did not impress me. I found a seat behind and between Dr. Brzezinski and the Vice-President. The President, in a blue blazer and gray slacks, walked into the room. Everyone jumped to attention. "Good evening, Mr. President." He looked good.

General Jones took the lead. After quickly introducing his party to the President's group, he stated that we were there to explain the rescue mission plan and to answer questions. With that, he nodded to General Vaught. In his detailed introduction of the General, he referred to him as the Task Force Commander, which he was; as an experienced and brave airborne officer, which he was; and as an old-time Green Beret, which he wasn't. I knew General Jones believed the information he gave the President, but I knew General Vaught had never served a day in his life in Special Forces. General Vaught did not correct the mistake once he stood up. Rather, he began to outline the proposed effort.

He took everyone through the rehearsal period of the Delta Force, how the Marine pilots had come into the picture, how the Air Force would perform, and his own beloved Rangers. He did really well. Obviously, he had done some hard work between his briefing to the Joint Chiefs that afternoon and this one in the White House.

General Vaught then launched into the actual plan. During this brief, Vice-President Mondale asked me for a pair of handcuffs, which we call flex cuffs; he played with these. It was a peculiar thing to do while listening to a vital brief.

General Vaught outlined all his areas of responsibility, General Gast's, and mine. He forcefully discussed the command and control of Desert One—the first stop in Iran of the rescue mission—and the Manzariyeh operation which brought into play the Ranger contingent. He concluded with an outline of the medical facilities and an assessment of the probability of success.

He had occasionally been interrupted for clarification, once by Dr. Brzezinski and another time by Vice-President Mondale. I don't believe either asked a key question. More important, I felt the President tracked very well with General Vaught.

General Jones then introduced me. "Mr. President, this is Colonel Beckwith, who will be the ground force commander."

Before I could begin, Hamilton Jordan spoke up. "Mr. President, Colonel Beckwith is a Georgian. He's from south Georgia, from Schley County."

The President looked interested. "Oh?"

"Well, sir, I was born in Atlanta, but my folks are from Ellaville."

The President beamed. "Well, that's right next to Plains. We must have been neighbors."

I began my brief by walking the President through the operation from Desert One to lift-off at Manzariyeh; how Delta Force would reach, before first light, the hideout area some fifty miles outside of the capital; and how it would lie concealed all day under camouflage material.

Next, I described how six Mercedes trucks and two smaller vehicles from Teheran would arrive after sunset and transport Delta to the capital. I said I was going to go ahead at a certain point, using one of the small vehicles, to check the last part of the route through the city and eyeball the embassy.

Once the trucks arrived at the east wall, which faced Roosevelt Avenue, Delta Force would climb over it. Then a high-explosive charge would be placed to blow a hole in the wall large enough for an 18-wheeler to be driven through it. The blast would also serve the purpose of blowing out all the windows in the surrounding neighborhood and causing confusion among the nearby Iranian population.

At this point I explained how Delta had been broken down into Red, White, and Blue. The Red and Blue elements would be the assault groups and contained forty men each; White, much smaller, would be used in support.

I described the task organization for each unit: how, once the explosive charge at the wall had been detonated. Blue would assault the DCM's residence, the Ambassador's quarters, the Mushroom, and the chancellery, freeing the hostages held in them: how Red would attack the commissary and the staff cottages to release the hostages there and to neutralize the guard posts at the motor pool and the power plant: and how, while this was being accomplished, White Element would neutralize Roosevelt Avenue and then seize and hold the soccer stadium which lay adjacent to the embassy compound.

Covered by three machine guns, two M60s and an HK21, the freed hostages, together with Red and Blue elements, would move from the compound, through the hole in the wall, and across Roosevelt Avenue to the stadium. From there they would wait until the helicopters could lift them out.

I then addressed the most troublesome part of the mission. "Mr. President, Delta Force's biggest problem is not going to be taking down the buildings—we've been training for two years as a counterterrorist unit. Our worry is the control and handling of the freed hostages. We intend to put yellow arm bands or sweat bands on the hostages so we can identify them. We have also assigned two Delta operators to each hostage. There is no way of knowing how they will behave. Will they try to protect their guards—that's a syndrome common to situations where hostages have been held a long time. Will they attack the guards and acquire their weapons, and put them in peril? I would like permission to use your name, to say, 'The President of the United States has sent us.' "

The President laughed. "I'm not sure that will mean anything to them."

Then I explained how the medics had been given the task

of counting heads at the stadium. No one would leave until all the hostages had been accounted for.

There was a chance we would lose one or two helicopters in the soccer stadium, but the backup would be sufficient to get everyone out. The first chopper should be able to carry all the hostages, but the second was a prudent precaution.

Red and Blue elements would leave next in the third helo, with White flying out last in the fourth. It was just a matter of rolling up the stick from the rear.

Once in Manzariyeh, the hostages and Delta would be met by a Ranger contingent, which would secure the airfield and protect the loading of everyone on large fixed-wing Air Force C-141 StarLifters.

That finished my part of the brief. I asked if there were any questions.

"How many casualties," the President asked, "do you see here?"

General Vaught spoke up. "Mr. President, we don't honestly have an answer for you. Perhaps six or seven Delta people might be wounded, and there's a chance that two or three hostages could be injured."

I said, "When we go into these installations I know good and well that when we turn a corner and start clearing out the rooms, there, in the dark, a hostage will probably have overpowered a guard and taken his weapon. There are military men in the embassy just waiting for that opportunity, and I know there's one CIA man who, given the opportunity, will do it. Once they have a weapon in hand they're going to run out into the hall or down a staircase to link up with us, and one of my operators is going to take them out. Delta is trained to kill anyone carrying a weapon in such a situation. This is going to happen. I hope it doesn't, but we gotta count on it happening."

The President said, "I understand. And I accept it."

Warren Christopher spoke up. He wanted to know what would happen to the guards. There was some confusion caused by my choice of words.

"Mr. Christopher, it's our objective to take the guards out."

"What do you mean? Will you shoot them in the shoulder or what?"

"No, sir. We're going to shoot each of them twice, right between the eyes."

This seemed to bother him.

"You mean you can really do that. In the dark, running—"

"Yes, sir. We've trained to do that."

"You mean you're really going to shoot to kill? You really are?"

"Yes, sir. We certainly are. We intend to put two .45-caliber rounds right between their eyes."

Mr. Claytor, the Deputy Secretary of Defense, interceded. "I've been down to Delta, Mr. President, and I've seen their shooting. I think it's very good."

It was obvious Mr. Christopher had a worry. I believe he thought Delta was going to go in and shoot everyone. We had the capability to do it, but that wasn't the plan. He might have thought some hostages would be killed if we went in shooting. But I think not. I'm convinced he was uncomfortable with our having to kill those armed Iranian guards. But *that* was precisely our plan. We were going to kill every guard in the four or five buildings and anyone who interfered in the assault. Any armed Iranian inside the buildings would be killed. We weren't going to go up and check their pulses. We would put enough copper and lead in them so they wouldn't be a problem. When blood began to flow, a lot of Iranians were going to turn and run for help, and when they did, Delta was prepared to hose them down. No question about it. That was the plan. Furthermore, I did not believe that the Iranians in the embassy would stand toe to toe and slug it out. Yes, there would be the odd person who would because of his religion and beliefs shoot to the death. We were prepared to help him reach his maker.

Mr. Jordan asked, "In your shooting exercises, Colonel, did your men ever hit the American targets and not the Iranian ones?"

"Sir," I said, "Delta's playing in the Rose Bowl, not the Toilet Bowl!" I explained that Delta expected to find roughly

70 to 125 people on the embassy grounds—not including the hostages. Twenty or 25 would be guards on duty, the others sleeping in a barracks. That building would be covered by machine guns. The only real threat was with the guards holding the hostages. They were all to be taken out.

I sat down.

General Gast was introduced and he covered the airlift portion of the operation: how we would fly to Egypt and to Oman and to Desert One, would be flown by helicopter to the hideaway and out of Teheran, and finally be air evac'd out at Manzariyeh.

General Gast was very thorough, but one aspect of the air operation, which he had not mentioned, still bothered me. Delta was going on this operation without tac air. I was confused. I had been told in briefings many, many times—and had been given call signs—that if something truly bad happened I could call in fighter support. But, I'd also been told, because of flying distances, not to expect such support for at least an hour. An hour to get on station was one hell of a long time. That was a hard bone to swallow. There was also no tac air support tasked to follow us out of Manzariyeh. It didn't make any sense to go through the entire raid only to get wiped out at the end by an Iranian jet jockey who happened to get lucky and knock down a C-141 carrying hostages and rescuers. General Vaught and I had had several discussions about this. The issue never seemed to get resolved. In the White House, it was.

The President spoke out: "There will be air cover from Manzariyeh all the way out of Iran."

Whew!

Someone said, "Mr. President, my agency now needs to know what your decision will be. Should we move forward and pre-position?"

The President answered in a direct way. "It's time for me to summarize. I do not want to undertake this operation, but we have no other recourse. The only way I will call it off now is if the International Red Cross hands back our Americans.

There's not going to be just pre-positioning forward. We're going to do this operation."

Charlie Beckwith almost fell out of his chair. I just didn't believe Jimmy Carter had the guts to do it.

A date to go over the wall was agreed upon. April 24th we would enter Iran, 25th we'd hide out and go over the wall, and early in the morning of the 26th we'd leave Iran.

The President said to General Jones, "David, this is a military operation. You will run it. By law you will keep the Secretary of Defense Dr. Brown informed; and I'd appreciate it if you'd do the same with me. I don't want anyone else in this room involved," and he gestured toward the table with his arm. At this point I was full of wonderment. The President had carved some important history. I was proud to be an American and to have a President do what he'd just done.

When the meeting ended, everyone stood up. President Carter looked at me. "I'd like to see you, Colonel Beckwith, before you leave." It was quiet in the room. He walked over and stood in front of me. "I want to ask you to do two things for me."

"Sir, all you gotta do is name them."

"I want you, before you leave for Iran, to assemble all of your force and when you think it's appropriate give them a message from me. Tell them that in the event this operation fails, for whatever reason, the fault will not be theirs, it will be mine."

"Sir, I give you my word I will do that."

"The second thing is, if any American is killed, hostage or Delta Force, and if it is possible, as long as it doesn't jeopardize the life of someone else, you bring the body back."

"Sir, if you've gone over my record, you know I'm that kind of man."

★ ONE ★

IT WAS JUNE of 1962. My wife, two daughters, and I arrived in Southampton, England. The instructions I had received in Fort Bragg requested that my family and I take a bus to London and, after checking into a hotel, to call the headquarters of the Special Air Service (SAS) and receive further information about where and when to report to the unit.

The dock was full of activity; but somehow, amongst the press of debarking passengers and the waiting crowd of homecoming well-wishers, I was found and greeted by an American major. He introduced himself as Bob Kingston and told me he had just completed a year attachment to the British Parachute Regiment. He'd come down to the pier to tell me how useful he thought I'd find my tour with the SAS. I tried to be polite and hear everything he had to say, but my mind was on collecting my luggage, clearing customs, and getting Katherine and the girls London-bound.

Settled into the bus, somewhere beyond the cathedral town of Winchester, I had a chance to think about what Major Kingston had told me. He'd been the second person to rave about the Special Air Service. The first had been Col. I. A. "Boppy" Edwards, the CO of the 7th Special Forces Group.

A few years earlier, Colonel Edwards had gotten together with an SAS officer, Lt. Col. John Woodhouse, and between them they had shaped an exchange program between the two elite units. The Brits would send the U.S. Army Special Forces an officer and a noncommissioned officer; and our Green Berets would reciprocate. A Sergeant Rozniak and I got into the program in 1962. We were selected to spend a year training with the 22 Special Air Service Regiment.

I knew a little about the SAS. I knew that it shared with the Brigade of Guards a deep respect for quality and battle discipline, but unlike the Guards it had little respect for drill and uniform, in part because it approached warfare in an entirely unorthodox manner. During World War II, in collaboration with the Long Range Desert Group, the First SAS Regiment had conducted raids behind Rommel's lines in the Western Desert on Benghazi, Tobruk, and Jalo. Then after the war, throughout the fifties, the unit had fought with distinction in Malaya. Working in small unit formations, some as small as 4-man patrols, the SAS had penetrated deeply into the Malayan jungle and there had hunted down, fought, and helped defeat a large, well-armed Communist guerrilla force. From this long campaign the Special Air Service had emerged with a reputation as perhaps the free world's finest counterterrorist unit.

This thumbnail historical sketch was all I knew. I had no idea how they assessed, selected, and trained their soldiers. Overflowing with the cockiness of youth, I was a hotshot Green Beret captain with Special Operations experience. I'd served a tour two years earlier in Laos. Our people in Fort Bragg had led me to believe I would lend to the Brits special skills and training methods we Yanks had learned. At the same time, I expected to pass along to our community information from the SAS. It didn't always work out that way—certainly not in my case.

In London, the adjutant of headquarters SAS, Maj. C. E. "Dare" Newell, told me he would drive us Monday to the Herefordshire home of the 22 Special Air Service Regiment, Bradbury Lines. Early Monday morning, Major Newell came by and picked us up. It was a hot summer's day, and the green English countryside, especially west of Oxford, looked lush. Toward midafternoon we drove into Bradbury Lines.

It was obvious the regiment had gone to a lot of trouble in making preparations to receive us. Several of the officers and their wives were waiting for us at our new quarters, which were situated directly across the street from the officers' mess. Our rooms were completely furnished, and once we had unloaded our luggage from Major Newell's auto, the wives took Katherine and the girls on a tour of the town that would be their home for the next year.

I felt very comfortable in these new surroundings, even if I was surrounded by men from Cornwall and Wales, Liverpool and Glasgow, whose various brogues, accents, and dialects I would have to learn. I expect they had as much trouble with my Georgia drawl.

After the second day, biting at the bit, I was called up to the regimental commander, Lieutenant Colonel Wilson.

Once the pleasantries were concluded, I was informed I would be going to A Squadron. This was disappointing. I had hoped I would go to D Squadron. It was commanded by a big redheaded Scotsman named Harry Thompson, who had been to the States and understood Americans. In the short time I'd been in Bradbury Lines I'd learned that Thompson was part of the team that had so successfully dealt with the CTs (Communist Terrorists) in Malaya.

A Squadron was commanded by Maj. Peter Walter. A small man and a very sharp dresser, he perceived himself—and was in fact—quite a ladies' man. He'd come up through the SAS ranks, beginning as a sergeant during the Emergency. Walter was a very hard man who had the reputation of being physically and mentally tough. He also wanted you to think he was without scruples. His nickname was "the Rat." At first I wasn't very comfortable with him.

There were four troops in A Squadron, and I would command Three Troop. I was taken by Major Walter to A Squadron Headquarters where I was introduced to my temporary troop sergeant, "Gypsy" Smith. Sergeant Smith then escorted me to Three Troop's billets.

Although the camp was World War II vintage, it showed none of its age. Bradbury Lines was, in fact, growing old graciously. The grounds and gardens were meticulously maintained by a crew of gardeners. The barracks had been recently painted on the outside a dazzling white with blue trim.

Straight lines, square corners, yes, sir, no, sir, three bags full. That's what I'd been taught. That's what I knew. I was a captain in the United States Army. Straight lines. Square corners. Yes, sir! No, sir! Three bags full!

I walked into Three Troop's wooden barracks. The long room was a mess. It was worn and dirty. Rucksacks (called Bergens) were strewn everywhere. Beds were unkempt, uniforms scruffy. It reminded me more of a football locker room than an army barracks. Two of the troopers—I never learned if it was done for my benefit or not—were brewing tea on the floor in the middle of the room.

I commented on the state of the room and on the men. I added, "What we need to do is get this area mopped down, the equipment cleaned, straightened, and stored, and the tea brewed outside." Two troopers, Scott and Larson, spoke up at once. "No, sir. That's not what we want to do. Otherwise, we might as well go back to our regular regiments. One of the reasons we volunteered for the SAS was so we wouldn't have to worry about the unimportant things." I didn't understand that. I thought I'd been given a group of roughnecks to command. Also, I suspected the troops were not comfortable with me. Who was this bloody Yank who didn't understand at all about freebooting behavior in a special operations unit? But I felt I had to bring the troop into line. My job, as I saw it, was to get them dressed smartly and to make parade soldiers out of them. Yes, sir! That was my job. I went home that night and told Katherine I felt I might not be able to handle this.

Peter Walter, my squadron commander, would normally have an officers' call at the end of each day. We'd go into his office and talk about the day. I found that whenever one of the officers addressed Major Walter he'd use his first name, and Major Walter, at his turn, would use the troop commander's first name. When I asked a question, I would address my commanding officer as Major Walter. This went on for several days and finally Major Walter called me in. "Let me explain the form." In a very precise and penetrating voice he told me that in the SAS system when an officer was in the midst of troopers or standing in a formation with what the Brits call ORs (Other Ranks), noncommissioned officers and enlisted men, they addressed each other using their ranks. "But, when we're in a room like this and there are just officers present it's always on a first-name basis. And that's the way I want it to be. Do you understand?" And I said, "Yes, sir!" "There you go again," he replied. That really made me uncomfortable.

I couldn't make heads or tails of this situation. The officers were so professional, so well read, so articulate, so experienced. Why were they serving with this organization of nonregimented and apparently poorly disciplined troops? The troops resembled no military organization I had ever known. I'm sure if I had been put in with a unit of the Coldstream Guards or the Household Cavalry I would have known what to expect. But the 22 Special Air Service Regiment! Well, this was too different, and for me the impact was too soon. I was adrift in a world that I thought I knew. I couldn't predict what would happen next in any given situation. Everything I'd been taught about soldiering, been trained to believe, was turned upside down.

I'd been in camp about ten days when I was told a sketch map exercise would be conducted. I was glad about this because I'd get an opportunity to observe the squadron in action.

Peter Walter told me I'd accompany Sergeant Major Ross, who would design and formulate the exercise. Life was full of surprises. In the American military system officers usually ran everything. But this was Britain. Major Walter jumped ino his flashy maroon Jaguar and took off for London, leaving Sergeant Major Ross and two or three other sergeants and me to go down to Wales, into the barren and harsh Brecon Beacons.

This exercise would test the soldier on his ability to navigate over very difficult terrain using only a compass and a simple sketch map. Ross, a large man with blond hair, was not particularly liked by the officers and most of the ORs. He was a Scot, dour and introspective, and his nickname was "Gloom." I found him very methodical and, not surprisingly, very professional. He and the other NCOs selected the proper area to run the exercise; it was quite difficult, and they discussed realistically how each trooper could solve the terrain problems they were setting up. Their aim was not to hand a soldier a complete, one-inch-to-the-mile military map, but rather a small sketch showing only major terrain features. A true magnetic north was also drawn in. To me this was realistic as a field exercise. We hadn't done much of this at Fort Bragg.

After we'd spent two days laying out this exercise, the squadron drove up in several 3-ton trucks. Major Walter and the other officers appeared and, as the sun went down, Peter told Sergeant Major Ross to get on with it.

After last light, as each trooper was dropped off, he was handed a sketch and told to get from where he was to somewhere else in a certain amount of time. I went on each of these briefings, holding Sergeant Major Ross's torch and clipboard. The instructions were very clear but very short. I remembered that if I were back in Fort Bragg, North Carolina, I'd be an hour answering questions. Sergeant Major Ross did not tolerate any questions. "This is your task. You are here and this is where your rendezvous point will be tomorrow morning and you bloody well better get hopping." That was it. The soldier disappeared into the night.

What I hadn't realized until the briefings was that each man had only a certain amount of time to get from one point to another. The men, if they were to make their rendezvous points, would have to run most of the night—while carrying heavy Bergens and individual weapons.

The next morning, when we began to gather up the men, we found them coming in pretty well shattered. Most were wringing wet. I looked again at the routes, remeasured the distances. Holy smokes, I thought, they've really covered some ground! If a trooper was late in arriving at his RV (rendezvous), he was not picked up that day and had to wait until the next morning, which meant there would be no rations for him that day. If a man not only missed his rendezvous but also got totally lost, he was severely punished. Peter Walter had him taken down to the nearest river, a rope was tied to his waist and he was thrown in with all of his gear, including sleeping bag. For the rest of the exercise, another day or two, this poor bloke stayed wet, day and night. That was the cost for not keeping up. I thought, "God, this is what we ought to do at home."

Little by little, I began to see the picture. The squadron was not playing games. They were deadly serious. They'd had a lot of experience, going back to World War II, whereas our own Army Special Forces hadn't actually been established until 1954. The Brits had made lots of mistakes, but they'd learned from them. We Americans had a ways to go.

A week later my free ride ended. I learned that the CO, Peter Walter, was up in Lincolnshire setting up an exercise similar to the one Sergeant Major Ross had run in Wales. This time, in Sherwood Forest, we would along with an extended timed march reconnoiter an objective and bring back information.

The first night we made a long forced march in groups of twos and threes. I selected two chaps, the very two who had been brewing tea on the barracks floor a few weeks before, Lance Corporals Scott and Larson. Larson was a proud Scotsman. He was never afraid to speak his mind and usually he had something worthwhile to say. Scott spoke with a thick Irish brogue and had a wonderful sense of humor. I'd learned to respect them and they now appeared to be comfortable with me. We made the march and we made the time. But my feet were a mess. My soles were covered with large blisters. In Sherwood Forest I got my nickname—Blisters.

The next afternoon we were given a forced point-to-point march, with the option of going in teams or going alone. Everyone chose to go alone. I studied the map all afternoon, memorizing my route. I said to myself, I've been to Ranger School and I'm a big boy. I'll be able to handle this if my feet'll hang in there. My feet were in terrible shape.

I started after last light. It was a tough go; the forest was dense and the tracks poorly marked. About 2:00 in the morning, wringing wet, hurt and tired, moving through a particularly thick area, I stepped off into a hole about six feet deep. I fell to the bottom in a heap. I sat for a while smoking a cigarette. I was running against time, and I didn't want to be embarrassed. Jesus Christ, I thought, you're all alone. What in the hell are you doing sitting here, boy? I got my Bergen off and by leaning it against the side of the pit I was able to climb out. I pressed on. My feet were bleeding by now and it was very painful for me to move. By first light I'd reached the rendezvous point. I wasn't the first man in. I wasn't the last man in. I was in what you'd call the lower third of the class.

That evening we went down to one of the pubs and drank a lot of warm beer. Although it hurt to walk, I walked anyway. I was too proud not to. Even the beer that night tasted good.

After we got back to Hereford, a day passed uneventfully. Then the regimental CO, Colonel Wilson, called me in. "You've been wearing that odd-looking American-made green beret around the area. We'd like you to wear a proper beret, the one with the SAS regimental symbol on it."

★ TWO ★

IF YOU'RE WHAT the Brits call an OR, you're issued a beret from the regimental stores. Officers, however, wore tailor-made ones. A couple of the officers went with me to London where I was fitted. I was very happy when the postman brought me my sand-colored beret. I wore it with a lot of pride. Nobody had given it to me. I'd earned it. Nobody gives you anything in the SAS. You have to earn it.

I hadn't "earned" my green beret. I'd just been handed it. I got assigned to Special Forces and put the hat on. Now I knew that wasn't right. Men ought to earn the right to wear a distinctive badge.

I joined the Special Forces in 1958. I arrived at Fort Bragg as a parachute-qualified officer. I'd just done three years in the 82nd Airborne Division. Not that I wouldn't have volunteered—that didn't matter. I was assigned to Special Forces because they needed officers. No one had been assessed. I knew a hat didn't make a good soldier. It's good to keep your head warm and useful to throw up in when you're flying and waiting in a plane to make a parachute drop and you get air sick. It's good for that. But in the SAS I realized the importance of a system that permits an individual to earn the right to wear a particular hat.

A month, maybe six weeks went by, and I saw that soldiers just didn't come down to Bradbury Lines, knock on the door, and join the regiment. I'd seen selection courses run without the SAS taking a single individual. Nobody! They'd sent all forty applicants back to their permanent regiments. And I mean applicants from the Guards Regiments, the best of the British Army.

I watched several selection courses. Blokes would volunteer and come to the SAS from their permanent regiments. For the first ten days the volunteers were put through rigorous physical training and map-reading courses. This was followed by another ten days when the recruits were required to endure long forced marches over the same terrain and against time. The men began to suffer from the continuous lack of sleep, with their judgment particularly affected. This phase concluded when the troopers marched forty-five miles in twenty-four hours while carrying a 55-pound Bergen and a 9-pound rifle. The tricky part was that the men were not told how long they had to complete the march—yet they all knew there was a time limit. This way, each volunteer had to go as hard as he could for as long as he could. The SAS was looking for men who would reach down within themselves to pull out those qualities they hardly knew they possessed. It's like the moment when a marathoner hits "the wall," when he's burned out, when there's nothing left, and yet he continues to push, to punish himself, and finds the guts to keep running. This phase is called "Selection."

The survivors then underwent ten to twelve weeks of additional training. During this period each man was subjected to rigorous mental testing. A board of carefully selected officers and NCOs put each man through a series of scenarios that required him to make difficult judgments.

A troop is on patrol in East Germany; the recruit is in charge, the mission to blow up a refinery. As they are moving to their objective, they stumble upon two little girls; one is fourteen, the other twelve. What would the leader do? Would he kill them? Would he take them with him? Leave them behind? Tie them up? Of course there is no right answer. The board was interested in how a man thought.

The candidate would be asked, "Who is your best friend?"

"Paddy So-and-So."

"Well, let's say Paddy gets into some serious trouble with

the police and he asks you to lie to the police for him or on the witness stand. Would you do it?"

Or, "You're off on a 4-man patrol and one of the troop disobeys an order and you determine that you will, on returning to base, report him. But on the way back, something happens: you are discovered, and during a fire fight he saves your life and is the most heroic individual in the troop. While they're pinning the Victoria Cross on this chap, do you report him for being insubordinate?"

At the end of this grueling examination the board would say, "Well, Tommy, you've obviously done well in this selection course. You've proven you're fit, and you should be proud. Now, tell us what you don't do well." Based on what I observed, men who could not articulate their inabilities did not become members of the regiment.

Finally, after all selection courses and tests had been run, the regimental commander personally accepted the individuals who were to be assigned to the SAS. As I said, whole classes washed out. In the SAS jargon, it was hard to be "badged."

What the regiment ended with, I thought, were men who enjoyed being alone, who could think and operate by themselves, men who were strong-minded and resolute. Those were the SAS characteristics I thought should be transferred to the U.S. Army's Special Forces.

Another noteworthy item involved the rank of an individual finally selected to join the SAS. In most cases he gave up his previous rank, the one he held in his permanent regiment. He would then have to work his way back up the promotion line. So, officers and ORs made a sacrifice to join the SAS. This was the case, for example, of my neighbor at Bradbury Lines, John Edwards. A permanent major in the Royal Highland Fusiliers, because there was no space in 22 SAS for another major, John in order to join the regiment had accepted the lower rank of captain.

There was one SAS custom totally alien in my own army whose importance I fully understood. Over pints of bitters in the Sergeants' Mess on those Saturday nights when the squadron was in Bradbury Lines, officers and sergeants would discuss freely situations that had developed during the week. The form here was that the regimental sergeant major would invite the officers in their mess to come to the Sergeants' Mess. This was important. The officers would then literally run down the two blocks separating the Officers' Mess from the Sergeants' Mess. And it was in their mess where it all happened. No one ever left before first light on Sunday morning. We stayed and drank beer all night. This was the opportunity for the officers and the sergeants to whittle away at traditional form and egotistical illusions.

This would be the time when my troop sergeant would say, "You know, Captain Beckwith, you made a bollix out of that inspection last week. Everyone laughed at you. You got too concerned about the missing button on Tommy's uniform. All you had to do was tell the man to get it repaired. You didn't need to embarrass him." The officers sometimes would accept the criticisms; yet, in some cases they wouldn't. Many times officers would argue amongst themselves, particularly between A and D Squadrons. These nights were filled with strong dialogue and many a good argument was had. Everybody got breathed on, even the regimental commander. A very intense scene, but it was a way of letting off steam. It was a very healthy environment. A lot got done.

One morning, shortly after returning to camp from a field exercise, I heard someone banging on my front door. It was nearly 3:00 A.M. and I went down half asleep to answer the door. A trooper in full combat gear stood facing me. "Sir! You are to report to the guardhouse as soon as you possibly can with the following equipment." And he handed me a piece of paper with the words "Crab Stakes" printed across the top. I started to get dressed. I was in a hurry but not in that big a hurry, because I didn't know what was going on. When I finally arrived at the guardhouse, my troop was waiting. They were livid. They wouldn't even speak to me. Down the road, a fair distance off, I saw another troop moving off. My troop couldn't leave until everybody had been accounted for. Obviously, I was the last man to get there.

Squadron Commander Walter gave me my instructions and

we took off. Well, we had to struggle through various events, including a long speed march on which we were graded. Because we were the last ones to start, we never caught up. We came in last in everything. I crawled into my shell and didn't say anything. I was just too busy trying to keep up. Saturday night in the Sergeants' Mess I caught hell.

"You bloody man, you. When someone knocks on your door, you better be ready and you better double-time next time. You were the last man in the squadron to get there and you live closer than most. Why didn't you ask for some help? Didn't you understand?" I didn't. I had no idea that "Crab Stakes" meant a contest.

Major Walter could have gotten me off to the side the day before and explained the form, but he hadn't. He didn't have to tell me what he was planning, but he could have said, "If you ever get instructions during the night marked 'Crab Stakes,' move in a hurry."

I was angry and embarrassed. Yet, Peter Walter was very keen, very clever. I began to recognize, maybe in the fourth month of training, what he was trying to do. It was when we went down to Corsica that I began to really understand.

★ THREE ★

THE SAS WAS invited by the French in September to undertake a combined exercise with one of their crack paratroop battalions located in Corsica. It was the famous Bérets Rouges, who had fought with gallantry in strongpoint Eliane at Dien Bien Phu and, three years later, had fought in the Battle of Algiers. For a time it had been commanded by one of France's great combat colonels, Roger Trinquier. The lessons learned at the hands of the Viet Minh and the Fellagha had not been wasted on their officers and NCOs. They were extremely professional.

We made the long drive from Ajaccio, north along the spectacular Corsican coast to Calvi, where the "paras" were stationed. On the right-hand side of the twisting road mountains rose, covered to their summits with evergreen oak. On the other side sudden glimpses of open sea or inlets and gulfs dotted the drive.

That evening, our first with the French, was one hell of a night. It was spent drinking cognac, and those Frenchmen were as professional in this as in everything they did.

The next morning, early, we were taken to a seventeenth-century fortress built during the Genoese occupation of the island. There a very rugged obstacle course had been rigged. Vertical walls to be scaled by climbing drain pipes and jumps from balcony to balcony, or turret to turret, were the order of the day. One particularly hazardous obstacle was a wide moat that had to be crossed by sliding along a single steel cable.

The French said two of their own troops had been killed when they'd slipped and fallen.

The 1st BPC (Bataillon de Parachutistes de Choc) gave A Squadron of the 22 SAS a free ride through the obstacles in the morning. Two troopers within the squadron broke ankles during the afternoon. The next day we Brits formed 4-man patrols and went out into the hills to hunt down French units scattered throughout the maquis. A useful exercise, it lasted four days.

We were then gathered in the boondocks. That night we were given plenty to eat and drink. In the morning we were stripped of our British uniforms and given coarse woolen uniforms on which were painted, in bold white letters, both back and front, the initials POW. The drill this time was to E and E (Evade and Escape).

Each of us was given time to study a map of this mountainous northern region and, if we could, determine a route that would take us to an RV. The object was to get to the rendezvous without being captured by patrols made up of French paratroopers and local gendarmes. Before being dropped off, we were expertly strip searched. Some tiny compasses one or two of the troopers had tried to conceal were taken away. I paired up with my troop sergeant, Gypsy Smith.

Loaded into trucks and taken deep into the wild Corsican countryside, we were dropped off and told to make for the RV. Visualize sixty 2-man patrols, every man wearing a POW jacket, fanning out throughout the granite mountain and rugged scrub country of northern Corsica, all making for an RV on the coast, all trying to avoid roadblocks, checkpoints, and roving patrols, and you'll have an idea of what was happening that night.

Sergeant Smith and I first tried to discover where we had been dropped. Once this had been determined, we chose a compass bearing, then climbed slowly through a jungle of boulders, evergreen plants, and shrubs. All night we moved over crude footpaths, climbed over granite outcrops, walked through oak groves and maquis-thinned fields, passed silent, dark, square stone-built houses surrounded by olive groves and ancient-looking villages hanging from hillsides. Northern Corsica is tough; very, very tough.

At first light, nearly at our limits, Gypsy Smith and I hit the beach. We headed for the RV, which, we were told, was a nudist camp during the holiday season. We were the second pair to arrive. Lance Corporals Larson and Scott, the two who had brewed tea on the barracks floor, had been the first in. A little time later, Major Walter and his partner, who had taken a particularly rigorous route, arrived. I hadn't even known the CO was out that night.

After everyone arrived or had been rounded up in the hills above the beach, we were taken back to Calvi where the squadron did some partying. Peter Walter and I went out to dinner. He talked and I listened. He said he recognized I'd been under a lot of pressure, and he explained that, because my performance had lived up to the squadron's standards, he and the men had accepted me as one of them. He felt that if I would relax and unwind I'd enjoy far more my year with the SAS. So when the unit returned to Hereford just before Christmas, I was as happy as I'd been for quite a while.

Following the holiday break, the regimental commander asked me to stop in. "Charlie," he said, "the regiment's off to Malaya in January and we want you to go. You need to visit London and find out what your side has to say about this."

Our side was the Army attaché in the American Embassy who was a bit wishy-washy with me. "I don't want to ask the State Department," he said, "because if they get in it, it will become very complicated. I think you shouldn't go. If something happens to you it will be difficult for us to handle. Think carefully about it, Captain. You ought not to go, but the decision really is yours." Well, hell, if the decision was mine . . . I returned to Bradbury Lines to tell Colonel Wilson I'd accompany the regiment to Malaya.

★ FOUR ★

IN MALAYA, THE Communists, known as the MRLA (Malayan Races Liberation Army), retreated into the jungle and in June 1948 began a campaign of full-scale violence. They had been unable to gain power by political means and now tried to seize it through terrorism. A state of emergency in Malaya was immediately declared. During the early stages of the crisis the MRLA, using tactics based on terror, met with considerable success. They followed the advice of the ancient Chinese general Sun-Zu, "Kill one, frighten a thousand."

The war rapidly escalated from isolated acts of terrorism to jungle battles between guerrilla bands and regular British Army units. Conventional military measures met with failure. The jungle, which covers four-fifths of the Malayan peninsula, simply does not lend itself to set-piece battles.

Recognizing by early 1950 that this strategy was not working, the British authorities decided to isolate the guerrilla force from the civilian community. Spearheaded by the SAS, small-size units penetrated the jungle, there to live like the enemy, moving freely from base to base, solving their own supply problems, and hunting down the guerrillas on their own terms.

When Britain moved Malay toward independence, the guerrillas lost their monopoly on nationalism. Deprived of their main sources of supply among the villagers—and losing their appeal among the people as a whole—the MRLA dwindled to a few hundred stragglers who hung on deep in the jungles of the north. In 1960, the Emergency was officially ended.

The SAS operation I was part of was to occur along the Thai-Malaya border. This was an area still inhabited by small guerrilla bands. It was going to be more than just a routine exercise. The old blokes in the regiment thought that because there was a chance, however slim, of getting a kill, this would be a very good training operation.

The regiment flew to Butterworth, which is across the strait from Penang in northern Malaya. I debarked with my troop, wearing complete British jungle kit. As we went through the terminal to get on the small planes that were going to ferry us to our base, Peter Walter came up to me. "Don't say anything, Charlie. There's some chap here asking questions about you. With your accent you're sure to give yourself away. For God's sake, let me do all the talking."

I caught a quick glimpse of an American embassy type up from Kuala Lumpur talking to Peter. I kept moving and didn't breathe freely until I was aboard the ferry aircraft and Peter had come up to tell me he had taken care of everything. I didn't ask how, and I didn't care. All I wanted was to get into the jungle.

We were flown to an old Gurkha camp carved out of the jungle a few kilometers from Gerik. The area had a few rubber plantations and one or two hard-surface roads. Some of the regiment had spent time there during the Emergency, and I could tell they were feeling good about being back. One was the Scotsman, Harry Thompson. He told me many stories about fighting in these jungles. In February 1958, hard on the Malacca Strait Coast, in the state of Selangor, Harry Thompson had led D Squadron in a hunt for two guerrilla bands led by someone known as "the Baby Killer." After nearly three exhausting weeks in the Telok Anson swamp, Thompson and his squadron finally cornered and captured the notorious terrorist. By then the men were suffering from their extended period in this huge swamp, and Thompson himself was walking on infected and ulcer-covered legs. No question he was an old hand. I had a lot of time for Major Thompson. A few years later, in Borneo, Harry Thompson would become second in command of the 22 SAS Regiment—and tragically die there in a helicopter crash.

In the morning, bright and early—the Brits were great for starting before first light—we packed our Bergens and were picked up and driven down to the river, loaded onto boats, and taken to the training site. There we were met by Sergeant Major Ross and the other instructors. We then marched forty minutes into the jungle, where we prepared a bivouac for that night. From piles of old parachutes we were expected to make hammocks. I'd frankly forgotten how, so one of the sergeants who was helping gave me a hand. You take three silk panels and sew up the edges, making sure you don't cut the shroud lines that attach the canopy to the pack tray. Then the shroud lines are braided, like a little girl's hair, and these are used to tie the head and the feet of the hammock to the holding trees. All this, including hacking out of the jungle a spot you could call your own, took no more than a couple of hours.

The following morning we were told we were going out on a land navigation exercise in groups of four. Sergeant Major Ross and I were paired. Ross had the reputation of being an outstanding navigator, and I'd liked the way he handled his job in the Brecon Beacons. I was to learn years later that Gloom, after leaving the SAS, took his own life. This morning, however, very much alive, he was in his element.

We started moving through the jungle and pretty soon began to climb a large mountain. Sergeant Major Ross pointed out game trails and places where elephants had come through. I learned you could usually find water along these paths where it collected in the deep footprints left by these huge animals.

For the first hour Gloom did all the navigating, explaining to us the terrain features we should be looking for. In jungle as heavy as we were in, it was hard to know where we were. The trees were so large that two men could barely join hands around them. Landmarks were difficult to see, so we were told to look for ridge lines or the tops of hills matching the contour lines on our maps. Streams were another matter. Sometimes we'd cross one and it wouldn't be on the map. Then there was the one on the map that had dried up and was no longer a part of the terrain. So it was a matter of keeping up with the contours and shooting azimuths and back azimuths. This was tough jungle. The leeches were very bad. There were more leeches in Malaya than I'd seen, or was to see, anywhere in Southeast Asia.

Following land navigation we did Immediate Action Drills (IADs). The Brits had had a lot of experience fighting the CT in Malaya, so they were good at this. We learned how to set an ambush, what to do if a troop ran head on into the enemy or into their flank, and how to respond if attacked while in bivouac. Drills for every eventuality existed. At first we walked very slowly through these drills. Gradually we got to go faster and faster and finally ran them with live ammunition. I'd never done this in the States. It was great!

Afterward, Sergeant Major Ross informed us that the next day, in pairs, we would navigate through the jungle, arriving at various RVs where vehicles would pick us up and carry us back to Gerik. I selected a trooper named Kilpatrick, and he and I spent the rest of the daylight hours choosing the route we would take. I didn't think it made any difference. I said to myself, "Knowing Gloom, hell, they're all going to be tough!"

We were released, and Kilpatrick and I took off. All day we climbed up and climbed down steep jungle ridges. There seemed to be an endless row of ridge lines, and much of that hot, steamy day we spent on all fours, pushing and pulling, sliding down one side of a steep river valley and struggling up the other. We went as hard and as fast as we could. When darkness fell and we still hadn't hit the RV, we continued to move even though there was a rule in the SAS, because of the danger, not to march at night. For another hour and a half we plodded on. We were bound and determined to make that damn pickup point. Finally, figuring out we were serving no purpose at all, we stopped and hung our hammocks. I didn't sleep very well that night. I know Kilpatrick didn't either. Next morning we got packed up and started moving before dawn. The first light was kind of smoky. We had moved no more than 200 yards through the jungle when suddenly we came out into a rubber plantation. We traveled for another half hour through the rubber trees before we struck a tarmac road. We'd been so close the night before, yet so far away.

We sat for ten minutes before we realized, "Hey, ain't nobody coming to pick us up now. We missed the truck last night. We better get moving." So we started walking, knowing we had another ten miles to hike. An old truck came along, which we hitched a ride on and rode the rest of the way to Gerik. In camp we learned we weren't the only ones who'd missed the RV.

Although others were still out in the jungle, I was sent off again immediately. As I walked into camp, Peter Walter came up to me and said, "I've got an aircraft waiting for you. You must get cracking. Get your gear, your troop is waiting for you. Straight away, get moving, right, right, right, and by the way, here's a beer and a sandwich."

The dense jungle canopy was a rich dark green, and I thought how beautiful it looked. A 2-engine aircraft flew me into a small grass strip that had been cut out next to a border security outpost along which a broad muddy river ran. I was taken to a big open-sided pavilion near the river. It reminded me of being a kid again, going to a church picnic.

I looked real bad. I'd changed my torn uniform for a new one back at Gerik, but my face and arms were cut up and there was dried blood all over me. Kilpatrick and I had busted our asses. I smelled bad and hadn't shaved in days. I began to get my kit together to shave and wash down in the river. Lance Corporal Scott said, "Begging your pardon, sir, you don't want to do that. What you want is to build up a good crust all over you so that even the bloody mosquitoes can't bite through. And, for God's sake, don't shave. That just gives the blighters more places to eat you." I said to myself, These guys don't understand hygiene. I whipped into this river and swam around a while, then washed all the crap off me and got a good close shave. When I dressed I felt great. The troops didn't say anything.

"Darky" Davidson had returned from the school he'd been attending and replaced Gypsy Smith as my troop sergeant. After I had cleaned up, he called Three Troop together in order to explain the next drill to the lads. Rations were issued and everybody began to load their Bergens with just enough, but not too little. We had to bear in mind that once we left this site we weren't going to get any more fresh food for ten days. I could take as much of anything as I wanted. All I had to do was carry it. There were also the loads that had to be carried for the wireless operators who were carrying the field radios. That night I slept on the wooden boards of the pavilion. Putting my head on the Bergen like it was a saddle, I slept very well indeed.

Next morning we got cracking. Since the packs probably weighed sixty pounds apiece, including ammunition, we helped each other put them on. You had to kind of lean over to carry it. We carried our weapons in our hands. No one in 22 SAS was ever allowed to sling his weapon on his shoulder. In fact, slings were not items of issue in the regiment. Experience had shown that in an ambush the time it took to unsling a weapon cost people their lives.

As we began to move out, the Malayan Security Police contingent, who the Brits sarcastically called Brylcreem Boys, quit right there. They were sweating already and weren't going to go any farther. They were obviously unfit. This was not too great a loss as we still had with us several Sarawak Rangers from Borneo who acted as trackers.

At first we paralleled a stream. Then we began to climb. There wasn't the trace of a track. We moved from rock to rock, holding on to trees and vines so we wouldn't fall. The people at the head of the column had a tough go as they were blazing the trail. They cut through thickets of bamboo, scrub, rattan, and thorn. We got fairly high up the first day and we stopped early. That was the rule. We needed two hours of daylight to set up camp in the jungle.

I looked around at the men as they came into the camp site. Dressed in battered soft jungle hats, sweat-soaked shirts, torn and stained pants, they looked like anything but members of an elite military unit. The first thing everyone did was light up a cigarette. In the jungle, where you could only carry so many, they were at a premium. If someone ran out, nobody would give him another. It was his tough luck. The next thing you did before setting up camp was to check your feet. Then there were the leeches. I'd go to my mate and he'd take his cigarette and begin to burn mine off. When I was clear I'd do the same for him. Often the leeches had gotten through your torn bush jacket and pants, and where you'd brushed against a tree you'd have mashed them. It wasn't unusual to have bloody socks from busted leeches. There might be fifteen or twenty of them on you. They're about an inch and a half long and a quarter of an inch in diameter, all filled with blood. Once you'd checked every part you could see, you'd bend over, spread your cheeks, and your mate would check that you hadn't any stuck up there.

The sun went down. One moment it was light; the next it was dark.

Tea began to be brewed, and tins of food were heated over small cookers. Although the sun had set, deep amongst the trees it remained hot, and the jungle was still and quiet.

The chief trouble at night was from insects. Mosquitoes were bad, but the midges were worse.

The second day of marching though the jungle was more of the first. No one spoke—we had learned to move silently. Visibility in places was down to several yards. The ground was spongy, wet with ancient leafmold. Heavy brakes of bamboo would suddenly bar the way, and we would be forced to slog around them. Cut off from the sun by the foliage overhead, the column moved between half-light and deep shadow.

Toward the end of the day, one of my troopers had a bad accident. Crossing a granite boulder covered with a layer of moss, his pack went one way and he went the other. He landed badly, breaking his leg. This was tough. We set it the best we could while a "recky" party went ahead, trying to find where we'd spend the night.

The third day was a matter of finding a place where we could get a small chopper in to take this trooper out. We spent the morning beginning to chop out an area. There wasn't any standing around talking about the problem. People knew what had to be done. We cleared out the brush, but there were still the trees to contend with. There was nowhere that didn't have these huge trees. The troops signals NCO got on the radio, and using Morse, dit-dit-dah-dah-dit, requested from headquarters an aerial drop of explosives. Around three o'clock a Royal Air Force 2-engine Valetta came in and looked us over. We popped smoke so he could find us. The wind wasn't bad so he made two drops, one of explosives, the other of blasting caps. We were in business.

The next day we continued with no slackening of effort to chop through the heavy undergrowth and notch the trees we were going to blow. It's not much of a problem blowing trees down. The trick was blowing them *away* from the platform we were building. I would have made some mistakes and blown some in. I was learning a lot. By last light on this day, the second full one since the accident, we'd blown down most of the trees. Any way you want to look at it, it was two solid days of the hardest work I'd ever done.

In miles and miles of dense green roof, our hole in the jungle must have seemed—to the pilot—no larger than the head of a pin. Nonetheless, on the third day a small helicopter with a litter tied to its struts flew into us. While we strapped the trooper in, he was making sure his rifle and equipment were going back with him. That's where I learned you keep up with your kit. The Brits didn't go off and lose anything. They didn't have a lot, so they accounted for everything.

Once the chopper lifted off, we got our packs on and, seeing we had the rest of the afternoon, resumed our march. That evening Gypsy Smith, Kilpatrick, and some of the others began to discuss the time we'd lost—we were then three days behind the rest of the squadron. I sent a signal to Peter Walter, and he replied we should press on. It was now a matter of time, of trying to make it up if we possibly could. I couldn't see how, since the going wasn't about to get any easier.

The following day, or the day after that, we came upon a very large river, and from the map we saw it was flowing in the same direction we were going. Some of the ORs recommended we raft down it, that being the only way to make up the time we'd lost. Others were concerned about our security.

The CTs could see us a lot easier on a raft than in the jungle. Based on the recommendations made by men I thought a lot of, I took the responsibility—we began to build three rafts. I'd never seen anything like this. These SAS troopers knew exactly how to do it. One group went out to cut and gather rattan while the rest of us began to cut good-size bamboo stalks. By last light we had three large, heavy rafts floating in the river.

The next day we on-loaded and poled our way down the river. We made up the time we'd lost.

It was about the ninth day in the jungle; we'd gotten off the rafts and were toiling cross country to our RV with another troop when I began not feeling well. I felt down, didn't have my zip. I'd run out of cigarettes so I blamed it on that. The tenth day we rendezvoused with First Troop. As we arrived, First Troop left to make another RV. The best I can remember, we didn't bring in a resupply that day. I continued to feel bad. The next day I felt worse. Four-man patrols were going out, and Gypsy Smith suggested I stay in camp. Obviously, I must not have looked too good. I had severe diarrhea. Lance Corporal Scott gave me a cigarette. I thought, Boy, I must be in bad shape if he's offering me cigarettes.

A resupply drop occurred, but the cigarettes didn't taste good to me. About then Darky Davidson and Gypsy Smith came over to see me. It was early in the morning of the day following the drop. I hadn't slept much that night. I was weak, and I'd shit all over myself. They said, "Sir, you're quite sick and we're worried about you. We need to send you out." I was embarrassed and didn't want to go, but I couldn't deny I was really sick. "We're going to call Major Walter and request you be medevac'd out." They got me up and helped me over to a tree where I waited for the chopper. I wasn't able to pack my stuff, so that, too, was done for me.

I was flown directly to the British hospital at Ipoh. I smelled very, very bad. An orderly took me to a tub and told me to clean up. I needed help, that's how weak I was. By late afternoon I was in bed and had been checked out pretty thoroughly. Toward dusk a doctor came in and asked me if I knew what was wrong with me.

"Yeah," I said. "I've got dengue fever," I'd had that in Laos, "and possibly a touch of malaria."

"Well, I'll tell you what you've got." He sat next to me. "You've got a very bad case of leptospirosis. In fact, you have one of the three worst cases I've ever seen, and the other two chaps never got over it."

I said, "Well, let me tell you something. I walked in here and intend to walk out. I'm going to make it."

"With that kind of attitude," he said, "you might make it." Then he told me he was going to start me on penicillin and that there'd be a reaction. "Just make up your mind that it's going to be a tough night. You're going to be uncomfortable for a while."

He was right. That first night was pure hell. I came pretty close to packing it in a time or two. The next morning I wasn't any better. For the next few days I kept getting penicillin, right in the ass. I got it every three hours. First one cheek, then the other. Day and night, every three hours for five days. I remember the last shot I got and I thought, Jesus Christ, what a mess. But I was so thankful it was over.

My strength began to slowly return. After ten days I took my first steps. Then I started to move around the grounds. The lieutenant colonel who was in command of the hospital came in one day and told me, "We've received information that there will be an aircraft in here tomorrow, and the Americans will fly you to a hospital in the Philippines." "Well," I said, "I don't want to leave here." "That'll be your decision," he said, "but I'll bring the colonel around when he arrives. Of course, if you want to stay here, we're glad to have you." He couldn't come right out and say it, but he wanted me to stay. They'd been good to me, and I couldn't see slapping them in the face by telling them I thought I'd get better treatment in an American hospital.

In the morning I looked through the shutters and saw my doctor walking with this short fat guy. I figured he was the official sent from the Philippines to fetch me. He was dressed all in white: had on white shoes, white socks that you pull up just below your knees, white shorts, and a white shirt. I rolled over on my side so my back was to him. I didn't want to look at him. "Captain Beckwith, I'm Colonel——" I forget his name. "I'm here to take you to the American hospital—" "Screw you," I screamed, "I ain't doing that!" I went on like that for several minutes. I want to presume that he thought I was crazy. I never turned to look at him. I just yelled and cussed. Finally he said some things to the British Army doctor, then he turned and left. Some time later the hospital commander came in and told me it had been decided I could stay.

It was the talk of the hospital, this crazy Yank who wanted to stay in a British hospital instead of going to one of his own. The nurses became so nice to me. They started serving me hot chocolate. I didn't even know it had existed before then. Word got back to my troop. The officers in the regiment heard. "For once," I thought, "I've done something right."

★ FIVE ★

WHILE I WAS recuperating, the adjutant of the regiment came down to talk with me and cheer me up. Along with the fruit he left, he loaned me a copy of Field Marshal Sir William J. Slim's *Defeat into Victory*. I browsed through it and then, while eating a banana, I came upon Sir William's Afterthoughts. The more I read the deeper I became involved. He laid it all out, how he felt about Special Operations. Although he concluded that most special units are wasteful and have more disadvantages than advantages, he believed that there was one type of special unit that should become an essential component of any modern army. This special unit is one that operates deep behind enemy lines, whose purpose is to disrupt the enemy, to collect information, to work with indigenous peoples, to sabotage enemy installations, to assassinate enemy commanders. The troops who made up this unit would require many qualities and skills not expected in the ordinary soldier and would use many methods beyond his capacity. Field Marshal Slim felt they could achieve strategic results if handled with imaginative ruthlessness.

All this stimulated me. What did I think about the SAS, their techniques, their training, their selection process? I did a lot of looking inside myself and a lot of comparing with the American Special Forces.

As soon as I could move around at will, I was sent to a recuperation hospital in the cool Cameron Highlands. There I began to put my thoughts together. I felt the U.S. Army needed a unit that could do what the SAS could do. It needed to be able to go out in small patrols and blow up bridges and dams and railroad lines, to take out an enemy commander, say, like Rommel, to collect information for air strikes or for attacks made by conventional forces. The American Army not only needed a Special Forces capability, but an SAS one; not only a force of teachers, but a force of doers. I'd been sent over to have a dialogue with the Brits, to learn and to teach. But I'd learned this was no exchange. Instead of showing them things the Special Forces did, I kept busy just trying to keep up with what I was learning.

I did recognize some things the SAS didn't do as well as our people. In certain areas we could plan better than they could; we could be more methodical. I felt the Brits went too fast. There wasn't always a need for their great haste to do things. I understood that if we could take the Brits' technique and combine it with our planning methodology we'd really have something.

Equally important with stating what a unit could do was articulating what that unit couldn't, or shouldn't, do. In the SAS, because of their fear of being misused, I learned that they were very sensitive to what they couldn't do. Needless to say, a rifle company can also be misused. It's no different in the field of Special Operations. It may be worse. Misuse a force that's taken years to put together and all that time, energy, and skill will be wasted. The SAS didn't want one of its squadrons to be plugged into an infantry battalion as if it were any ordinary replacement unit. It would be a total misuse. Another misapplication of the Special Ops principle is to give one of these units terrain to hold and defend. The outfit is mean and lean, and a large investment has been made in the training of its people. It needs to be used in a strategic offensive role. You want to use it where it can hurt the enemy the most when he isn't looking.

The SAS had a very broad definition of what it does and remained flexible. The American Army was quite the opposite. We would go to a great deal of trouble to frame a Field Manual. The FM for Special Forces is 31–21. We'd gone to a great deal of trouble and expense to spell out very, very clearly what the mission of the Special Forces is. If it doesn't happen to be in the FM, no matter how good an idea it is, it won't get done. All our demolition recipes are recorded; all our communication procedures are spelled out. The Brits would never do that. They kept everything in their heads. If you aren't smart enough to keep it up there, they felt, you get your hat and go somewhere else to work.

My tour in England was up. I departed 22 SAS. I was a totally different person from the brash, regimented Green Beret captain who'd arrived a year earlier. I felt I had more confidence in myself than ever before in my life. I felt I had captured a new world. I knew in England I had stumbled upon a concept that, when welded with the American system, would improve many of the things we did in the Special Forces. I was enthusiastic and elated with all I'd learned and was eager to share it.

I expected to be welcomed with open arms when I arrived home. People would sit down with me and pick my brain. I'd be asked to write reports, draft papers. My debriefing period would be two weeks, maybe three. It had cost money to send me to England, and I knew our people would want to know what I'd learned.

I requested to go back to the States by ship. Those five days at sea could be devoted to writing a paper that would be the basic document for everything I wanted to accomplish. I had so much in my mind and needed the time to sort everything out. I worked long and hard putting together my report, confident in the knowledge that people were going to be anxious to read it. My idealism was boundless. Midway across the Atlantic I suggested to Katherine, "Why don't you take the girls and pay a visit to your mom and dad. I'm sure I'm going to be very busy for the first few weeks." I knew I was going to be really jumping, getting things moving, making myself available to everyone who was waiting to talk to me.

★ SIX ★

KATHERINE AND THE girls went to Michigan and I caught the first train for Fort Bragg. I'd shaved the morning we docked but not again. I rode all night, arriving in Fayetteville, North Carolina, around 10:00 A.M. I took my bags and grabbed a cab to Smoke Bomb Hill, the location of the 7th Special Forces Group. It had been a year since I'd been in my old headquarters and I saw many new faces. I told the adjutant who I was and that I had, just the day before, returned from England. "Well," he said, "you need to see the deputy commander."

I was still in civilian clothes and probably looked somewhat scruffy. But I really didn't care. I was a man with a mission. I found Lt. Col. Ed Mattice seated behind his desk. I don't remember exactly how he put it, but his meaning was clear. "Captain, you've been gone for a year and we got things here that are happening every day. I'm going to assign you down to A Company and you can sort of put your report in when you want to." In other words, "We don't really care where you've been or that now you're back." I spent a lot of time listening and he did a lot of talking, trying to impress me with his experience. The only thing he impressed me with was that he seemed to be an old man who was worried about getting promoted to full colonel.

A few minutes later Lt. Col. Mert Kelty, who commanded A Company, came along followed by his little Dalmatian dog. This particular officer was a bachelor who lived with this dog.

Colonel Kelty immediately told me that I needed a shave and a cleanup. He said I was to accompany him down to the Company area.

We started across the parade ground. I said to the good colonel—he, too, seemed a somewhat elderly gentleman—"It's a beautiful day, sir. Why don't we drop down and knock off fifty push-ups? Which hand, sir, right or left? You just make the choice." Colonel Kelty was flabbergasted. I'm sure he thought to himself, How in the hell did I get this buffoon hung around my neck?

We marched into A Company's headquarters building, and behind a desk sat a forty-pound-overweight sergeant major who I'd casually known in the 82nd and who, I knew, had never been in the mud of the Special Operations business. The sergeant major immediately snapped, "It'll cost you fifteen cents, Captain, for having your hat on." I told the sergeant major I wasn't paying no goddamn fifteen cents for having no hat on.

In Colonel Kelty's office I said, "Sir, I don't think A Company is big enough for me and you, and since you are the commander here, I think I should leave." He said, "I think you should, too."

I marched out of A Company about five minutes after I'd arrived. I suspect at that moment Lieutenant Colonel Kelty called up Lieutenant Colonel Mattice and the two of them tried to figure a nice way, without embarrassing themselves, of drumming old Beckwith out of the 7th Special Forces Group.

I went back to Group Headquarters and said to the adjutant, "I would like to have permission to look around and find a home somewhere out of the Special Forces community. I'm disgusted." All this happened within half a day. I was disillusioned and frightened. After lunch I sat back and thought that this was the most ludicrous thing in the world to have happen. I said, "Hey, boy, you're too smart for this."

I remembered that Col. Clyde Russell, who had commanded the 7th Special Forces Group for about nine months while I was in England, had just been reassigned to the XVIII Airborne Corps as the operations officer. I'd known Colonel Russell and always gave him high marks. I determined I'd go see him to get some guidance. I couldn't see him that afternoon, but made an appointment for the next day. The rest of the first day I spent going around visiting some of my old friends, sharing my feelings with them. Most of them didn't really understand where I was coming from. Instead of a year, it felt as if I'd been away from Bragg for a lifetime.

Late the next afternoon I met with Colonel Russell. I explained what had happened—my year in England, my return to Fort Bragg, and now how I was very disillusioned and upset. He made it clear to me that he'd made four combat jumps with the 82nd Airborne Division in World War II and that he didn't have much time for the Brits. He further explained that he thought the exchange program with the SAS was a big waste of time inasmuch as only one officer got the benefit of the program and not the entire Special Forces. Dead end! Now, I didn't know which way to run.

The next day, back in the 7th Special Forces Group area, I was walking across the street on my way to one of the mess halls to get a cup of coffee, when a lieutenant colonel who I'd never met before walked up to me. "My name is Buzz Miley, and I'm the commander of B Company. I understand you're just back from England. I've got the responsibility of setting up an exercise that's going to involve some of the Brits, and I need some assistance. Will you help me?" It was like someone had just picked me up out of the gutter. "Come on," he said, "let's go have a cup of coffee and talk about it."

Over the coffee, Lieutenant Colonel Miley explained, "I have to leave tomorrow to make arrangements for an exercise up in the Pisgah National Forest. There's a small contingent of four or five people going with me. I'm told you know the Special Forces business and that in England you obviously learned something. I could use you. What do you say, Captain, want to help?" I was so happy I wanted to hug him. I explained my situation, and he told me he'd take care of everything with Colonel Mattice. And he did. I wasn't assigned to B Company, but I was attached for the duration of the exercise. I suspected Group Headquarters was just going to watch to see what I would do.

Crossing the Atlantic I'd finished my big report, the one stating what I'd learned from the SAS and how this information could assist our side. The recommendation I made in this report was that the United States Army organize as soon as possible a unit along the lines of the British SAS. But now, in Bragg, I didn't know what to do with this report. I knew if I gave it to Colonel Mattice it could end up in the trash can. The new Group commander of the 7th Special Forces, Colonel Evans-Smith, who was coming out of the Army War College and had never served a day in Special Ops, had not yet arrived. I nevertheless felt that Evans-Smith was my best bet, so I determined the clever thing to do was to hold the report until he got on post, then get him to read it. I had to hope he was the kind of senior officer who would listen to me.

Then I outsmarted myself. Johnny Johnson was the 7th Special Forces Group operations officer. He'd served in Korea with a Ranger unit. I trusted him. Johnson's assistant, Bud Sydnor, was the officer who had preceded me as the SAS exchange officer. Bud had been the first officer to be exchanged, so I felt I had one friend up at Group and no doubt two, because Bud would by now have converted Johnny Johnson. I felt confident. I knew that Johnson, being operations officer, had some clout. So I gave my SAS After Action Report to Major Johnson and asked him to read it. This proved to be a mistake.

The next day I went up into the Great Smoky Mountains of western North Carolina with Lieutenant Colonel Miley. We were there about a week, and I had a hell of a good time. I never will forget how one night, pretty late, we wheeled into this motel. Everybody was worried about what it was going to cost Uncle Sam to put his officers up. The discussion went on about how many officers could share one room. Aw, shit! I thought, so I grabbed my sleeping bag out of the back of the jeep. I found me a tree, and I crawled up under it and went to sleep. American Army staffs often worry about piss-ants when elephants are stomping them to death.

The exercise went well. We found a very good place near Andrews, North Carolina, up in the Nantahala National Forest, to set up our base. What didn't go well was that most everyone spent one hell of a lot of time worrying about creature comforts; where the troops were going to sleep, how their bowels were going to be taken care of, whether the tents were in good shape, would the visitors have a nice place to sit and watch from? We were even directed to go as far as to bring in a Special Forces Demonstration Team, which rehearsed each of the parts it was going to play. If we had visitors from Washington, D.C., it was thought we should look good. But that was phony. This particular team's actions were canned. I couldn't come to grips with that. I was disgusted. It was like being in show biz.

About that time, maybe fifteen days had gone by up there in Andrews, when one SAS squadron reinforced arrived. John Woodhouse, who I'd met in Aden on my return from Malaya, brought them over, and Peter Walter was with him. Boy, was I glad to see them. I really had more in common with them than I did with my own people. The Brits laughed at the size and magnitude of the exercise. All they wanted were tents—didn't need any floors in them. As for water, they found their own.

Brig. Gen. William P. Yarborough, the commander of the Special Warfare Center at Fort Bragg, found the time to talk to John Woodhouse about me. I'd gone earlier to General Yarborough and told him, "Sir, you know you're really missing something if you don't take a good hard look at this SAS concept." General Yarborough was a great guy and a very polite man. "Captain," he said, "you don't understand. I have a full plate here handling what I got." He was very nice to me, but not at all sympathetic. I was making waves, no question about it. Anyway, General Yarborough talked to John Woodhouse and told him I was getting unmanageable.

John buttonholed me one evening. "Charlie, you need to slow up a little. I know what you're going through and I'm sympathetic with you, but you gotta live here and we don't. What I'm saying, old chap, is that you want to take your time with this. You're going to catch more flies with honey than you are batting them around."

I appreciated what John said. Yet, no one wanted to hear one goddamn thing I had to say. It was like being hit in the ass with a canoe paddle. I'm a very emotional person, so it took some time for me to get over my disappointments. I also knew I had an ace up my sleeve. My report. When it was read it was going to be acted upon. I was sure of that. No one would misunderstand the importance of my message. But I had to wait, had to have patience.

When the exercise ended, Lieutenant Colonel Miley got me off to a corner and said, "When we get back to Bragg I'd like to get you assigned to B Company as my S-3 [operations officer]." I said, "Boss, I'd love to have the job."

★ SEVEN ★

LATE SUMMER OF '63. My report was with Johnny Johnson, who I knew had forwarded it to the new 7th Group commander, Colonel William Evans-Smith.

I'd met Evans-Smith up in the Nantahala National Forest. Just out of the War College, having no real experience in Special Ops, he'd been given command of the exercise. I felt sorry for him. The system had made a mistake, in my view. Colonel Evans-Smith was obviously a fine officer, but he didn't appear to me to have the qualifications to command a Special Ops unit. The day Colonel Evans-Smith arrived at the base site, I was the officer ordered to go out to meet him. After helping him with his luggage, I noticed something different on his uniform. Not wanting to embarrass him, I whispered, "Sir, your Special Forces patch is sewn on upside down."

It didn't surprise me to learn that Colonel Evans-Smith did not understand my SAS After Action Report. He did forward it to General Yarborough, and about two months later I heard from the general. "Thank you very much," was the message. That was all. I was very disappointed to learn that my report had begun its rounds with Maj. Johnny Johnson and Capt. Bud Sydnor recommending disapproval to any consideration of organizing an SAS capability within the U.S. Army Special Forces. My report, which was going to change the world, went nowhere. It just limped around in circles. Some staff people who read it said it sounded good to them. Others said, "Bullshit!"

On weekends I worked on a larger report. I laid out a whole proposed TO&E (Table of Organization and Equipment). I described the mission, the roles, everything. I told Lieutenant Colonel Miley what I was going to do. He smiled and I knew he thought I didn't have the balls to mail it. But I did. I did something an Army officer is not supposed to do. I made a left-end run. I mailed my report to my senator from Georgia, Richard B. Russell.

About three weeks went by before General Yarborough received a telephone call from the Army's legislative liaison people telling him that Senator Russell of Georgia was making inquiries about the void I had pointed out in Special Forces, which an SAS type unit would fill. Never underestimate the cleverness of the Army bureaucracy. General Yarborough, in order to deal with the congressional action, asked the Combat Development people, who worked for him, to study my proposal. Four months later the study was complete. The recommendation to General Yarborough was the same as Johnny Johnson's: that the U.S. Army Special Forces not undertake the development of an SAS capability, that the Special Forces could in fact do the same thing.

I was frustrated; oh, was I frustrated! And I was a vocal young officer. I was still a captain. But I didn't mind saying that I thought we were fucked up, that we didn't do certain things very well. I kept hammering. We were carrying garbage. I shouted until I was hoarse that we were too hung up on being trainers, whereas what we needed was doers. I argued that we were too big. We needed to get smaller. I said these things to my peers, to my bosses. I didn't give a rat's ass who heard me. Frequently I was called in and chastised. But I felt I was qualified to say the things I said. I was always being disappointed by officers with my rank who sounded off in private about how right I was, but in public, in front of the boss, didn't have the balls to say it. They weren't my cut of cloth and we parted company. In some cases, friends became enemies.

I think if there had been any way to get rid of me during this '63–'64 period, Ed Mattice and Mert Kelty, among others, would have pulled every string to do so. But Buzz Miley protected me. Then there was the left-end run to my senator. I spoke my mind. I was a rare bird. So no one really knew what I'd do. They were not afraid of me as a captain, but as Charlie Beckwith I was something else. Some people would say I was like a misguided missile. They were afraid. They were threatened by what I'd seen and what I knew. But I was frustrated and it was getting to me. At the bar, at happy hour, I would intentionally take an officer who I knew didn't have any balls and I'd insult him for his ignorance. He'd go away mumbling, "Beckwith's crazy." I needed somebody to take it out on. I would do that because I'm that kind of person. Yeah, I ain't perfect.

I began to run some unique training exercises in B Company. I sent radio operators home. I'd say, "Go home and play with the baby's momma all you want, but you're going to make four radio contacts a day. If you miss one I'll have you picked up as AWOL." Then I'd give these operators basket leaves, and they'd go home with their radios and wait to receive what was sent. First thing I'd do every morning is have our communications center send, in Morse code, the front page of the *Fayetteville Observer* newspaper. The operators in their homes throughout the country would have to copy it, the whole front page; then they'd have to send it back at a rate of not less than fourteen words a minute. Some said this was harassment, but I knew if I could get an operator to receive and send the front page of a newspaper at good speed, we'd have a pretty good radio operator.

In January '64, Buzz Miley got orders to go to MACV (Military Assistance Command, Vietnam) in Saigon. He was very popular in the 7th Special Forces Group, not because he was easy, but because he was fair. I had been very fortunate to have stumbled into him. I felt that when he left I was going to be in real trouble. He told me, "Charlie, you know, I keep a lot of people off your ass. Some of the people up in headquarters, the old man and Mattice, in particular, don't care for you. You're going to have to watch your p's and q's. I wish there was someone here to watch you, but I don't know of anyone. So, be careful. Be particularly careful of who you trust." I understood that kind of language.

After Buzz left for 'Nam, I was offered, of all things, the job as the 7th Group's operations officer. If I took it, it would mean working up in headquarters and that, as deputy group CO, Ed Mattice would be my boss. Naturally, I hesitated. On the one hand I was scared, I saw a trap. On the other I saw the challenge. Sergeants came to me, and other officers, saying, "Charlie, if ever you're going to get this goddamn show on the road, this is the time. You can influence the direction we need to go in." I said, "No. They're not going to listen to me up there. I know them." "Try!" they said.

Then I remembered something I'd read that Teddy Roosevelt had said: "It is not the critic who counts, not the man who points out how the strong man stumbles, or where the doer of deeds could have done them better. The credit belongs to the man who is actually in the arena . . . who strives . . . who spends himself . . . and who at the worst, if he fails, at least he fails while daring, so that his place shall never be with those cold and timid souls who know neither victory nor defeat."

So I went up to Group Headquarters, and I went to work.

★ EIGHT ★

IT WAS SPRING 1964. I tried to be cautious at first. I knew B company, so I looked at the three others, real slow. Then I welded together a plan which actually was a rehash of part of my SAS paper, the part on training—but with a wrinkle. I took it to Colonel Evans-Smith. I told him I thought the Group was not well trained, that he was failing in his responsibilities, that I was failing in mine if I didn't point this out, and that he ought to look at my proposal, which would enhance the training posture of his Group. I handed it to him, he skimmed the high points, screamed, threw it at me, and ordered me out of his office.

I then perceived that what Charlie Beckwith should do was go find himself a gray flannel suit and a briefcase and an insurance job. I'd just been promoted to major the week before, but now I figured I was finished. I went back up to the office and gathered around me the officers who worked for me and described what had taken place. They, too, thought it was all over. I remember that I got very little accomplished that day. That evening I had a couple of big drinks of bourbon and shared my troubles with Katherine.

I was in the office as usual the next morning around a quarter to six. We did our PT, and Colonel Evans-Smith was out there with us. "I'd like to see you in my office after this formation," he said. I showered quickly and reported to him. Looking at me, he picked up my proposal. "Implement the damn thing. You're right."

I was shocked.

What my proposal did was articulate the principle that before a Special Forces Green Beret soldier could become a good *un*conventional soldier he'd first have to be a good conventional one. He had to understand what a rifle squad was all about, what a rifle platoon was supposed to do, what a rifle company needed to know. To break the rules you need to know what the rules are. You can't be unconventional until you're conventional first. So to get down the road where we'd teach unconventional warfare, we needed to go back to blocking and tackling—the basics. Because I had commanded rifle and weapons companies, I was appalled on arriving in Special Forces to find officers who had never commanded conventional units.

Many people didn't support me. "Beckwith's reinventing the wheel. He thinks he's back in the 82nd Airborne." Evans-Smith understood conventional soldiering. So when I laid out squad-platoon-company attack exercises, or night withdrawals, or delaying actions, he knew what I was talking about.

We ran rifle companies in the attack and we used live ammunition. Sergeants participating in the exercises would come up to me and say, "Sir, this is the best goddamn training we've ever done." I felt great. We went through this conventional period for about three months, restructuring the training of the 7th Special Forces Group. From there we returned to unconventional training.

I got to know almost everyone in the 7th Group by his first name, and I learned what each could or could not do. I knew who the performers were. I knew who the duds were.

About this time Capt. George Chapman from 22 SAS came to Bragg as the exchange officer. George had been in D Squadron, and I knew him to be a switched-on officer. Some strings were pulled and George Chapman was assigned to B Company. It was comforting knowing an SAS officer was on post. Maybe the two of us could fight the battle.

The other officers in the operations office shared my feeling that we should set up an exercise back up in the Pisgah National Forest near Hickory, North Carolina. I got George Chapman over to the house one night. We began to talk about going up to Pisgah and running some skill station training. In this case we'd run a mountain climbing station and a communications station. Additionally, we'd teach everyone sketch-map reading. Then we agreed as a grand finale we'd have an E and E (Evade and Escape) exercise. George and I almost talked in shorthand, because we'd done these things before.

We selected some very sharp officers and noncoms to go with us up to Pisgah; and while we were in the mountains, I received word that Colonel Evans-Smith was being replaced as CO of the 7th Group by Col. Ed Mayer. As soon as Colonel Mayer had settled into his new headquarters, he came up to Pisgah to see what we were up to. One morning he grabbed me. "Charlie, I want to see some more training. Just pick out something you want me to look over and let's go do it."

That was fine. Grabbing two 12-foot sling ropes, I drove him over to Wilson Creek, high over which had been rigged a 1-man cable bridge. "Follow me, Colonel," I said. I whipped on my Swiss seat, tied it around my waist, put the mountaineering snap link in, hooked it onto the cable, and pulled myself the full sixty feet across. I unbuckled and looked back to the other side at Colonel Mayer. He shouted over to me, "Hey, Charlie, come back over here." "Yes, sir." I put my rope back on and slid back across. "Now, let me tell you something," Colonel Mayer said. "The name of the game is to train the soldiers. The name of the game is not to train the group commander, so don't play these kinds of tricks on me." I burst out laughing, "You caught me."

The grandiose final exercise, following the skills training, was an E and E maneuver. We'd gotten the 82nd to burp up a rifle company that was going to act as aggressor and try to round up the Green Berets. We figured if these escaping groups did some real humping they ought to make the final RV in two days, but we also felt we needed to add something else to slow up the exercise and give the Green Berets some problems. So George and I decided we'd make them hit an RV between Blowing Rock and Linville Gorge. There we formed them into 4-man groups and introduced them to footlockers containing sandbags. Of course the men were told they were carrying important equipment. These teams then had to move their footlockers on over to Linville Gorge.

I gotta tell you, when four guys have to get a heavy box from one point to another in a day and a half, going up and down mountains, it causes a lot of problems. We wanted to see how it affected their unity and their fitness. It was a stress test and we wanted to evaluate those men on how well they handled it. Everyone got to the other end. But at the debriefing for this phase of the course, George Chapman and I were highly criticized. The men who participated were tired and very angry. They hadn't liked being put through a physical and mental wringer. Colonel Kelty, whose A Company had gone through the course first, was just livid over the exercise. He felt his men had been mishandled and abused. This kind of criticism didn't bother me a goddamn bit.

Before the exercise ended and I had returned to Fort Bragg, I received orders to report to the U.S. Army's Command and General Staff College at Fort Leavenworth, on a permanent change of station. A few months later, about halfway through the course work at the Staff College, I began to receive letters from Vietnam from noncoms who had gone through the Pisgah exercise. "All the time up there we thought you were crazy. I cussed you at the time, but now I realize what we trained for."

★ NINE ★

NO SURPRISE—I wasn't a good student at the University of Georgia and I wasn't one in Staff College. The course I was in was nine months long and its aim was to teach the officer how to be a staff officer within an infantry or armor division. I wasn't interested in logistics, not at that level, and I wasn't interested in being any kind of a staff officer. I muddled through.

One of the requirements at Leavenworth was to write a term paper. I dug into my trunk, dusted off the old report, brought it up to date, and had Katherine type it for me. I also changed the name: "The Need to Organize in the United States Army—A Special Operations Force." I figured I should stop beating the name Special Air Service to death, so I gave the unit a shiny new name. There were two grades given on this paper. One was for the concept, the other was how well you could verbalize your argument, and this grade had nothing to do with the concept. I got a good grade in public speaking, but only an average mark on my paper. The Army still wasn't listening.

I learned more, actually, from my peers than I did from the faculty. I sat next to an old boy who knew a lot about artillery. I used to ask him questions. Then I talked to several armor officers about tanks and how they should be used. I learned a lot but finished near the bottom of my class.

The biggest thing in Kansas—it worried everyone—was where we were going to go when we got out of school. I volunteered for Vietnam. I was afraid the war would be over before I got there.

The Personnel Assignment folks from Washington came out and spent a couple of days talking to us about our new assignments. I had orders to go to Vietnam all right, but I was going as a sector advisor, which meant I was being assigned to a village where I would work with the local Vietnamese people. I thought I was better than that and told them, "With all this Special Operations experience I have, there's gotta be a place for me. I know there's a Special Forces Group in 'Nam." I was angry, mad. Again.

I immediately sat down and wrote some letters. One of them went to Irwin Jacobs, a close friend who was then adjutant of the 5th Special Forces Group in South Vietnam. "Here is a copy of my orders. I'm being assigned as a sector advisor and, damn it, I want to go to the 5th Group. If there's going to be a Special Forces Group in Vietnam, then Charlie Beckwith is going to be a member of it."

Time went by. I got a letter back from Irwin, "There's a good chance your orders will be changed." Three weeks before graduation from Staff College I received a call from Washington telling me I was going to Nha Trang, where the 5th Special Forces Group had its base. It was like coming back from England all over again. I kept telling myself, I gotta get over to Vietnam. They need me over there. I'd been shot at in Laos while on duty there in 1960, but I hadn't really come to grips with a WAR. I was hungry. The whole Army was lying at my feet.

Irwin Jacobs met me in Nha Trang at the end of June 1965. Earlier in the week. I'd gotten Katherine and the girls settled in Birmingham, Michigan, near her parents. I'd cut my leave short. I'd had a whole year in Fort Leavenworth with my family. I figured if I was dumb enough to get to 'Nam early, the Army would be dumb enough to get me in sooner. I was in a hurry to get my whistle wet.

Irwin took me in to meet Col. Bill McKean, the CO of the 5th Special Forces Group. Like Evans-Smith, he'd never been in Special Forces, not one day. In spite of having a face that looked liked a clenched fist, McKean, I was to learn, had a heart big enough to fill a bucket. Colonel McKean told me they were going to give me the DELTA Project, Detachment B-52. "Yes, that's fine. Yes, sir." I didn't know what Detachment B-52 was, nor did I know what the DELTA Project was.

Irwin had briefed me from the airport to the colonel's office: "I've been politicking to get this for you. It's the best job in the Special Forces. But these guys need some help and the Group needs help." I heard I was taking my command over on Monday. I decided to spend the weekend around the Special Forces Headquarters, sort of looking things over. I ran a few miles up and down the beach, which was quite beautiful, swam back and forth, making sure I still had my perk there. Then I went back to headquarters, drew my gear, test-fired my weapon, and saw some old friends. That killed Saturday.

Sunday I got up and looked around. Nobody was about. A few officers but not many were in camp. I went over to Group Headquarters. "Anybody here?" I shouted. McKean, who had only been in country one week longer than I, spoke up from back in his office, "Yeah, I'm here. What the hell's going on out here?" "I'm not sure," I said, "but I don't think there's anybody here except you and me."

Through the discussions I'd had the night before, I got the impression that there was a lot of shacking up downtown; a lot of people were getting their ashes hauled by the Vietnamese gals.

"Colonel," I said, "I suspect most of the headquarters' personnel are down in Nha Trang proper. Let's get a jeep and ride in." This was about 1300 hours. We drove in the town and saw all kinds of things. We saw officers who'd been living down there all weekend. We were waved at out of windows by some of the officers, gals under their arms. I said, "What kind of goddamn war are we fighting over here?" "I don't know," he said, "but it ain't gonna be like this no more. On Monday I intend to stop all this bullshit cold. We're gonna start manning the store."

I began to think more of Col. Bill McKean. He thought, as I did, that we should be in the compound, not shacking up or soaking up rays on the beach or being fitted out by the local tailors for new rags. I figured we went to Vietnam to kill the enemy. What I saw was a lot of guys going native. "Hell," I thought, "this ain't no way to run a railroad."

On Monday morning I went looking for my new command. I found them down by the beach. They were living in Nha Trang at the Jockey Club, which looked to me like a small, dirty hotel. There were girl bartenders and the usual number of whores hanging around. Some guys were obviously living here. I got hold of the senior sergeant, named Dougherty. He didn't know me and I didn't know him. I asked him if he would assemble all my people back at the compound, because I wanted to speak to them. He was a little put out and suggested we do it right there over a couple of drinks and that afterward, if I wanted, he'd arrange to procure some companionship for me. I made it very clear to him that I didn't come to Vietnam to go to bed. I'd come to get on with the war. I knew right then I was going to fire Sergeant Dougherty as soon as he got to the compound.

A short time later all thirty members of the DELTA Project, Detachment B-52, stood in front of me. Sergeant Dougherty began our meeting by explaining to me the economics of the Jockey Club. "When we're off on an operation, sir, other people move in, but we get to keep the profits."

I became livid. "You don't understand. You're not over here to make money. You're here to kill the enemy!" I told them that the Jockey Club was off limits and they would be living from now on in the 5th Special Forces Group compound. "And," I added, "if you fucking well don't like it you can pack your bags and go somewhere else."

Dougherty spoke up, "I think this is the wrong thing to do." I said, "Sergeant Dougherty, you have been here too long, and you are to be the first one to get your hat and go." Most of his entourage decided they would go with him. Then their mistake became apparent. There really wasn't anywhere else to go except to some godforsaken Special Forces camp way out in the boondocks. That afternoon Project DELTA went from a force of thirty to a force of seven.

Major Charlie "Tommy" Thompson, my second in command, gave me some advice about some of the men who had chosen to leave. "Major, you might look at this one twice. He's good. We should keep him." I said, "You go get those that you think we should keep. I'm going to lay the axe on the rest of them."

For what I had in mind, this was just the beginning. I went over to see Colonel McKean and told him what I'd done, but I added, "I can't expect my men to live in the mud out here in the compound. I want your permission to build a camp here. I want it to be nice. I'm gonna spend some money." The tents the men were expected to live in were in poor shape, with no floors; in the monsoon season the mud was knee deep. No question, the living conditions had been better down at the Jockey Club.

That night I really got sparked. I wrote a little flyer. It said, "WANTED: Volunteers for Project DELTA. Will guarantee you a medal, a body bag, or both." I took it to Irwin Jacobs. "Shit, this is good, Charlie. You'll rally a lot of people around you with this. The best will come." I listed the qualifications the man had to have for him to see me. He had to volunteer; he had to be in country at least six months; he had to have a CIB (Combat Infantryman's Badge); and he had to be a sergeant—otherwise, don't even come talk to me.

McKean said, "You won't get a swinging dick. But go ahead, what have you got to lose?" I stuffed fifteen or twenty flyers into each of the mail sacks that went out to the ninety or so detachments of Green Berets spread all over the country. The next week my problem was turning people away. I was inundated with replies. Commanders in the field screamed, "My best guys are trying to get to go to work for Beckwith in Delta." Damn, they howled. I would have, too. Their best men were leaving.

This was my first real opportunity to test the SAS concept. I began by assessing this huge group of volunteers and trying to select the right men. There was a good-size island across the channel from Nha Trang. I knew it was a tough sonovabitch, because I'd already walked all over it looking for a place to do IADs (Immediate Action Drills). I sent an E-6 by the name of Walter Shumate there to set up a mini-selection course that we could run the volunteers over. When we got them there we made them move from one point to another, fast. No high trees, but tough scrub country, very difficult terrain. And they had the heat leaning on them, because there was no canopy keeping the sun out. Many collapsed from exhaustion. Then we learned if they could read a map. The third test was when they fired their rifles; could they hit what they fired at? The last thing was whether they could follow concise, clear orders. It was that simple.

Those who busted out were sent back to their original detachments with a nice letter. Those who didn't bust out I looked at again. I didn't do much psychological testing, because I didn't have the time. I needed people. Certainly DELTA got some duds, but I was in a hurry. I began to build from the original seven men and within three weeks had twenty-five. Then I went up to forty. I organized them into 4-man patrols. Didn't call them Troops. Called them Recon Teams.

The mission of Project DELTA was to conduct with the Vietnamese Special Forces (LLDB) long-range reconnaissances inside South Vietnam. We were tasked to go ahead of large operations—division or two-brigade size operations—and test the water. We were to go in a week or ten days before and look the country over. If we were discovered and got into a heavy firefight, we'd know we were in a hot area. Then, it was up to MACV in Saigon to decide what the big operation did. DELTA also did bomb damage assessment, hunter-killer missions, and special-purpose raids. Our job was hairy. A guy could get killed.

In addition, Project DELTA had the job of working with four companies from the 91st South Vietnamese Airborne Ranger Battalion. The recon elements were to go out and if they found an enemy target of opportunity, they'd call back and we could slam in the Rangers. The concept looked good, but the Vietnamese didn't belong to me. They belonged to General Quang who was based down in Nha Trang City.

I also had to supply American advisors to Vietnamese patrols and this was a hard role. I learned Charlie Beckwith made a very poor advisor. My Vietnamese counterpart in the LLDB was Major Tut, a nice guy I felt sorry for. I must have been the third or fourth guy he had to put up with. I tried to be as prudent as I could. This Vietnamese special forces unit had lots of equipment, lots of money, and the troops looked smart. On paper things looked good. But I didn't know what they could do in a crunch.

About the last of July in 1965—I'd been in country a month—we were asked to go up and do a small operation southwest of Pleiku, around the Special Forces camp at Duc Co. This was Indian country. Bad. We were supposed to put teams on the ground and report enemy sightings back to II Corps. Col. Ted Mataxis was the senior American advisor there, but Maj. Gen. Vinh Loc was the ARVN (Army of the Republic of Vietnam) commander in the area. Although the war at this time was still a Vietnamese show, the Americans were beginning to elbow themselves onto center stage.

The first mission I went out on was run by the Vietnamese. Although ostensibly I was only going to tag along, I had been warned that once on the ground, if we Americans didn't take control we would all be in trouble. The recon team I went in with included three Vietnamese and Sergeant Weber. Major Thompson was a little uneasy about this. I said, "You don't need me sitting back here. Hell, you run this show. I need to know what's going on in the field. I gotta see how the Vietnamese operate."

We boarded Sikorsky H-34 helicopters, and I thought I'd shit. There was a leak somewhere and oil was all over the floor. I thought we'd crash for sure. But somehow they always managed to fly. This was when I was first introduced to the Vietnamese helicopter pilots. They were some of the bravest men I'd ever met. They were handpicked, the cream of the Vietnamese Air Force, and they were the finest pilots in the country. In my view, there wasn't an American pilot who could wipe their asses and take the risks these little guys took.

Our senior Vietnamese pilot was named Khoi. We trusted

him. If he said he'd put you down somewhere, you could be sure it was exactly where you should be. On operations like those we were running, to be put down in the wrong place would have meant disaster. When Khoi went back to camp after inserting us, I'm sure he walked into Major Thompson's office, picked up a colored pin, put it in the map, and said, "Here is where I inserted Major Beckwith." That was reassuring.

We were put in late in the afternoon. On the ground we ran as quickly as we could away from the LZ (landing zone). Intelligence indicated the area was pretty saturated with the VC, the Viet Cong.

The job was to look at two large trail complexes coming out of the Tri-Border area and hitting Route 19. When we were about four kilometers away from one of the junctions, we decided to stop. There were mountains to the west, but where we stood it was hilly. We spent the night in a thicket. I thought the Vietnamese made a good choice. We sat there all night. I didn't sleep a damn wink. You couldn't have drilled a flaxseed up my ass with a sledgehammer. I was scared.

Before first light, sixty or seventy yards out in front of the thicket, I spotted the biggest pussycat I have ever seen. I'd seen a tiger before in Malaya, but just for a flash. This one, which was as pretty as a picture, I watched for what seemed an hour. He didn't pay any attention to me, but I tracked him over the sight of my rifle. I wasn't going to shoot it, because the shot would have told the enemy where we were, and, besides, what was I going to do with a tiger? I felt good about seeing it. If that big old cat could come through there, obviously ain't nobody else around.

We moved out a short time later. I heard Thompson buzzing near us in a single-engine Otter (U-1). He called, "One Zero Foxtail, this is Big Bear. Do you read?" Quickly we snapped the talk button on our HT-1 three times, click, click, click. "I have authenticated your position," he said. "You're on course." We moved carefully, slowly. Around noon we hit the first trail. There was nothing moving, but looking at the ground we could tell there had been a lot of activity in the area.

The Vietnamese lieutenant in charge said we should break up in a circle and observe the trail from hidden positions. This was a good little drill I'd learned in Malaya. I climbed into a large bamboo brake adjacent to the trail. I figured, shit, ain't nobody going to see me in here. I felt I could even smoke. I had just settled down for a long quiet wait, pulled out some rations, added a little curry powder to my plastic bag of rice, when all of a sudden, directly over my head, I heard an ear-shattering scream. I nearly pissed all over myself. An enormous black gibbon ape swung down and looked me straight in the face. He scared the living daylights out of me. My heart just pounded. I was told I didn't scream. Weber, who was in another part of the thicket, said he heard the gibbon but didn't hear me. It happened so quickly. My heart returned to my chest, and I caught my breath. I don't remember whether I enjoyed my lunch or not.

We watched the track until the middle of the afternoon, then decided to move along to spend the night in a location that was very close to the second trail. We found another good spot to spend the night. Suddenly, I felt all worn out. I was at the point where I really didn't care whether the VC walked up on me or not. I'd been under a lot of stress because I wanted to do well. Weber watched me. He said, "Did you get any sleep last night?" I told him I hadn't and asked him if he'd take the first watch. That was O.K. with him.

About 0400 Weber woke me up. "Boss, I can't keep my eyes open any longer." "Go ahead and sack out," I said. "I won't get you up till 0730. We'll leave late. Screw it." The rest of the night I fought big black ants. They nearly ate us alive. Big old black ones able to bite your ass off. Eventually the sun came up and scattered the clouds to the horizon. Shortly afterward we left the hiding place.

Around 1300 hours we came up on the second trail. No one ate lunch that day. Walking in the morning, Weber and I made up an E and E plan in case something happened. I wasn't impressed with the Vietnamese as we proceeded. They weren't too slow for me, just nonchalant. When we got to the trail, the Vietnamese weren't keen on following the footprints we found. I felt we needed to find out where these prints entered the trail and where they left it. They didn't like that idea, so Weber and I ended up doing it ourselves.

The second night was spent uneventfully. We got up early the next morning. Thompson came up on the radio. We passed our intel to him very quickly. We had accomplished what we'd set out to do, and everything was quiet. Tommy told us to find an LZ, and that afternoon they'd come in with a chopper and extract us. That is when you really become vulnerable, because you get antsypants wanting to get out. When the Vietnamese learned we were leaving to go home—man, you could see them perk up. Things got even more lax. The Vietnamese began to want to walk too fast, to take shortcuts, to move through some open areas.

Weber chastised the little lieutenant: "We ain't going through here that way. We're going to bend way around here; we're going to take the long way."

"Not necessary. Nothing here."

Well, you never knew.

We found a helicopter landing zone around 1530. The Vietnamese swept the area, looking, listening. Then it began to rain like hell. That didn't stop us. Weber and I did most of the chopping. Nothing fancy, just a platform an H-34 could land on. The rain quit suddenly. Everything I had was wringing wet, but I didn't care, because I wanted to get out of there. By 1630 we were ready. I heard a chopper way off. We gave him our location. Didn't even have to pop any smoke, we just put up a mirror that he caught. Came straight down, picked us up and took us out.

In Vietnam I began to learn the art of compromise. One of my biggest concerns was trying to get a handle on what the Vietnamese were doing. Bill McKean—his radio call sign was Bulldog—was just like that name implies. He was always biting everybody in the ass. Particularly the Vietnamese. He was anxious to get them off their asses and moving. He wanted to kill some bad guys, and he wanted to look good. Sometimes people don't need to be bitten in the ass, just for the sake of biting somebody. I felt that way. And particularly the Vietnamese, because in my opinion McKean didn't try to understand them. He'd just walk down and tell General Quang, who was the overall commander of the Vietnamese Special Forces, "This is what I want done!" You don't do that with Orientals. You've gotta gradually get their confidence, bring them around slowly. There has to be some compromise.

I had a real concern. I wanted to be able to use those Vietnamese Ranger companies without going through General Quang. Thompson explained to me. "We can usually get one company without any strings being attached. Two is like pulling teeth, and we ain't never going to get three." I said, "It has to be arranged so we can get two." I liked a good-sized force. Shit; get in trouble out there, you want some help. I started thinking about my counterpart, Major Tut. I tried to put myself in his shoes. Would I go fight my boss for something the other guy wants that doesn't mean anything to me? Probably not. Thompson had an idea. He said, "Captain Kong, Tut's operations officer and my counterpart, is the smart one. Why don't we try to manipulate him to manipulate Tut?" Kong, I knew, was sharp.

Thompson and I, one evening, took Kong to dinner at Francois, which was the fanciest restaurant in Nha Trang. You could get a huge lobster for a dollar and a half and a bottle of Algerian wine for fifty cents. We talked to Kong about a number of things, then, "—Oh, by the way, how about the use of these Ranger companies?" I said, "We got four companies here. I want to be able to commit two, and the compromise will be on three." I knew I'd never get four anyway.

Captain Kong, who enjoyed the dinner, politicked with Major Tut, and Tut worked on General Quang.

★ TEN ★

NO MATTER HOW badly October ended, it certainly began innocently enough. You might even say it began auspiciously.

In the middle of the month I was asked to go to a place called Phu Cat, which is up above Qui Nhon in Northern II Corps. DELTA was to run a recon operation in order to find out how many bad guys there were in the area. This was a very important mission, because we'd just gotten permission to take along two Vietnamese Ranger companies.

In October the weather was bad in Northern II Corps: fog that hovers in the hot air, then lots of rain and low-hanging clouds. All this makes it tougher to get a recon team out if it runs into trouble. Then Lt. Col. John Bennett, who was the group deputy, came up to see us. As the road was normally closed from Qui Nhon to Phu Cat I recommended that he parachute into our location. I did that really hoping he wouldn't, but the bloody man did. He looked over our operation and wasn't at all impressed. He felt we were wasting a lot of time for the little we had discovered. John Bennett wasn't really interested in recon operations. What John Bennett was interested in was body counts. He couldn't see any advantage in just going out and looking at the VC without shooting them. I wasn't interested in running out, getting into a firefight, then returning to a big "attaboy" for ten VC killed. I never was one for trying to kill more than anyone else. My mission was to find the enemy and report that to the big boys, but I understood Bennett's point of view.

The next morning, Tuesday, October 19th, a helicopter came in and picked up Colonel Bennett. Later in that same day, toward dusk, I got a call on the radio informing me that the Special Forces camp at Plei Me was under heavy attack and that I should get my force to Pleiku as quickly as possible.

Plei Me, in October 1965, was defended by 400 Montagnard tribesmen with their families. Also, there was an "A" Detachment of twelve Green Berets, and an equal number of Vietnamese. The compound, perched precariously along National Route 6C, twenty-five miles southwest of Pleiku, was one of several civilian camps that kept tabs on enemy movement in the western highlands. There were about ninety similar camps spread throughout the country. The concept was a good one. The camps gave protection to the villagers in the area, prevented the VC from recruiting them, and helped to establish an American presence in the region.

Attacking just before last light on the 19th, the enemy surrounded Plei Me, and it appeared that rather than hitting and running they were there to slug it out toe to toe with whatever the South Vietnamese and Americans could throw at them.

On the morning of the 20th—after the fog had burned off, Project DELTA's four recon teams on the ground were extracted from the Phu Cat area. I selected fifteen Americans who had not been deployed earlier to go with me, and they, along with the two South Vietnamese Ranger companies, were shuttled back to Qui Nhon. On the airfield tarmac there were parked a C-130 and a C-123. The two planes were already heavily loaded with equipment, and I was worried about getting our 175 men on board. I pointed out that at Fort Bragg we felt we could only load so many men on an aircraft before it got dangerous. The Air Force types reassured me they could handle anything. We were not to worry. I did. We loaded up; people were packed in and standing on top of each other. The two aircraft somehow got airborne and in about thirty minutes arrived at Pleiku.

I was met by Colonel Bennett and Bill Patch, a lieutenant colonel who commanded the American Special Forces advisors in the II Corps area. The two men quickly explained the situation—that Plei Me had been attacked by an unusually large Communist force and was now under siege, that heavy casualties had been sustained by both sides, and that it was important for me to get my force into the camp and give the defenders some help.

Colonel Bennett thought the best way for us to get on with it was to parachute into Plei Me right before last light—that evening! John was the sort of fellow who pushed you along. Hey, man, I said to myself, this ain't the way to go. I couldn't see hanging from a parachute and being shot at by the Communists as I floated into that little old camp. I thought other courses of action were open to us.

Bennett kept saying, "It's going to be all right. Charlie, we've thought about this." I said, "Yeah, but I haven't." I was very happy, therefore, when the senior American military advisor in the region, Col. Ted Mataxis, who was listening to our conversation, turned to Bennett and said, "There'll be no parachute operation this evening. In fact, there won't be one at all."

That Wednesday evening things really got going. Colonel McKean flew in.

The obvious way to get into Plei Me was to conduct an airmobile operation. In other words, we should be put down by helicopter as close to the camp as possible, then fight our way in. The problem was that an operation was planned elsewhere in II Corps and the helicopters we needed had already been committed. McKean and Mataxis really went around the axle on that one and had one hell of an argument. Colonel McKean said, "What if the weather is bad, Ted, and these choppers can't get to the other operation's staging area?" Mataxis said. "Then, Bill, the helicopters would be made available to you." "Then, goddamn it," McKean said, "the weather's bad!"

The other operation was finally canceled when Plei Me became the region's number one priority, and the helicopters were made available to us.

I worked all night, studying maps, looking for LZs, determining routes. My bones told me this was not going to be any piece of cake. I talked to the Air Force forward air controllers who had been flying over the camp. There was a lot of our enemy down there. This was going to be an operation where a lot of our people would get hurt.

Bill McKean and I, the next morning, flew near the camp trying to find an LZ. The trick was finding one not so close to the camp that it gave our position away to the enemy, and not so far away that we would wear ourselves out working our way to the camp. As we were flying around looking at the proposed LZ the Hog (helicopter gunship) that was escorting us threw one of its rotor blades, crashed, and exploded in the jungle. A bad omen.

The two Vietnamese Ranger companies and fifteen American Green Berets from Project DELTA climbed into the helicopters at Camp Holloway and took off, flying south toward Plei Me. After the LZ had been prepped with two air strikes flown by bombers and gunships, we landed about 0900 of the 21st. The day was another hot one. Major Tut, who commanded the Ranger companies, and I agreed we'd go along very slowly, carefully. I didn't think we should sacrifice speed for security. The elephant grass we were moving through was shoulder high. In some areas, where the foliage was particularly heavy, we had to crawl on our hands and knees.

Around noon we crept up to a small Vietnamese village. We learned it was deserted, but that villagers had been there no more than eight to ten hours before. The cooking fires were still smouldering. Somebody had come through there and taken these people with them. This bothered the Vietnamese. I didn't give it much thought since it was only a matter of time before we hit something. About then Colonel Bennett, who was flying in a Bird Dog (0-1), one of those small forward control aircraft, came up on the radio. He first asked me to mark my position with smoke. I refused. Then he tied into me. "Major, you're moving too slow. You won't get there in a week the way you're going." I answered him respectfully, but thought, That's nice, but why don't you go to your room, boy, and let me get on with this operation. You're not on the ground, and you have no idea what we're trying to negotiate.

We continued to move through the jungle in single file. The column stretched out. Toward the middle of the afternoon I heard two shots up ahead of me. I ran forward and found one of my guys had shot an enemy soldier wearing a pith helmet and a khaki uniform. He'd been carrying a box of 75mm recoilless rifle ammunition. Another enemy soldier with him had managed to escape in the dense undergrowth. Major Tut came up and went through the dead guy's uniform looking for papers. Tut was getting nervous. He told me that this man was not a VC, but rather from a regular North Vietnamese unit. Our people had suspected the NVA had regular units in the south at this time, but this was the first time anyone had actual proof of it. The next time one of the communications planes flew over I got on the air and passed the news along.

Major Tut then came over and informed me he and the Ranger companies were going to turn back. This was as far as they were going to go. I told him my mission was to get into Plei Me, and I intended to do so with or without him. I preferred to do it with him, but I didn't really give a shit one way or another. I intended to reinforce the camp. Tut said that when we shot the NVA soldier it had become a new ball game. I didn't have enough sense to be frightened. Probably, I should have. It was getting late now so I didn't argue with him very long.

I called together the fifteen Americans and told them what had happened, and that I intended to push on. I told Major Thompson and my two sergeant majors we would lead the relief force.

I had with me the Group's sergant major, Bill McKean's right arm, John Pioletti. Sergeant Major Pioletti had convinced McKean to let him go. I had mixed feelings about this. I knew if anything happened to John, McKean would string me up alive; but I also knew that if I needed support McKean would not leave me and his sergeant major dangling out there. On top of it, Sergeant Pioletti was a first-class guy. I trusted my life with my own sergeant major, Bill DeSoto. I was glad he was along for the ride.

I also had with me a new operations officer. Tommy

Thompson was to go home in two weeks, and Major A. J. Baker had just arrived in country. He was a great big boy we called Bo who had played football at the University of Arkansas. He had arrived in Nha Trang on the 19th and on the 21st he was with us in the jungle outside of Plei Me. What a way to get his whistle wet! I asked him to bring up the rear of our small column. We moved out.

At approximately 2000 hours we were close enough to the camp to hear the shooting. I got the camp on the radio and they came in clearly. Someone said to me, "Come on in and join the party." That made me angry. I knew people were dead and more were dying, and I didn't perceive this to be a goddamn party. I had also decided not to go into the camp that night. My sixth sense told me if I attempted to enter the camp, those inside might take us for the enemy; and if anyone on the perimeter was trigger-happy, it would end badly. I radioed back to Pleiku and informed Bill McKean that I would enter the camp at dawn. Bill DeSoto and I did a quick recon of the unimproved single-lane dirt road we'd been moving parallel to, which ran into the camp. When we returned to the column, Bo Baker ran up and said, "Major, Tut's back." I followed him—there were the two Ranger companies. Tut said words to the effect that he would have lost face if he'd left me.

We went on half-alert that night, that's half the force awake and half asleep. I slept for three hours and was awakened on the 22nd before the sun came up. After Bill DeSoto got the column up we eased on about 300 yards to our left flank and began to slowly go down the side of the road. We hit a ridge above the camp, maybe 800 yards out, and from there I could look down into the NVA positions. I noticed a position the Communists had set up to ambush any relief columns that tried to enter the camp. For some reason it was unoccupied. I was damn glad. I told my guys and Major Tut it would take us too long to reach the camp continuing through the jungle. "My plan is to veer off to the east, hit the road just as it goes over the hill, then run like hell to the camp gates."

We evidently caught the enemy by surprise. Once on the road we dashed for the camp and took some light fire. A Vietnamese lieutenant was killed. So, too, was a newspaper photographer who, without permission, had gotten on one of the choppers back in Pleiku and had come with us. He had long blond hair. The bullet took him through the side of the face. Four or five others received minor wounds. Within a half hour everyone was in the camp. The first thing I noticed on going through the gate was the Montagnard tribesmen who had been killed while defending the camp; they were still lying in the wire. I mean everywhere. Dead people. Oh, shit, I thought, there's going to be a lack of discipline in here. If they can't pick up that kind of thing then, man, there's some problems in here. I was right. There were about sixty other dead Montagnard soldiers stuffed into body bags and stacked up like cordwood. The smell was terrible.

The Special Forces captain in charge of the camp was Harold Moore. I let him know quickly that I was the new mayor of Plei Me. Shaped like an equilateral triangle, the camp sat in a slight bowl and was surrounded by barbed wire. There was a trench system that ran throughout the inside of the camp. About ten wooden buildings with corrugated metal roofs made up the interior. The outside of the camp was usually occupied by the Montagnard soldiers' families. Needless to say, under siege the families were now all inside. The camp was crowded and it was dirty. A thick red dust covered everything. It was in turmoil. The Vietnamese camp commander, Captain Moore's counterpart, stayed in his deep bunker. I never saw him once the whole time I was there. Outside the barbed wire there were a hell of a lot of Communists.

I called Pleiku and explained to them that we should fortify the camp first, to make sure we could hold it, and then find out how many of the enemy we were facing. We shouldn't do anything until we knew for sure. Bill McKean did not agree with me. He said, "I want you to get outside the camp, rummage around, clear the enemy out of there. Then, obviously, if you do that you can hold the camp."

I said, "Sir, that's not a good idea."

He said, "Well, Major, I'm ordering you."

In the afternoon we mounted up both Ranger companies.

Captain Thomas Pusser, a West Pointer I thought a lot of, was the advisor to the Vietnamese Rangers. I got him and the other American advisors who were going out on the sweep operation together. "I want you all to be very careful out there. Don't take any chances you don't have to take." Then Pusser and I discussed the two Vietnamese companies. The leadership of one of them was stronger than the other. I suggested to Tom he go with the stronger unit. He felt because he could kick ass and get it moving he should go with the weaker one. I finally agreed with him. He went out with the weak company. I shouldn't have let him do that.

The plan was to begin to clear the northern slope area from which most of the heaviest fire was coming. The NVA waited for both companies to get outside the gate. Then they came out of their holes and hit us with everything they had. About fourteen men were killed, including Tom Pusser. Many more were wounded. I felt fortunate to get any of those Rangers back inside the camp. They had been very badly mauled. I immediately got on the radio, and got Bulldog to agree that we should fortify the camp. I then asked for an air drop of a couple hundred 5-gallon water cans, since we were running out of water, and a basic load of ammunition. I didn't know how much we had, but I wanted to make damn sure we had enough. I also asked for a couple of boxes of cigars, some cigarettes, and a case of whiskey. "I don't care what it is, anything assorted." This got McKean a little bent out of shape. Then I asked to have a chopper come in and get our dead. I felt that many dead were bad on morale. Reportedly, McKean asked for volunteers in Pleiku to fly in to us, but no American chopper pilot stepped forward.

The first Air Force resupply drop, in order to avoid the enemy .51-caliber machine guns that ringed the camp, flew too high and dumped most of its ammunition outside the wire. The second drop landed in the camp. It was all ammo. The third drop contained water, cigars, and the other things I'd ordered. It, too, landed on top of us.

Late in the afternoon of this first day, after the Ranger companies got back and we licked our wounds and took our resupply drops, I got together with Tommy Thompson, Bo Baker, Bill DeSoto, and John Pioletti. We were all beginning to realize that we would be damn fortunate to get out of this camp alive. We were receiving a lot of 81mm mortar and 75mm recoilless rifle fire. I was very concerned that we hold that first night. I had our people go out to all the crews manning the machine guns to make sure they knew what their instructions were. I didn't want them picking up and running away scared. That night I thought we were going to get hit. We took heavy mortar and recoilless rifle fire all night long, but were not probed.

The next day we began to strengthen the camp's fortifications. The mortar and recoilless rifle fire fell in spurts. Occasionally a lone enemy soldier would jump out of a hole and rush the wire throwing hand grenades. Around 1030 hours Bill DeSoto got hit. One of those heavy machine gun slugs nearly tore his arm off.

From the intensity of the fire Plei Me was absorbing, I made an estimate of the enemy force besieging us. When I reported I thought there were at least two, maybe three, large forces of regimental size surrounding the camp, I got some people in Pleiku really shook up. After that I got priority on all air strikes. I don't deserve credit for the damage those strikes did to the enemy. My deputy, Major Thompson, organized and directed the strikes. Air Force fighters and naval aircraft flying from the carriers off Yankee Station pounded the jungle around us. They hit the enemy with napalm and 250- and 500-pounders all day long. We learned later we were surrounded by two regular North Vietnamese infantry regiments, the 32nd and 33rd.

That night I received a telegram by radio from President Johnson. It said something like, "We're thinking about you. Hold out there as long as you can. God bless you all."

The nights were worse, far worse, than the days. Ropes of green and orange tracers flew into and out of the camp. Overhead, circling C-46 Flareships kept the area illuminated. Multicolored parachutes, which had been used to resupply us, were strewn here and there and gave the camp a raffish appearance.

The pounding intensified. Mortars and recoilless rifles fired relentlessly. Amazingly, during these terrible nighttime hours the camp rats, oblivious to the havoc they were a part of, continued to come out and run over the ruins just as if everyone was asleep.

Bombers came over again on October 24th and began to eat up the NVA. I'd say our side flew seventy-five to one hundred sorties a day. We just walked these air strikes all around the outside of the camp. We used a lot of air, and we broke the enemy's back with it. Many of the strikes were so close to the wire we took shrapnel in the camp. One particular string of bombs hit very close. Major Thompson, who was calling in the strikes, kept hollering, "I like it! I like it!" Captain Moore had wanted to take a photograph of one of these strikes. I tried to warn him to keep his head down. A piece of shrapnel from one of the hard bombs ripped half his shoulder off.

During the daytime, between the air strikes. I tried to sleep. Besides the newspaper photographer who was killed during our run for the camp, I had two other unauthorized newspaper people with me in the camp. We taught them how to shoot a .30-caliber machine gun and gave them one to man in the south corner of the perimeter. They did a first class job for us.

The situation on the third day: We were putting in a lot of air strikes and I wasn't sure what was going to happen next. We learned by radio that a South Vietnamese armored column trying to reach us had been pinned down and stopped cold by an enemy ambush.

Sometime, I'm not sure when, Khoi, the Vietnamese helicopter pilot I thought so much of, flew into the camp. I told him he was crazy, and he should fly his ass out of there. "You know, Boss," he spoke perfect English, "your problem is you worry too much." He loaded up a lot of dead. We had problems keeping the Montagnards off. They wanted to get out too. Khoi made two flights in and out. He took fire the first time but not the second. His luck held that day. Sometime later, though, he was killed in Military Region I when his chopper crashed into a mountain in bad weather.

With the napalm and bombs doing their work, the NVA

began to relax their hold on us. The mortar barrages fell off, so did the small arms and machine gun fire. It got so that even a couple of Huey slicks (small troop-carrying helicopters) flew in. We were then able to get a lot of the kids and women out. We also began flying out our dead. Some of the dead had been lying in the jungle heat for six days. They were ripe. I know that John Pioletti, while loading one of the choppers, was throwing up over the body bags.

There was another problem that worried me. The first day in Plei Me, Captain Pusser had been killed with the Ranger companies outside the wire; in the melee that followed, they hadn't brought his body back. I knew I had to recover his body. We mounted an operation. It was on either day four or five. I asked for volunteers. "The Vietnamese," Major Tut told me, "will get his body for you. We want to do this." Some Vietnamese went out and brought Captain Pusser's body back. He could only be identified by his dog tag. The heat had distorted his body terribly. It was a damn shame.

We received word by radio on Monday, the 25th, that the relief force of tanks, armored personnel carriers, and troops was on the move again. A slick arrived and left a forward observer in the camp who would help direct artillery fire down the road, walking it just in front of the slow, chugging armored column. As the sun went down the first tanks finally clanked into view and took up a defensive position around the camp's perimeter.

The following morning the 2nd Battalion, 1st Brigade, from the 1st Cavalry Division (Airmobile) was helicoptered into Plei Me. I was asked by their liaison officer where I would recommend he put his unit. I selected an appropriate area for the Cav to land in. Around and beyond the north slope there were a lot of dead enemy soldiers and the stench was terrible. Landing there would be an instructive introduction for the 1st Cav, which had only arrived in country a short time before. No better way to let them know war is hell. After the battalion landed, because his people were throwing up all over themselves, their CO asked if they could move somewhere else.

Before I left I walked around the outside perimeter of Plei

Me. The ground was pitted by bomb craters and blackened as far as I could see by napalm. There were also a lot of dead out there. In one case I noticed two enemy soldiers who were actually chained to their machine guns. It was later estimated there were 800 or 900 dead North Vietnamese regulars in front of the camp. I don't know the exact number and I didn't run around counting them. Eventually a bulldozer came in and just covered everything up.

★ ELEVEN ★

WHEN I GOT back to Pleiku. I had some people to thank. I personally expressed my appreciation to the Air Force forward air controllers. Then I found the senior Air Force office at Pleiku and told him if it weren't for his people obtaining and directing the air sorties I wouldn't be there talking to him. Then I went to bed.

About midnight, Lt. Col. John A. Hemphill, the assistant operations officer of the 1st Cav, knocked on my door, "Charlie, they want to see you at the command post. The Cav's ADC [assistant division commander] wants to talk to you." When I got to the command trailer I was introduced to Brig. Gen. Richard Knowles, a great big tall fella. He had a problem. The 1st Cav was going to stage out of Plei Me and go on westward into the Ia Drang River Valley to find, fix, and defeat the NVA regiments that had just withdrawn. Lt. Col. John Stockton, who commanded the division's recon squadron, had asked to have a rifle company from Harlow Clark's 1st Brigade assigned to him to guard his parked helicopters. When Stockton ran into trouble near Duc Co, at a place called LZ Mary, he deployed this company in a combat operation. They were deeply engaged and now General Knowles was asking if there was anything Project DELTA could do to help them out.

While I was standing there General Knowles got Colonel Stockton on the radio. Knowles's call sign was Longstreet and Stockton's was Bullwhip Six. "Bullwhip Six, this is Longstreet. I do not appreciate that you took that rifle company and used it for a purpose other than the one you stated. I don't appreciate it a bit. Now we have to mount an operation to get it out. What have you to say about this?" Bullwhip Six, Stockton, came back with some kind of bullshit. When he was done the general put the radio down, looked at me and said, "That's what you call really telling him, isn't it?" I looked at him and said, "Sir, if I was a general and an officer under my command disobeyed an order, as that colonel has, I would tell him to put his hat on backward and start marching in an eastward direction till he hit the China Sea. That's what I would do." Well, the general's mouth fell open. John Hemphill told me later the general had not appreciated my thought. I felt, if this is the way the Cav's going to operate, then I don't want to fool with them. They made me nervous. I didn't sleep anymore that night.

But, the choice wasn't mine, and the Cav needed DELTA's assistance for Operation Silver Bayonet in the Ia Drang Valley. Colonel McKean was running around wanting to know what we could do. At this time Major Tut informed me that his instructions were to stand down and prepare to go back to Nha Trang. He had been told by General Quang not to participate in anymore combat operations. The Vietnamese Rangers had run out of gas and were not going to do anything more.

General Westmoreland was in Pleiku and asked me what we could do to help the Cav. I told him I had four all-American teams back in Nha Trang we could deploy, but we needed his authority to use them. He said, "You got it!" That made my day. Now that Project DELTA could use all-American teams, I felt we'd taken another giant step forward.

Then there was the fight over who owned the helicopters that inserted DELTA's teams. The Vietnamese Rangers had taken Khoi and their choppers back to Nha Trang, leaving me naked. I stated my requirements to the Cav and was told that Colonel Stockton's helos would support DELTA, but that they would remain under his operational control. I became very hard-nosed over this point. I'd stood there and watched that general take crap from Stockton, so I wasn't comfortable with

Stockton. He took too many risks to suit me. I wanted to control all my own parts. The argument went all the way to Maj. Gen. Harry Kinnard, the division's commander. The Cav finally agreed to attach the helicopters to me, but they didn't like it. They didn't like it at all. Stockton was very angry. But I got my way.

As things turned out, the Cav's choppers weren't much to brag about. Their pilots couldn't find our LZs. They couldn't come back, put a pin in a map, and say for sure that's where they'd put a team. The first time they tried it they put the teams in twenty kilometers from where they were supposed to. We went out, found the teams, brought them back, and reinserted them the next day. This time the pilots were only ten kilometers off. It was just a damn mess. The teams on the ground, when I asked them if they wanted to be airlifted out, told me they'd rather walk out. It was just ludicrous. In fairness to these pilots, it has to be pointed out that they had recently arrived in country and Silver Bayonet was their first large operation.

When our part of the Ia Drang campaign was over, I didn't even ask permission to leave—I just scrambled us up a couple of C-130s, loaded everybody up, and moved on back to Nha Trang. Later Colonel McKean told me the 1st Cav hadn't been impressed with DELTA. We were too expensive and required too many of their assets. From that moment on, whenever I was around Colonel McKean he'd keep talking about the relationship between Project DELTA and the 1st Cav, "We gotta get this patched up." I finally decided he was more concerned with the fact that maybe this general who commanded the 1st Cav, Harry Kinnard, might sit on one of his promotion boards.

Anyway, Plei Me was over and Project DELTA had done well. We could go anywhere now and people knew who we were. We were proud of ourselves. We had had a successful operation. We helped save the camp and had killed some bad guys.

★ TWELVE ★

IN EARLY NOVEMBER we were asked to support and do some reconnaissance work for the 1st Division, which was just coming into country. One time, after being on the ground all day working on a 1st Division operation, I was pulled off a chopper at Bien Hoa and told to call Saigon. I was bushed. I got on the phone, then I jumped into a jeep and took off for the hour-and-fifteen-minute drive to the city. I arrived at MACV headquarters having come right off a field operation. I was wearing my jungle costume and was filthy.

After I reported to Colonel Gregory, he showed me some aerial recon photos. "What does this look like to you, Major?"

"It looks to me, sir, like a road with a pile of gravel next to it."

He showed me another photo.

I said, "That's a road with no gravel."

Colonel Gregory agreed. "We want you, Major, to go up to Pleiku, find this road, and tell us why the VC is using gravel." I became angry. I told him I didn't have a hundred DELTA teams: "I have only a handful and right now I'm in the middle of an operation. Damn it, don't you think it's sort of dumb to call me up here tonight. All you've got to do is pick up the phone, call II Corps and ask Colonel Mataxis to task the Special Forces right there in the area to do the job."

All of a sudden I felt a hand come around my shoulder. I turned around and there stood Brig. Gen. William DePuy, MACV's ops officer. He was wearing a T-shirt, fatigues, and jump boots. I had a lot of respect for this no-nonsense general who soaked up work like a sponge. DePuy quietly told me to go into his office. After I'd shut the door, I heard him take this colonel apart. He told Gregory he'd used poor judgment and that he should have called Pleiku instead. Then it was my turn.

General DePuy came into his office, closed the door, and tore my ass up. He made it clear he didn't appreciate my coming into his shop and conducting myself the way I had and that I should never talk to a senior officer that way. He went on like this for several minutes. "Sit down," he said finally. Then he smiled and asked how Project DELTA was doing. The special recon project was actually his baby; his office gave us our missions. We talked for a while about DELTA, and then he asked me if there was something I needed. I thought for a moment, then asked for two Air Force FACs (forward air controllers) to be assigned to me. I needed them to work for me. Wherever DELTA went, it seemed we always had to borrow someone else's. These were the guys who directed the fighter sorties when we were in trouble. They were fellas you really wanted in your pocket. General DePuy agreed, and DELTA got its own FACs.

Christmas came and went and we continued to do business with the 1st Division and with Timothy's Traveling Troubles—the 1st Brigade (Separate) 101st Airborne Division—named after their CO, Brig. Gen. James S. Timothy. During this time I tried to make DELTA as autonomous as the 5th Special Forces Group would permit. I wanted my own reaction rifle companies, my own choppers and pilots, my own FACs. I had learned that from the SAS. They taught me if I was going to do something unique, something very dangerous, then I better have all my own horses. When your life and those of your people are the stakes, you don't want to have to depend on strangers. I ran my small DELTA ops center on each operation precisely the same way 22 SAS would have run it in Malaya. I ran it out of a little tent. Nothing fancy. Just efficient. I wasn't interested in eyewash.

I felt you led a unit two ways. I'd seen commanders who

led by persuasion, and I saw leaders who led by example. I thought the best was a combination. I had a rule that I wouldn't ask anyone to do anything I hadn't done or wasn't prepared to do. I also worried a lot about my guys. Coming back from a mission briefing in Saigon my guys would always meet me at Nha Trang. "What's the form, sir?" "The one we've got coming up," I'd say, "is going to be a bad one. We're gonna get some people hurt, I'm afraid. We gotta look at it closely." "Aw, shit, sir," they'd say, "you say that every time."

We came back from Christmas. We'd had a big cookout. We somehow came up with a couple of hogs, located some beer, and invited all the nurses over from the evac hospital. The camp we were building was nearly completed. The 5th Special Forces Group's executive officer, Jim Vail, accused me of spending too much money. I thought it was a cheap shot. He was living on the fat side of the group headquarters. Some things in the Army never change. I learned early to look out for my own unit. No one else would if I didn't.

When I arrived in Project DELTA I noticed we didn't have but a couple of vehicles and the ones we had were in bad condition. So I put the word out to the guys. Whenever we'd go on an operation in another corps area, we'd usually go in a C-130 aircraft. We would never fill up the entire aircraft. In the new area everyone would sort of look around at all those new jeeps, just sitting there, unlocked. Whenever we came back from an operation we'd always return in the C-130 with one or two new jeeps. Before you knew it, we had a pretty good-sized motor pool. Of course, we had to change bumper markings and things like that. I was finally told, in a real nice way, that my motor pool was large enough and it should stop growing—at once.

I don't guess we were the neatest unit in the Army. All I cared about was making sure everybody had sufficient uniforms. When I first entered the Army, I used to spend hours polishing boots. After I left England I wasn't the same. In Project DELTA I couldn't care less for spit and polish.

We were a fraternity of the cream of the crop in the 5th

Special Forces. We had a very tight bond. I believe that loyalty runs up and it runs down. I learned that presenting someone a 9mm Browning pistol or a Rolex GMT watch with his name on it wasn't the name of the game. You should reward people with a promotion, with another stripe.

I learned something at Plei Me: Human life is the most precious thing on earth. I didn't want to waste any of it by being stupid. This didn't cause me to be too cautious, but it did teach me to sit down and weigh the risks. If you were going to lose lives on an operation, that operation had better be worth it.

In the New Year of 1966 I looked around, surveyed where we were. I learned DELTA had obtained a very good reputation. DELTA had gotten away with a lot. It was just a matter of time before the percentages caught up with us. You didn't have to be a riverboat gambler to know that. When you hung your ass out as often as we did, it was just a matter of time. I believed this about the guys, but not about myself. I'd become convinced that I was indestructible. After Plei Me I figured I could walk through fire with impunity.

★ THIRTEEN ★

ABOUT MID-JANUARY OF 1966, Bulldog McKean heard about an operation that was going to be run by my good friends in the 1st Cav, up around the An Loa Valley in Binh Dinh Province. This was Indian country. "Why don't you go up there, Charlie, and talk to them. Let's see if we can get back on a good footing with the Cav." "Sure, sir," I said, "I'll be happy to."

I went up to An Khe, got briefed, and was surprised that everyone was as nice as they could be. But, when I came back to Nha Trang I still hoped they wouldn't use us on this operation. I knew we'd have the same support and helicopter problems all over again. We'd argue and their staff officers would get mad. But the operation gained momentum. Colonel McKean told me that one of the Cav's brigades wanted to work with DELTA. I told him, "I know how they operate, so I've got a bad feeling about this. What do I do if they misuse us?" McKean said, "I'll set up an appointment for you to go and discuss this whole thing with General Larsen. I knew "Swede" Larsen when he was assistant commandant of the Infantry School at Fort Benning and I was a student. He'd come into 'Nam and was the field force commander in the II Corps Tactical Zone. I liked and respected General Larsen. He had a tremendous combat record.

He understood how I felt about the 1st Cav. "General, Colonel McKean wants me to go, but I ain't keen on it." He said, "Well, that's up to you, but they do need you." Well, he just stroked me around until I said I'd go. But before I capitulated, I asked the general to do something for me. "If I get up there and they ask me to do things I can't do, if they use me totally outside of my capabilities, I want your permission, or someone's, to pick up my marbles and come home." "Absolutely," he said, "and I will fix that."

I took about thirty-five Americans from DELTA to Bong Son. The weather was bad, with a little bit of rain. There was a lot of artillery going off and the 3rd Brigade was sort of busy. I got a few minutes in a coordination meeting with Lt. Col. Hal Moore. I told him, "I'll have teams on the ground by last light tomorrow. Three will go in first to test the waters, then I'll send in others. I believe the An Loa Valley is full of VC." "That's fine," he said. "You go find them and I'll come kill them."

This is Operation Masher. The idea is to sweep the coastal plain, drive the Viet Cong back up to Bong Son and into the mountains, then trap them in the An Loa. Project DELTA's mission is to find the enemy units. Once they have done this, the 1st Cav will be called in.

January 27th and 28th we ran some reconnaissance flights, and then late in the afternoon of the 28th I put three teams on the ground. The An Loa Valley is surrounded by high rugged mountains covered with double canopy foliage. Everything is quiet that night and I get some sleep. At first light one team comes up on our communication net and tells us that they've not made contact but there are VC all around them. They think they should come out. I agree. Ten minutes later the other two teams come up and they're in contact. One man is hit. Both teams are taking heavy fire. It's now about 1000 hours and it's raining. I can't do anything but wait for the weather to clear. I sit in the communications tent. I can't fly. These teams out there are in serious trouble and I can't help them. Everyone is very worried.

Finally it stops raining and the clouds break up a little— not much, but a little. Major Murphy, the helicopter commander, runs over to me. He's quite emotional, "Charlie, I think we can get up there." What I have in mind is to get onto the ground with my teams. I'm going to take my sergeant major and two radio operators. I feel if I get on the ground, then my ops officer, Bo Baker, will have some leverage to get the Cav to react more quickly.

Before we leave, I hand one of the guys my GMT Rolex. It's new and I don't want to get it banged up. We take off at once. We're forced by the weather to fly at treetop level. As we get close to the teams, we start receiving fire. Almost at once a .51-caliber machine gun bullet comes through the helicopter. It goes in one side of my abdomen and comes out the other. I pass out.

The next thing I remember I'm lying on a stretcher back in Bong Son. A Green Beret medic gives me a shot of morphine. Some of the guys are standing around me. I ask. "Tell me how I am?" Lonnie Ledford says. "You're in bad shape, Boss." People are running around. The slick that brought me back can't take off. It's shot up too bad. As luck has it, a chopper comes in right then. The guys grab the pilot. "Major Beckwith's been hit and we need to get him to the hospital in Qui Nhon." Because of shock and the morphine, I don't yet know exactly where I've been hit, and I don't feel pain. I remember the helicopter ride, the litter, the hospital. I don't know its number. (I get it later, the 85th EVAC.) My brain clears for a while. Triage. A big red-headed nurse major comes up and looks me over. Then two doctors. One of them says, "He'll bleed to death before we can do anything for him." They agree, I'm not worth fooling with. I'm not going to make it. I grab the big nurse, she's closest, "Now let's get one thing straight here. I ain't the average bear, and I didn't come in here to pack it in." That gets the two doctors' attention. They begin to prepare me for surgery. This part's as clear as a bell. I become very violent and very profane. It's taking them too long. I know I'm dying. "Goddamn it, let's get on with it." The nurse starts fooling with my arm. I still have a scar where she cut me trying to type my blood. I curse her. "I have to find out what type blood you have." "Goddamn it," I yell, "I'm A-positive. Look at my dog tags." They aren't real happy with me. They keep farting around. "Goddamn, let's move. Let's go!" I'm rolled into surgery. I start counting down from 100 and get to 94.

In the recovery room when I came to I knew I was in bad shape. I had hoses running in and out of me all over. A doctor came in and told me he'd had to remove my gallbladder and twenty-one inches of my small intestine. They'd cut me from the top of my chest all the way down to just above my penis. They had sewn me up with what looked like piano wire. They'd also done a temporary colostomy. The doctor told me I was fortunate to be alive.

I was very thirsty, but the nurses couldn't give me any water. Every couple of hours I got an ice cube to suck.

That evening a Hawaiian boy, shot up worse than I, was rolled in from the operating room. The duty nurse came over to me and said, "Major, this boy next to you is in a bad way." He'd been gut shot as well as having been hit in the shoulder, the hip, and the leg. He lay on the cot next to me. I reached over and grabbed his hand. "It's up to you," I told him. "If you want to make it you can. It's all in your mind." I squeezed as hard as I could. "If you want to quit you'll be dead by morning. If you're strong you'll live. Goddamn, son, make up your mind." He barely squeezed my hand back. Just a little pressure. As it turned out, he was up and out of the hospital long before I was.

I stayed in the recovery ward for thirty days. Again, they thought I was going to die. Bullets are not clean and I was severely infected. At first no one knew what was wrong with me. I went way down. I had a terrible fever. They called the chaplain and I had a last little conference with him. The doctor came around in the morning. I told him, "I feel like shit. I ain't sure I'm gonna make it. I'm losing strength." He said, "We can't figure it out." I said, "You know, I got a lump over here." He put his hand under my right armpit. "That's all pus!" Within a half hour I was back in surgery.

February 1966. I was sort of in charge of the recovery room by right of being there the longest. I was also the senior officer. There weren't a lot of majors getting shot up at this time. The doctors would bring other doctors around and they'd show them my operations. I was sort of, I guess, a showpiece. One doctor came looking for me. He wanted to see himself this man who had gone through twenty-three pints of blood during surgery.

There were many people coming in and out of that hospital. You could tell there was a war going on. Being next to the operating room I often saw doctors just come in, find a cot, and fall asleep for an hour until it was time to go back to work. They worked around the clock. The nurses were good to me. At night, when I couldn't sleep, they'd bring me a small cup of Kool-Aid. Goddamn, I really appreciated that.

One day a boy, just out of the OR, came out of his anesthesia and began to howl. I tried to encourage him, but he just laid there and shouted and moaned. This went on all night. He began to drive everyone in recovery crazy. Finally, about four o'clock I said, "You're the noisiest sonovabitch I've ever heard." About six o'clock he stopped hollering—when he died.

Another time, the nurses and orderlies came around sweeping, washing and cleaning. "What the hell's going on," everyone wanted to know. No one knew. All they'd heard was a code 7 or something was coming up for a visit. They knew the code number was the highest they'd ever received. That afternoon General Westmoreland paid a visit. He sat by my bed for a while and asked if I needed anything. He talked to every soldier there.

My guys came around to see me. Lonnie Ledford returned my Rolex. I had known Lonnie a long time. He'd been my old ops sergeant back in Buzz Miley's B Company at Fort Bragg. I'd told the guys that if anything ever happened to me I wanted them to divide up the weapons I'd collected and stored in my footlocker. I'd picked up a couple of folding-stock carbines and bolt-action rifles—things like that.

"How about the weapons?" I asked Ledford.

"We've divided them up."

"Can I have my 9mm Browning?"

"Nope. Sorry, sir. They're all divided up."

Lonnie also told me what happened to the three recon teams after I was hit. The first team that had come up on the radio early, the one which was not engaged, got out O.K. The other two, the ones I tried to reach, were not as fortunate. The 1st Cav made no effort to help them after I went down. Seven men were killed. The others hid in the jungle and eventually made their way out.

Hal Moore, the CO of the Cav's 3rd Brigade, the guy that had said, "You find them. I'll kill them," came around once and visited with his soldiers. I knew damn well he knew I was in that hospital, but he never said a word to me. I was wounded while supporting his brigade.

Soon I was flown to the Philippines. Then, with a large batch of wounded. I was moved to Letterman General Hospital in San Francisco. The next morning, early, 4:00 A.M., they woke all of us who had come in the night before and moved us to the loading area outside the hospital. We began to wait for the ambulances. We lay on our stretchers and waited. I'll tell you, San Francisco in March is cold. I began to hear guys up and down the line: "You know, I'm freezing my ass off." I was too. Finally, I started hollering. A nurse came out after a while, "What's your problem?" I said, "My problem is I want to see who is in charge of this hospital and I damn want to see him now! If you don't get him, I'm going to raise more hell than you ever thought about." A lieutenant colonel came over to me. I reached up and got hold of him by the hand. "You're the dumbest sonovabitch I've known. We've been lying out here over an hour, freezing to death. You get some blankets out here." In less time than it takes to tell it, we had blankets.

I eventually arrived at my final destination, Great Lakes Naval Hospital outside of Chicago. Katherine came over from Michigan, where she had taken an apartment near her parents, and was there to welcome me with her loving care.

Of course, all during this period I was really concerned about where I was going next. I requested that I be sent to the 10th Special Forces Group in Germany. Then, one day while

I was sitting in bed reading, the phone rang. I picked it up and heard, "Is this that snotty-nosed motor pool officer I sent to England?" It was Col. Boppy Edwards, who was now Director of the Ranger Department at Fort Benning. "Where you going to be reassigned?" I told him Germany. "I don't think you want to do that. I think you want to come on down to Benning and run one of the Ranger camps for me. Charlie, do you object if I sort of put my oar in the water and get your assignment changed?" Within a few days I was ordered to report to Fort Benning, Georgia.

In early May 1966, the doctors finally cleared and released me. After some more rest I went over to Detroit and bought a black Harley Sprint motorcycle. I planned on riding it from Michigan to Fort Benning. I like to feel the wind in my hair.

★ FOURTEEN ★

TIME BEGAN TO slip by now. Some years moved quickly. Some slowly. I'd decided at last they were not going to listen to me. The U.S. Army could see no possible reason why they should have a unit with an SAS capability. My wheels came off the track. I'd broken my head once too often on the bureaucracy. Even I learn. I stopped charging. The flame flickered. Those years I spent earning my keep, paying my dues. I kept soldiering.

This period began in the summer of 1966 when Colonel Edwards asked me to run the third phase of the Ranger training course. I realized this would give me a chance to implement principles learned in the SAS and with Project DELTA in Vietnam. I decided it'd give me a chance to state my philosophy. First, the training should be a learning experience. Second, each candidate had to earn the right to wear the Ranger tab. Lastly, every Ranger would have an insurance policy that the training he received might save his life in combat.

The purpose of Ranger training at this time was to teach an extremely high quality of leadership at the small unit level—squads and platoons—primarily to junior officers and NCOs. The first phase, which was basic in nature, was taught at Fort Benning. The Chattahoochee National Forest, near Dahlonega. Georgia, was the site of the second phase. The students there were taught how to conduct patrols, raids, and ambushes in a mountainous setting. The third phase, taught in northwest Florida at Auxiliary Field 7 at Eglin Air Force Base, conducted small unit commando-type exercises in marshy swampland.

Realism was so important, and it was necessary to put the Florida phase of Ranger training into a Vietnam mode. The course needed instructors who were recent Vietnam returnees, men who'd been in the mud, had seen combat, guys who knew what it was all about. Colonel Edwards supported this, and whenever possible he'd send down officers and noncoms who, coming into the Ranger Department, had combat experience. Eventually, some very good instructors came on board, men like Dave Bramlett and Jim Daily, who'd seen action and knew how to prepare soldiers for war.

Colonel Edwards gave me a free hand in Florida. Along with upgrading my instructors I attempted to update and modernize the Ranger training exercises. Going through the files I found all the exercises thoroughly locked in on paper. It gave the bureaucrats something to do. I found antiquated exercises that hadn't been changed in years. I said, "To hell with this." Changes had to be made and no one had the time to write everything up. Within six months the staff changed every exercise in the training phase. People came down from Benning and observed what was happening. The recruits were put through combat-simulated exercises. Everybody was happy and everything was on track. Finally, a staff officer came down to inspect the vault files. "None of these files," he said, "match anything you're doing." "Yeah," I said, "that's right. These exercises are dynamic and are constantly being changed." This caused a stink for a while and I was told to update my vault files. I never did. Didn't have the time.

A tombstone was put up in front of the briefing shack where each Ranger class gathered for its welcome to the three weeks of training. The epitaph read:

Here lies the bones
Of Ranger Jones,
A graduate of this institution;
He died last night
in his first fire fight,

sing the school solution.
Therefore, be flexible!

I also, occasionally, did something else to get the trainees' attention. Fully dressed in a field uniform I'd jump into Holly Creek, then soaking wet I'd dash up the hill and confront the class as they sat on the bleachers. "If a man is bloody stupid," I'd tell them, "his mother will receive a telegram and it will say, 'Your son is dead because he's stupid.' Let's hope your telegram only reads, 'Your son is dead.' With the training we're going to give you here maybe your mother won't receive any telegram at all. So pay attention!"

We always tried to remain current in our training. This was done by floating new Vietnam returnees through our staff. Every time we got an instructor who had recently finished his combat tour, we'd usually have added a new VC booby trap to our curriculum. The war continuously twisted and turned and changed. We tried to keep up with it in Florida. I wanted to save lives.

In the spring of '67, I received a call from Colonel Edwards.

"Charlie, get your ass up here to Benning. Bring everything you can on the SAS with you. There's a chance we can put a Ranger unit together and send it to 'Nam, and I'd like to see you command it." So, boy, I'm vibrating now, I'm back on the crusade. The flame, again, burned bright.

At Benning I learned Colonel Edwards wanted to propose a Ranger battalion to go to Vietnam, and he didn't care how I organized it. I sat down at once with one of my officers, Capt. Dave Bramlett, a very bright young West Pointer, and we skillfully wrote up an SAS unit proposal using Ranger nomenclature—the selection process, the training, the evaluation, goals, missions, everything went into our proposal. Colonel Edwards flew to Saigon with it and briefed General Westmoreland. Although impressed, he was only a few days away from deciding to reactivate the Long Range Patrol Companies, which was an entirely different concept. In other words, there wasn't any justification now for activating a Ranger battalion along SAS lines. The proposal was put on a back burner. The light burned dimmer. After that training cycle, Katherine, recognizing a difference in me, asked what the trouble was. I told her straight out, "I need to go back to Vietnam. I was wounded and I want to find out if I can handle it again."

I'd heard a rumor that the balance of the 101st Airborne Division out of Fort Campbell was going to 'Nam. I said, "If the 101st is going, I'm going with it." Since I'd just made lieutenant colonel, I thought I could get a battalion.

Katherine said, "That's up to you, but I think you're crazy."

★ FIFTEEN ★

AFTER TET, ON February 10, 1968, I took command of the 2nd battalion (327th Airborne Infantry) 101st Airborne Division. This was straightforward infantry work; pure yes, sir, no, sir, three bags full; square the corners, straighten the lines, sweep the fire base, search and destroy the enemy. This is chain of command administration, don't stop and talk to the old man, take it to the first sergeant.

The tempo of the war at this stage was much faster than when I was here last. There were a lot of bad guys running around now. You could get killed very easily. I felt it was my job as a battalion CO to come to grips with the enemy and destroy him. I went looking for fights and anybody didn't feel the same way shouldn't be around me. When Col. "Rip" Collins commanded the 1st Brigade, each of the Division's battalions shared equally in the hard jobs. Later, when "Doc" Hayward had the brigade, I felt that whenever there was a nasty job to be done the 2/327 got it. I liked that. We were known as the "No Slack" battalion.

During the nine months I had the battalion, I saw some very brave men in the 101st Airborne Division. We had a good track record, many successes.

After Hue, we cleared the area around the Division headquarters in what was known as Operation Mingo. Then came action while the 2/327 was attached to the 1st Cav for Operation Jeb Stuart. Operation Nevada Eagle cleared the Hue–Phu Bai area. Somerset Plain swept the southern portion of the A

Shau Valley. The toughest job the battalion had was clearing a seven kilometer stretch along Route 547, which ran west from Hue. There were no VC here, just NVA regulars! The road faced steep mountain and thick, nearly impenetrable jungle. The cost was high. We got clawed and we clawed back. Eventually, the road was won and Fire Support Base Bastogne established.

I learned if you command an infantry battalion in combat in Vietnam for nine months it's going to grind you down. We took a lot of casualties. All losses are bad. Some still stay with me. Much of what happened haunts me to this day.

Toward the end of the tour I became very tired. I was offered the Division's operations shop but turned it down. I did that for several reasons. The bombing of North Vietnam had been discontinued and that turned me off. If we were going to hang our ass out over there and they were not going to continue the bombing, then I was confused.

I'd also learned that Maj. Gen. Melvin Zais was replacing Gen. Olinto Barsanti as commander of the Division. Barsanti, whose call sign was Bold Eagle, was a wild man. He literally terrified his battalion commanders—ate lieutenant colonels for breakfast. Hard as he was on officers, Barsanti was always good to the troops. I somehow got along with him just fine. Mel Zais was a different story. In my opinion, he didn't trust his subordinates. The 2/327 was being extracted from the A Shau Valley. The weather was bad, heavy fog drifted across the valley floor, and because of the timing necessary to lift the troops, my plate was full. It was a complicated but not impossible job. I'd done it numerous times before. What I didn't need was someone else on my radio net offering advice. Nevertheless. Mel Zais came on my frequency and began to tell me how I should do my job. So when my tour was up, I felt it was best for me not to return to the 101st. I had paid my dues. I'd done two tours in Vietnam. It was time to go home.

My next assignment was in Hawaii at CINCPAC (Commander in Chief, Pacific). I was thinking that this was a place where they could use my expertise. I had my family with me, it was Hawaii, and I was looking forward to the new challenge.

Eventually I went to work for Col. R. C. "Butch" Kendrick. No finer officer ever defecated between a pair of jump boots. The general officers in CINCPAC called Butch a "fountain of knowledge." Whenever the answer to a tactical question was needed, they'd go to him. The Army made a terrible mistake when they didn't select him to be a general officer. He, like Boppy Edwards, was very straightforward, intelligent, and someone who knew how to take care of his troops.

I began my work by monitoring a couple of Special Operations programs. I was responsible for watching the 1st Special Forces based on Okinawa, the 5th Special Forces Group in 'Nam, which I knew well, and cross-border operations conducted by MACV-SOG (Military Assistance Command, Vietnam Studies and Observation Group).

Kendrick had an Air Force colonel named Bill Christian working for him. Bill Christian didn't know anything about Special Operations, but this guy really knew how to put pen to paper. I was required to write a lot of papers. Unfortunately, it was a task at which I had little skill. Colonel Christian spent a lot of time crossing my t's and dotting my i's. He'd get so disgusted. But he worked with me and what he appreciated most was that I wouldn't give up. He taught me the King's English, how to organize my thoughts, how to write, how to prepare a staff paper. After about six months of teaching and learning, instructor and student, I began to feel comfortable with words on paper. I owe Colonel Christian for that.

This job also gave me the opportunity to go back to Southeast Asia. I made many trips to Saigon and Bangkok and Phnom Penh. We made every effort to develop a good viable UW (Unconventional Warfare) campaign in Cambodia. I was on sort of a fast train and learned a lot being on the CINCPAC staff. It always made me feel good when I was asked to serve on special studies groups. They'd ask for me by name; they recognized my experience. I felt very productive. Promotion time came. When the list came out my name was not on it. I hadn't made full colonel. I felt I had earned it. I got hold of some people in the personnel business at the Pentagon. "Well, first of all," they told me, "you don't have a college degree.

Second, you've stepped on a lot of toes, boy."

I decided to get my act together and go get a college education. When I left the University of Georgia after four years, I lacked thirty hours of graduating. I'd had my nose in a football, not in the books. I decided to change my major from physical education to political science. At Chaminade College in Honolulu I undertook a full year, carrying a full load of courses, to earn my degree. The Army gave me the year to bootstrap. I found I loved school and I graduated with a 3.5 grade average.

In June 1973 I took an assignment with the JCRC (the Joint Casualty Resolution Center) operating out of Nakhon Phanom, Thailand. Its purpose was to search for the bodies of men who'd been killed in Southeast Asia. The Special Forces were going to supply people who would go out in small patrols to places where there was thought to be remains of dead Americans.

The commander of the JCRC was Brig. Gen. Robert Kingston. He was the same officer who had met me at the dock in Southampton just as I was beginning my exchange tour with 22 SAS. I was greatly surprised to learn that General Kingston was not pleased to have me there. He has a tremendous memory and he remembered I wasn't very cordial to him that summer morning in England eleven years before. "But, sir," I told him one night, "I was a captain and you were a major. I didn't think I should *embrace* you." We became very good friends once we cleared up the misunderstanding. Kingston has a Boston accent which belies his two nicknames, Barbed Wire Bob and War Lord. He'd won a DSC in Vietnam. I found him to be ruthless when necessary, aggressive, intelligent, and one of the best friends I've ever had.

The mission was a tough one. We were not permitted by the North Vietnamese to go into certain areas to search for the remains of the men who had paid the supreme price. Then, in December 1973, one of the teams searching south of Saigon was ambushed by an NVA patrol. We were ordered to stand down. We remained idle and had nothing to do but play sports and stay out of trouble.

Before leaving Thailand, I wrote the Military Personnel Center in Washington asking them to assess what possible military assignments might come my way. Was there a future for me in the Army?

I received a real nice reply. "We've gone over your record very carefully and recognize you have some unique skills. We think you should stay in the Army. Because you've been passed over once for promotion, we feel your possibility for command again is remote." The letter explained how I could help in staff areas.

When I showed the letter to Kingston he said, "They're trying to give you a message. Next time you'll get promoted." Because so many people had been passed over the last time, the new promotion list came out in ten months. I was at the top of this one. I had made full colonel.

After the tour in Thailand ended in May 1974 I asked to go to Fort Bragg. General Healey was the commanding general of the United States Army John F. Kennedy Center for Military Assistance, usually called The Center, and had formerly been known in the early sixties, when I was at Bragg, as the Special Warfare Center. General Healey didn't know me well, but some others there did. One officer urged Mike Healey to have nothing to do with me. Others told him I would be an asset to his staff. Healey was confused until Butch Kendrick, who Healey had worked for and liked, gave me a sterling recommendation.

One day General Healey called me down to his office. "I have been directed to run a sports program for ninety Mexican officers. This is a project," he said, "that the Air Force didn't want, the Navy didn't want, and the Marines didn't want, so they pawned it off on the Army. The Army pawned it off on General DePuy, at TRADOC [Training and Doctrine Command], and General DePuy pawned it off on me. Damn it, Charlie, I don't want it but I'm stuck with it. And now you're stuck with it." That was the way Healey operated.

I was an old jock and knew how to organize things. Looking around I found the experts. We lined up our coaches, administrators, and interpreters, and we taught ninety Mexican Army officers how to organize and conduct sporting events such as track and field meets. The training conducted at Lackland AFB in San Antonio received some recognition, and was considered a huge success.

Healey came to me afterward and in essence said, "You did well. Now I've got to show you my appreciation." I said, "Yes, sir. I've served my time in purgatory." He asked me what job I wanted although he'd already made up his mind what he was going to do with me. There really was only one job that fit me perfectly. I knew it and everybody else did, too. I became commandant of the Special Forces School.

General Healey left Fort Bragg shortly afterward for an assignment in Turkey. His replacement, who after leaving Thailand, had been the ADC with the 1st Infantry Division, who had just received a second star, who was known as Barbed Wire and War Lord, was Bob Kingston. Things, I said to myself, are picking up. When General Kingston arrived at the JFK Center, we had several meetings about what the school should be doing, and found ourselves in perfect accord. In the evenings—the Kingstons had moved in across the street from Katherine and me—we had many long discussions about the military. He reminisced about the Parachute Regiment, and I'd talk fondly about the 22 SAS. We had the Brits in common. He had told me on my first day in England, "You're going to love this year with the SAS. I envy you." He felt about the SAS the way I did.

He came to see me one day in late 1975. "Charlie. I'm going to Washington. I want you to put together a paper for me on the SAS." Well, just like that, out of nowhere—I felt like, well, you know, damn . . . !

★ SIXTEEN ★

THAT EVENING, AFTER digging out all my old papers and rereading them, I wrote another fact paper on the 22 SAS Regiment.

After showing it to my immediate boss, Col. Dave Presson—I owed him that courtesy—I walked it over to General Kingston. Because "Shy" Meyer and Kingston are good friends, it was natural for Bob to take it to him. Lt. Gen. Edward C. Meyer, who was then the Army's Deputy Chief of Staff for Operations and Plans, was considered to be the smartest man in uniform in Washington.

On his return to Bragg, General Bob told me he'd had some conversation in the Pentagon about the formation of a unit that could operate along SAS lines. He thought, maybe, somewhere down the road, the Army would get serious about it. Since this was nothing new, I didn't think a lot more about it. But Kingston did. Whenever he entertained a visitor, especially if it was someone with clout, he never hesitated bringing up the SAS and their successes.

The subject began to take on a life of its own.

Then, in late August 1976 General Kingston was asked to attend a conference chaired by Bill DePuy at the Army Infantry School at Fort Benning. The object of this meeting was to examine the role of the light infantry division and Kingston was tasked to explain what Special Forces could do in support of conventional forces on the tactical battlefield. General Kingston requested I accompany him and Colonel Henry.

The VIP conference room in Building Four at Fort Benning is typical. A large round walnut conference table takes up most of the space and is surrounded by large overstuffed swivel chairs. These are for the general officers. The action officers who occupy the other half of the room sit in less comfortable straight-back chairs. Two screens hang on one wall and there's a lectern, complete with carefully mounted switches and buttons controlling the 35mm slide projectors, in the front of the room. Briefers normally receive a quick lesson on what the many switches control. It would be unfortunate for some colonel to change a slide in the middle of his performance when all he wanted to do was adjust the PA sound. On three walls hang prints and paintings of American infantrymen in combat—Gettysburg and Shiloh, St. Mihiel and Belleau Wood, Anzio and the Bulge. This is a very comfortable room to be in.

The conference appeared to be another straightforward capabilities brief. Several presentations were made before it was General Kingston's turn. When he was through, General DePuy began a general discussion.

"You know, Bob, you didn't articulate your position as well as I thought you would. What you said, however, I agree with. You used the term 'indigenous forces' several times. Thirteen times to be exact. Special Forces is responsible for the training of these people, whether they be on our side of the lines or on the enemy's side, and we need it to do that job." He went on a little while longer elaborating on this idea. Then he leaned back. He looked around the room. "How come we don't have a unit like the British Special Air Service?" I almost fell out of my chair.

"Those people went into Indonesia through Borneo and conducted operations which were so successful the Indonesians were too embarrassed to take it to the United Nations." This referred to an attempt by Sukarno to liberate the Sultanate of Brunei, one of the three British dependencies in Borneo, through the use of Indonesian-supported terrorists. SAS squadrons had operated very successfully against their bases, which were located well within the borders of Indonesia.

Bill DePuy continued. "The Brits did very well in that operation and they did it with very little fanfare. Why can't we do those kinds of things in our Army? Where is the force which will do that? We have never been able to do special operations well. Special Forces—yes, they teach and train, but we've never really been able to do special operations very well. We didn't do them well in Korea. We didn't do them well in Vietnam and I'm concerned about it. Maybe what we really need to do is carefully examine the British SAS model, see how they do it, and then organize a similar American Army unit."

I sat there ready to burst, thinking, God, I'd like to hug this beautiful general. He's got it all in one sack.

Lunchtime arrived.

In the hall I spoke to an old friend, "Shali" Shalikashvilli, the Director of Instruction at the Infantry School. General DePuy joined us and complimented Shali on his Long Range Patrol Company presentation, which had been delivered earlier in the morning. After some small talk, Shali changed the subject. "General, back at Bragg, in 1962, Charlie here wrote a paper proposing that we create and organize an SAS capability in our Army. He's been beating that drum ever since." General DePuy answered. "Someone ought to have been listening to him."

During lunch I was like a string going to snap. I told myself. This is going too smoothly; something's got to happen. After lunch I wasn't sure where the morning discussion was going to lead. DePuy, in his own smooth articulate style, began where he'd left off an hour before. The results were the same as in the morning. Everyone agreed the Army needed an SAS capability.

"All right, Bob," General DePuy swiveled to look at my boss, "go back to Bragg and develop a proposal on how we can accomplish this. We have to take this all the way up to the Chief, and it won't be easy. When you and your people have it in a manageable form let me know and I'll review it. I don't want to go to Washington and fail with this."

At this point I was so damn excited I couldn't believe it.

When we were alone Kingston and I hugged each other. During the plane ride back to Fayetteville. General Bob talked about how he wanted the task organized. "Charlie, you're the prime guy; you know all about the SAS, but I want Tom to help you." Tom was Col. Tom Henry, who ran Combat Developments for Kingston. "Because you still have to run the school, you'll not have sufficient time to devote to this project. Since doctrine belongs to Combat Developments, the action really belongs there. I'm going to get Tom to help you."

Henry had been the ops officer in 'Nam for the 5th Special Forces Group and I had a lot of time for him. He was anxious to work on the project and in this he proved to be unusual. Most people at Bragg, when they heard what we were working on, felt we were wasting our time. "It's too new," they said. "It'll get watered down!"

All through September and October, despite these dour predictions, Tom Henry and I worked scores of hours getting the proposal to stand on its own. We were very, very thorough. Every conceptual point was clearly stated. Tom had his concerns, though. If you asked him about this period he'd tell you, "The biggest problem I had was translating Charlie's British jargon into American. I couldn't use 'bloke' or 'the lads' or 'bloody' or 'bonnie.' 'Bergens' had to be 'rucksacks,' 'lorries' had to be 'trucks.' " Tom recognized the problem of overselling the Brits. The idea had come from them, but now it had to be all American. The proposal needed to be carefully developed and sold without overdoing the SAS. We defined the problems and created the solutions—at night, on weekends.

When Kingston thought everyone was ready he made the call, and in mid-November we went up to Fort Monroe, Virginia, to brief General DePuy and key members of his staff, including his deputy, Lt. Gen. Frank Camm. The briefing room in this historic post is smaller and less elaborate than the one at Benning. The brief itself was very formal. General DePuy gave it his total concentration.

He was not enthusiastic. A wise old bird, he knew better than most how the Army worked. "There's something here I don't like. I want you to change specific areas of the brief and, more important, I want you to credit all the other services. Talk about how the Special Forces train indigenous people and do it better than anyone else. Describe how the Rangers excel in special-purpose raids and how the Marines conduct amphibious operations. Point out what the Navy SEALS do, and the Airborne, and the Infantry. Give everyone equal credit. Then show that amidst all this expertise and excellence there exists a void, a task that cannot be done by any one of them, or combination of them. Then introduce the proposed SAS unit. Bob, you've some more work to do."

He repeated what he'd said at Benning: "I don't want to lose when we go to Washington. We're going to get their attention only once and once has to be enough. If we fail to get it, the idea is finished. The Chief and the people around him are going to have to be convinced. I'm afraid it's not going to be an easy job."

Back at Bragg the changes were put in and the fixes made. The briefing was restructured as General DePuy had directed. Toward the end of January 1977, we went back to General DePuy, and this time, for extra clout, I convinced General Kingston that he should deliver the brief. General DePuy sat silently a few minutes. Henry and I were sweating. Then he began to talk to the points he had scribbled on his yellow note pad. Further changes were to be made. We were surprised to hear that some of the areas, things we had fixed specifically on DePuy's November instructions, had to be changed again. Much of what we had done, structure and comparisons in particular, had been done exactly as General DePuy had requested. We knew this because we had taped, with permission, the previous briefing. He directed that they be changed again.

"I want to point out to the others who will have to hear this brief the critical tasks that members of this unit will have to perform: for example, freeing hostages in buildings or on hijacked aircraft; being able to operate with a low visibility and, if necessary, to dress in civilian clothes or in disguises. Put all that in. Once you have outlined the tasks, the void will appear by itself. Even the most obtuse staff officer will be able to see the obvious."

We were told to go back to the drawing board and do some more work. What he wanted done was again very clearly stated. I really wasn't that sure what the hell was going on. Obviously, between the November and January briefings the political winds had shifted slightly and DePuy had adjusted to them.

The Joint Chiefs of Staff is composed of a chairman, appointed by the President, and four chiefs who represent the Army, Navy, Marines, and Air Force. Created in 1942, the JCS is the primary military committee responsible for the armed forces. It is the military interface with the Congress. It integrates strategic plans.

It was possible that petty concerns, special interests, and internecine battles—nurtured not necessarily by the Chiefs but within the process itself—could kill this new unit's chances for approval. The proposal could easily be short-circuited by people having nothing at all to do with the counterterrorist concept itself.

General DePuy, therefore, had the unenviable and difficult task of surgically maneuvering the proposal through some rough country. For the small team working on the proposal at the JFK Center, it meant more work needed to be done. Both Majors Odorizzi and Buckshot (pseudonym) had been assigned to the Special Forces School and, shot through with enthusiasm, they became part of the new organization and were models for the type of men I was looking for.

Chuck Odorizzi had been my communications officer in 'Nam with Project DELTA. He was a real achiever and loyal. A Texan, he was a no-nonsense type of officer who was also good with a pencil. Another southerner, from Virginia tidewater county, Buckshot, had he a smaller nose, could have passed for Robert Redford. Quickwitted and daring, he could be trusted with your life. I trusted him with mine. Buckshot had just departed for the U.K. to undertake the SAS selection course; and I awaited his return to the JFK Center with some eagerness.

The winter squalls never affected our enthusiasm. Kingston led the bandwagon. "You know, Charlie, we're going to eventually get this proposal approved." His exuberance was contagious.

Then, from a totally unexpected source, we received some additional help. On a flight back from the Staff College at Fort Leavenworth, DePuy's deputy, General Camm, had an inspired idea. "What we need to sell this idea," I'm told he said to DePuy, "is a real bright officer off our own Training and Doctrine Command staff. He doesn't have to know a thing about Special Operations, but he has to be able to articulate their ideas. We need a salesman, a professional talker. Kingston and Beckwith will teach him everything he needs to know."

General Camm was a hard guy to figure, and Kingston and I didn't like him very well. Now we began to see him in a new light. Bill DePuy liked the idea because it carried an added bonus. By using someone from his own staff, he got the proposal out of the Special Forces arena and made it somehow less Green Beretish. If an officer wearing the TRADOC shoulder patch did our briefing, he would subtly carry with him DePuy's approval and clout.

The officer chosen was an engineer who'd never served a day in Special Forces. Although you couldn't have filled a thimble with what Lt. Col. John Devens knew about Special Ops, he was, we were told, a wonderful briefer—and he was ours. A nice-looking fella and very intelligent, at first we might as well have been speaking Urdu to him. But he had the ability to memorize everything we explained, and he wasn't afraid to ask questions if he didn't understand something. We found Devens to be truly silver-tongued. Then it was show time again.

The briefing room at Fort Monroe was growing familiar. Our briefer stepped forward and adroitly did his thing. The slides and graphics were very professional. I gotta tell you, it went well. "Well, I'm not totally satisfied," DePuy said, "but I think we're probably as far down the road as we can go. I'm going to go with it like it is. The packaging is good, so let's move it forward. By the way, what should we call the unit?"

"Delta," I said. "Call it 1st Special Forces Operational Detachment—Delta [SFOD-Delta]. We have an A Detachment commanded by a captain, a B Detachment commanded by a major, a C Detachment commanded by a lieutenant colonel; so why not have a D Detachment commanded by a colonel?" I wanted to establish that right away and try to get my oar in the water.

"Fine," General DePuy said, "I have no problem with Delta. What's the SAS commanded by?"

"A half colonel."

"Well, we'll use a full colonel."

Maybe DePuy knew more than I did—maybe he knew I was going to get command of Delta—but in any event he never let me in on any of that. I just had high hopes.

Then General DePuy said, "What we have to do now is brief FORSCOM [Forces Command]. I'll call Fritz and make the appointment." It was nervous time again.

Gen. Frederick "Fritz" Kroesen commanded all the Army Combat and Combat Support Forces in the United States: all the rifle companies, battalions, brigades, divisions, and special forces stationed in this country—are responsible to him, DePuy, who commanded the Army's schooling, and Kroesen both wore four stars, so they talked to each other. I was nervous because another barrier had been put in our way. The thought was we'd go directly, now, to the Chief of Staff. But we realized, the manpower pool Delta would draw on would have to come from FORSCOM, so having their support was vital. Without it the unit had nothing.

One morning in early May 1977, Kingston, Henry, John Devens and I went to Fort McPherson, which is in Atlanta and is FORSCOM's headquarters.

I was very familiar with Fort McPherson as I had grown up just two miles from its main gate and had visited it often. There were few Sundays that I missed seeing the polo games at Fort Mac. Being a very small post I knew exactly where Patton Hall was, the location of General Kroesen's headquarters and where our brief would be presented.

Arriving, we were surprised to learn that we would be required to deliver a prebrief that afternoon for the benefit of FORSCOM's operations staff.

The briefing room at FORSCOM is not very fancy. From the furniture, which was Army functional, you could tell this was a working area.

The atmosphere was much less formal than at TRADOC. It was obvious to the party that had just arrived from the JFK Center that the purpose of the prebriefing was a rubber stamp affair to prepare key FORSCOM officers with information so they could respond to General Kroesen's questions the following morning. They were wrong.

Maj. Gen. Robert Haldane, Kroesen's deputy for operations (G-3), ran this session, which also included FORSCOM's G-1 (Personnel) Maj. Gen. Phillip Kaplan, and Haldane's deputy, the guy who looked out for the Ranger battalions, Brig. Gen. Guy S. Meloy III. There were also two colonels in attendance. One was G. G. Thomas Jr., an airborne officer and another big Ranger fan, and the other, a Colonel Spinks, I recognized as a "yes, sir, no sir, three bags full" type of officer. Our silver-tongued briefer got under way beautifully. By this time I knew the brief by heart. Haldane was paying close attention. He has only a small amount of white hair around his ears. Notwithstanding, I felt he must have been a ball of fire when a young officer. "Sandy" Meloy, a nice-looking small man who, having just returned from a trip, was wearing a smart-looking blue blazer, gray flannel slacks with a crease that would cut your hand, white shirt, and tie. Unlike the other officers in the room, Meloy seemed uncomfortable.

The briefing was slick. On its completion, General Haldane said, "I'm not qualified to make comments on this. I understand what you're trying to do, but I lack the background experience to make relevant comments." Haldane was a conventional soldier and was not trying to cop out. "Therefore, I'm going to yield to members of my staff. Any comments, Sandy?"

Meloy sat up and said, "I'm not at all comfortable with this briefing." General Kingston jumped up. "What in the hell makes you uncomfortable, General?"

Kingston has a bad temper and he was angry.

Meloy said, "I don't think, General, you can get the kinds of people you're looking for to fill the organization. Based on your criteria I don't believe you'll be able to find those kinds. The two Ranger battalions are having trouble finding people to maintain their strength." General Kaplan, FORSCOM's Personnel man, whom Kingston had prepped earlier, spoke up. "I believe we can find in our command the people needed."

Kingston turned to Meloy again. "What else makes you feel uncomfortable?" Meloy said, "It looks like you're duplicating Ranger functions in some areas." Kingston said, "General, you just didn't listen." The two of them went at it tooth and nail. But the argument was between a two-star general and a one-star general. Kingston was sure to win. Finally, Haldane interrupted, "Well, I've heard enough. We'll continue this tomorrow when you brief General Kroesen."

It was after dinner when we met to discuss the day's proceedings. Kingston was worried. He'd known Meloy would be protective of the Ranger Battalions, but the degree of resistance to the Delta Plan had been unexpected. It was obvious General Meloy thought we should be involved in a high-visibility counterterrorist activity that included an illuminated night attack involving a Ranger battalion-size force that had either parachuted or rappelled into the target area. We were speaking another language. Our concept of a low-visibility counterterrorist action was viewed as a nonilluminated night attack involving a company-size force (Delta) which infiltrated the target area in civilian clothes with unique weapons and equipment. Delta had come so far, but perhaps now they were going to turn off our lights. Without FORSCOM's concurrence, Delta could not proceed to Washington. There was just no way we could approach the Chief of Staff of the Army and say, "We have people out there who don't believe in the proposal."

Our briefing was scheduled for 10:00 A.M. At 9:00, Sandy Meloy, who I saw as a conniver, gave a classified Ranger briefing to General Kroesen. Neither Tom nor I was allowed in the brief. Ostensibly it was a status report on an exercise that one of the Ranger battalions had conducted and done well in, but the suspicion lingered that the timing of this report, one hour before Delta's, was intended to stonewall us.

Our briefing began on time. Our salesman, the lieutenant colonel who didn't know the difference between a parachute and a pillowcase, was beautiful. He pointed out that nowhere in the United States armed services was there a small force of handpicked volunteers who were thoroughly trained for the counterterrorist job they were expected to undertake. Normally, in any infantry unit, makes no difference if it is Ranger or Airborne, the smallest integral force is a 40-man platoon, which is broken down into squads. Delta advocated a unique organization that used as its building blocks 4-man patrols. This was David Stirling's thesis when he designed the Special Air Service for the British during World War II. He argued for a 16-man troop flexible enough to permit it to be broken into two 8-man patrols, four 4-man patrols, or eight 2-man patrols. The secret, the key, was modules that could change easily within any situation. John Devens deftly described the number and variety of skills Delta required, particularly in terrorist scenarios: people who could get into buildings or planes held under siege, shooters and snipers, explosive experts, locksmiths, medics, electricians, drivers, men who could hot wire a Ford or a Ferrari, soldiers with skills to climb mountains or buildings, men who spoke other languages, men with resolve who could operate decisively in the absence of orders. The void was pointed out. There was no unit in the military that could, with these unique characteristics and skills, act in the event of hostage situations or aircraft hijackings.

A single factor that sold the future Delta Force more than any other was terrorism. The unit was dedicated to coming to grips with it. One of the weaknesses in other organizations is that they are only part-timers in this field. Semipros or gifted amateurs, no matter what their individual abilities or potential are can be no match for international terrorists. It takes full-time professionals, who spend as much time on the subject as the enemy does. In fairness—and following General DePuy's guidelines—our briefer acknowledged that the Rangers were primarily a commando-raid-type organization and were young in age. What was needed, he suggested, was not youth but mature professionals. Also, staff structure and intelligence-collecting mechanisms would be designed to handle terrorist incidents. Devens began to really warm up.

Suddenly—the briefing wasn't half over—General Kroesen interrupted, "I've heard enough." Oh, God, I thought. Sitting next to G. G. Thomas, I could see every note he had written was either negative or derogatory. Here we were, dead in the water. Kroesen turned to Kingston, "Bob, you should have been doing these things long ago." Oh, *wow*! I thought. General DePuy's representative said, "My instructions, sir, are to ask if you will support this proposal when it's taken to the Army Chief of Staff." General Kroesen stood up. "Absolutely," he said as he walked out of the briefing.

Round Two was over. One more to go. Meloy's staff officers tore up their notes and left the room.

★ SEVENTEEN ★

DELTA ENTERED A critical period now. General Depuy had to make an appointment to get on the Chief's calendar. You just didn't do that tomorrow.

We finally received word that that briefing was scheduled in the Pentagon for 2 June 1977.

I wasn't sure what my role in Delta would be. As a once-passed-over colonel, my chances at command ranged from slim to nil. But, hell, I was as happy as I could be. The team's batting average was 1.000. Everyone was floating.

Chuck Odorizzi. Major Buckshot and I spent many nights sketching out a proposed Table of Organization and Equipment (TO&E) as well as skills which Delta needed to acquire. One evening, it had to be near nine o'clock, the weather was unusually warm even for spring and the windows were open, we began again to discuss skills. Chuck, who'd been going nearly fifteen hours, thought we should visit some large manufacturing operations to see the various skills they utilized. He thought we might equate some of these civilian skills with ones we could use.

Buckshot asked him for an example.

Off the top of his head Chuck said, "Well, why don't we go up to General Mills and see what various skills are involved in making cereal."

"Chuck." I said, "We ain't making no goddamn cornflakes here."

Buckshot nearly broke a gut laughing.

After that when anyone would complain that a course was too tough or a skill too difficult, someone else was bound to say, "Well, you know, we're not making cornflakes here!"

The end of May approached. We were days away from doing what we all fervently hoped would be our last successful brief when the world took a full turn.

All of a sudden a requirement surfaced in U.S. Forces Korea for an operations officer (G-3). Two generals had been contacted and because they refused to move their families, both were turned down for the assignment. On the first day of June the word reached Bragg. Maj Gen. Robert Kingston was ordered to report to Seoul, Korea, no later than the 7th of June. Kingston was disappointed, because he believed the formation of Delta was vital to our country and he wanted to be involved with it. He discussed the matter with General Meyer, but eventually, being a good soldier, he accepted the assignment.

I was as upset as he was by this change. Why now, when we were so close? No one could predict what would happen to Delta at this juncture. Jack Mackmull, a major general who I didn't know, a former ADC (assistant division commander) to the 101st Airmobile Division, was nominated to replace Kingston as the new JFK Center Commander. It made sense for General Mackmull to attend the Pentagon briefing of Delta, and he was invited.

I spent the next few days with General Bob—he lived just across the street—helping him sort through his belongings. Once we left for Washington, he would not return to Bragg but fly directly to Korea. Katherine and I promised Bob's wife, Jo, we would help her clear quarters.

I had peeked into the Chief's briefing room at the Pentagon a month or so earlier. Along with the familiar battle paintings that ring the walls, there are portraits of men who fill America's military pantheon. The space is larger than any similar facility I've seen anywhere else. The room at that time had been empty. Today, June 2, 1977, it was full of general officers. General Meyer was there, so were Generals Kroesen and Meloy from FORSCOM. A small group from TRADOC led by General DePuy already sat around the large rectangular table. Tom Henry and I sat out of the way against the wall near the door. Pershing and Patton were hanging next to each other on the opposite wall.

This briefing was for the Army's Chief of Staff (CSA). I'd seen him in photographs, but this was the first time I saw him in person. A Rhodes scholar, Gen. Bernard W. Rogers has pure white hair and looks like the officer Central Casting would have sent over to fill the role of CSA.

General DePuy stood up. The room became very quiet. "What I want to do is describe and reflect on a void I believe exists in the Army." He nodded to John Devens, who walked to the podium. I said a little prayer. It was a variation of one I had used many times before in other crisis situations: Oh, Lord, we have worked so hard and come so far. What we propose we believe is right, and if You can see yourself clear, help us obtain approval. If You will help me today. I'll make tomorrow on my own.

When Devens had finished, General Rogers spoke right up. "This is all very illuminating. I had no idea we had this void. . . ." He went on for a little while, he thanked General DePuy for bringing the issue to his attention, before he got to the moment of truth. "We have, I can see, a real problem here. We have the Rangers, we have the Special Forces, and now we have a need for this capability. Rangers, you know, are damn good men. I've been out and looked at them. On the other hand, they're expensive."

General DePuy saw things were getting off the track. "General Rogers, for the past forty-five minutes we've pointed out an existing problem having nothing to do with the Rangers or with Special Forces. I agree the problems you raise are real but they should be addressed at a later date. What we need to do today is address the problem of the void as presented to you. We could sit in here the rest of the day and talk about it. But there's one officer in this room who knows more about the kinds of operations we have briefed you on than anyone else, and he knows more about the British Special Air Service Regiment than anyone else in the Army."

General Rogers asked, "Who is it?"

"Col. Charlie Beckwith."

General Rogers looked around the room. "Please stand up, Colonel." I stood up. He looked me over and I sat down. It was like being in another world. It had to be a dream. I then flashed on the number of years it had taken to get to this point. I quickly counted the fourteen years I'd been pushing to get the Army to recognize it had the void.

I learned later why my name had been brought up. When DePuy was told that Kingston had been assigned to Korea, he and Bob had discussed who it should be then that ran with the ball. I had been agreed on as the logical choice and to give me the clout to go along with the responsibility General DePuy had introduced me to the Army's Chief of Staff.

General Rogers spoke to General Meyer. "O.K., Shy, what I want from you now is to tell me how we're going to get this together and how much it's going to cost."

I didn't know it then, but it was General Meyer who all along had orchestrated the plan. It was Meyer who early on had seen a need for a counterterrorist force; it was Meyer who Kingston had taken my paper to; it was Meyer who had chosen DePuy to manage the movement and development of the proposal; it was Meyer who had decided they needed Fritz Kroesen; and it was Meyer who had understood the politics and plotted the moves. DePuy and Kingston had been vital, but General Meyer had made it all happen.

After the briefing, General Meyer asked Kingston and me to his office. General Bob immediately asked General Meyer to get the Chief of Staff to change his orders. "Let me stay here and help with the formation of the unit. This is so important." Meyer would have none of it. He was sympathetic but it was not his decision to make. The die had been cast. Kingston was going to Korea. Before we left, General Meyer asked me to complete a cost estimate and a proposed TO&E within ten days. This had already been done. Now it would be a matter of double-checking it.

Kingston and I went over to a friend's apartment. After pouring ourselves some Jack Daniel's, we laughed for joy. We cried a little, too. This was good-bye. Bob Kingston believes there is more to friendship than just paying it lip service. He believes there is a responsibility involved and I agree with him. I've had many fairweather friends, but few real friends. Now, one of them was leaving. Had he stayed, had he been able to mother it along, this infant unit would have gotten on its feet a lot faster. If Bob Kingston had remained at the JFK Center, Delta wouldn't have had half the problems I was soon to learn it had.

"You have the responsibility now, Charlie, to complete this assignment. If you have any problems talk to Shy. God bless you. I wish I could be here to help you, but I can't. You're going to have to fight some tough battles and you're going to have to really use your head."

I didn't know then how much there was to do. Not only wasn't Delta in the ball game, it wasn't even in the park.

★ EIGHTEEN ★

THE GREATEST DANGER, in this kind of situation, is that one may get caught in a hostile or indifferent environment. I had asked the question, "Where does this unit belong?" This was during the second TRADOC briefing at Fort Monroe. General DePuy had replied that it should fit, he felt, under Special Forces. I wasn't sure this was appropriate. He'd said, "Well, initially, let's do it and then maybe down the road we'll move it." That meant there would be problems caused by jealousy. Had Kingston stayed, then maybe; but with Jack Mackmull, who knew what to expect? During the briefing in the Pentagon I'd carefully watched him. I never thought he focused long enough on any of the slides to get their meanings. I felt "This guy may not understand what he's hearing and he may not think it will ever happen."

Mackmull had played football at West Point. In spite of this, if you were to put a white beard on him he'd look like Santa Claus. He was prudent and businesslike and wanted everyone to like him. He went out of his way to be nice to others. At the Academy his nickname had been "Bobo."

When he came in and took command of JFK Center, I went over and briefed him on the activities of the school. I stuck the fire hose down his throat and gave him the whole nine yards. He didn't know anything about Special Forces. He'd commanded helicopter units in 'Nam. "You know, Charlie, when I was at Can Tho, I supported Special Forces a lot, so I got a pretty good feel for them." He'd flown into Can Tho and had gone over to the Special Forces headquarters where he'd probably had a beer with the guys; so he knew what they looked like and what kinds of weapons they carried, but this is no way of getting a feel for what they could or could not do. I thought to myself, Oh, my God!

When I'd finished the briefing on the school, I brought him up to date on my newest activity. I showed him the proposed TO&E and the budget which had been worked up with the Fort Bragg comptroller people. We grossly underestimated the budget, because at the time I was afraid that if Delta carried too big a price tag we'd scare the Army off—but it was better than nothing. I told General Mackmull I planned on taking everything up to the Pentagon. He didn't look at my table of organization or my figures. He wasn't interested. "Fine," he said, "you take them on up." I did, however, get permission to use Special Forces School money to cover my expenses. Remember, this new unit had no money, no authority, no nothing. It wasn't even established on paper. We had only the results of a decision briefing and a name, Delta.

After General Meyer had reviewed my paperwork, indicated we were on track, and told me he'd pass it on to General Rogers for his approval. I began to look around for some more people to join Chuck Odorizzi, Buckshot, and me. I received approval to employ Maj. Curt Hurst. Shortly afterward he became Delta's first operations officer. But what I really needed was a sergeant major. Actually I'd found him, his nickname was "Country," and it was a matter of getting him away from the Special Forces School where he worked.

Country was a tall, raw-boned, very strong man who'd come out of the coal mines of western Pennsylvania. He was a hard man, articulate, and, unlike Buckshot, laid back and unemotional. His strengths were loyalty, intelligence, and experience. He approached problems dispassionately and impartially.

General Mackmull, for the moment caught up in our enthusiasm, let me have him on temporary duty. He also let me have two little buildings the Special Forces School wasn't using. These buildings were vintage World War II, needed a lot of paint, and, if the truth be known, were ready to be torn down. Mackmull's enthusiasm had its limits.

The month of June went by. I heard nothing from General Rogers or General Meyer. July went by and still no word arrived from the Pentagon. I was formulating plans, making overtures, and, frankly, spending more time in the Delta arena than I was in School business.

Sometime later I found out from an old acquaintance of mine, a lieutenant colonel who worked in General Meyer's office, what had become of my TO&E and budget. He told me that General Meyer passed them up to the Chief of Staff's office where they stayed a couple of days. Then Rogers had them sent back to Meyer. My source explained that Meyer had three boxes on his desk. An "in" box an "out" box, and a "too hard" box. When Rogers sent my papers back to Meyer, he had attached a short note, "Shy, please see me." So, Meyer thought there was something wrong and put the papers in his "too hard" box until he could figure out what to do. Meanwhile, I was getting antsy and nervous at Fort Bragg. I don't know if it would have made me feel better or worse knowing my papers were sitting in the "too hard" box.

Days had gone by, then weeks, now months. Finally, I had to do something. Anything. I went to see General Mackmull. This was in August.

"You know, it's very difficult for me to do two jobs and do them right. It's not fair to the school. I'd like you to consider finding someone else to run the school and let me get on full time with this Delta business."

"I'm not convinced in my own mind, Charlie, that this Delta thing is going to get off the ground. I think if it was, we would have heard by now. I'll consider relieving you as you request, but I can't guarantee you a job if Delta collapses."

"I'll take that risk, sir."

I submitted some recommendations for my replacement and began working on Delta full time. This also meant I could worry full time. My frustration level had reached my ears. I couldn't get anything moving. General Mackmull had gone as far as he could in giving me Buckshot. Odorizzi, Hurst, and

Country. He didn't have the authority to give me any funds. Delta couldn't move without written authority from Department of the Army.

I remembered what Bob Kingston had told me about being smart. I made another left-end run. Instead of writing a normal letter that should have gone through General Mackmull at JFK Center, then to XVIII Airborne Corps, then to FORSCOM, then to the Pentagon, I wrote directly to General Meyer and had the letter delivered by safe hands.

On a Friday evening in mid-September, the telephone in my home rang. The call was from one of General Meyer's administrative aides. "Charlie, the General asked me to tell you that the package you sent has been approved and you better come up here and get the wheels moving." I was so excited I couldn't talk.

Monday morning General Meyer told me, "Start framing the necessary documentation for my deputy, General Snippens, and his staff. We need to determine the total number of personnel spaces required and where these will come from. Also, we need to determine your funding. Take the TO&E down to TRADOC and get it approved." I began to learn. "There are people in this building, Charlie, you should talk to. Find out how the Ranger Battalions were activated, find out the mechanics necessary to activate a new unit within the Army structure. Go downstairs and get to work."

In the Army it's spaces, not faces, that are crucial. Because the Congress puts a manpower ceiling on the Army, there is no magic drawer in Department of the Army where you reach in and pull out spaces. They have to come from trade-offs. The Army might be in the process of establishing another new unit and cut from it a specific number of spaces. Or, there may be a unit on the rolls that doesn't have sufficient personnel to fill its spaces. There might also be a unit the Army has recently reorganized and some extra spaces surface which can be used by someone else. Personnel spaces to a new unit are almost as critical as funding. Delta Force received its spaces from various recently reorganized units and from another one unable to recruit the necessary personnel to fill its organization.

Planning and activating a new unit in the Army force structure is necessarily a difficult task. It's a big business with built-in checks and balances; and it requires expertise. The Pentagon was pretty much an unknown territory for me. I lacked a chart showing where the power bases were. These I'd have to find for myself. The CSA approval of the Delta concept was no more than a key that opened the door to the Army's structure and its bureaucracy. Without the necessary maps, blueprints, diagrams, dictionaries, and schematics, the key would mean nothing. It was easy to get lost in the labyrinth that lay open to Delta. I located officers who could assist me and they sent me on to other people and to other offices. I walked down all the halls and around all the rings asking questions of anyone who could help. General Snippens and his staff pitched in and offered assistance and support. There was more than a month of walking, getting lost, being put back on the proper path, stepping off again, being put back on; of talking, arguing, cajoling, fighting. Spaces and funding. Funding and spaces.

Slowly I began to fill in the chart, the deep water and reefs were marked, so were the lagoons and safe anchorages. I learned that General Meyer had not merely given me a ring. It was, in fact, a golden ring. In his wisdom General Meyer gave Delta a high-priority unit status. To get it he had to have it justified and approved by a specific section in Department of the Army. Without it the lines would have been endless.

Equipment was a good example of how high-priority status worked. A list was drawn up of what we thought Delta would need: transportation, arms and ammunition, communications, office equipment, and uniforms. The questions began. How many do you need? What kind? What model? Who has them? Can they be borrowed, bought, leased, or transferred? When you have what you need, who will maintain it? How will you account for it? When will you need to replace or upgrade it?

Ammunition. "What will it cost?" "Can you get it cheaper?" "Can you use less of it?" "Where is it located?" "How will you move it from here to there?" "How will you reorder?" "How will you pay?" "Can you use this instead?" Without a high-priority status Delta would still be waiting in line outside the Depot Supply Office.

Money. The unit was funded in a unique manner. The money flow went directly from an operating agency in Department of the Army to Delta. I'd learned in Vietnam that straight lines were best. There I'd seen how a program had been funded by the Navy directly out of CINCPAC, and how other paramilitary programs had been financed directly from the CIA. The key to funding was not having to rely on money that reached you through layers of bureaucracy. That way there is a good chance every level of command above you through which your money must travel will hold out a certain percentage for unforeseen events. What you finally receive will not match what you were given; the difference ends up in various other units' budget accounts. Very carefully, we structured our funding channels directly from Washington to Delta—not Fort Bragg. Money gave Delta autonomy and autonomy is what Delta needed.

There were many irons in the fire and there were some mistakes made. "You're piecemealing us to death, Charlie." This from the comptroller shop in Department of the Army who had come down to Bragg to straighten out some of Delta's eccentricities. "How about sitting down, taking the time and figuring out what you need and coming to us once." This seemed fair. "Tell us Delta's billet requirements, tell us its range requirements, its logistical requirements. Put a dollar price on all of it. But do it once, not once every week. We don't care what it is, but give us your best shot."

The necessary paperwork to launch Delta took hours, days, weeks, to manufacture. Nothing happened without it. Sometimes it seemed the more the better: weight seemed more important than quality. General Snippens, for example, before he did anything, needed justification for doing it. He didn't invent the system, but the system existed and it needed to be stroked. With Majors Odorizzi and Hurst, I wrote hundreds of papers. When we weren't writing, we were talking. Whenever someone had to make a big decision, when a trade-off was complicated or someone didn't like giving up funds, an appointment had to be made to see General Meyer. A talking paper is prepared. It goes up to his horse-holder (executive officer). Meyer is filled in. Another meeting is scheduled, there is a wait, then the briefing, then another wait, then a decision. Very bureaucratic up there. But it's the only way the system will work.

Delta began to bulge at the seams. Suddenly there was no more space in our original location to put all the matériel that had been ordered and now began to arrive. General Mackmull talked to the Corps commander, General Warner, and Delta was told to find three alternative locations on the post to which it might shift its activities.

Our first choice had already been located—the Fort Bragg Stockade. It was large, isolated from the rest of the post, and surrounded as it was by a double chain linked fence topped with barbed wire, secure.

In the event the Stockade was not available, our second choice was some building being used by the ROTC (Reserved Officers Training Corps).

The third option, and one down at the bottom of the list, was a group of World War II buildings which were located in the 82nd Airborne's area and in close proximity to the post's drug rehabilitation clinic.

General Mackmull didn't know whether the Stockade would be available or not, but he would do some checking. Days went by, then a week. The answer came back. "The Stockade is out of the question!"

We started looking very hard at the ROTC buildings. Meeting after meeting was held. Finally, Mackmull recommended I see Brig. Gen. James J. Lindsay, the XVIII Airborne Corps' chief of staff. Lindsay said, "Colonel Beckwith, this doesn't make any sense to me. Here we've got a nice Stockade facility where we're keeping eleven bad buys. On the other hand, you want to use it with a bunch of good buys. Why don't we take the eleven and put them downtown in the Fayetteville jail? Your use of the Stockade is better than the use it's being put to now. Colonel, you've got it!" I was impressed. I said to myself, This general will never get promoted again. He's too practical. He solved my moving problems in less than four minutes.

Delta's future headquarters, the Fort Bragg Stockade, covered about nine acres of fenced-in real estate. The concrete building itself is a long corridor from which various wings or blocks extend on either side—six major ones in all. Most of these long wings contained beds which had been secured to the cement floors. One of our first jobs was to saw the beds off the floors.

The one wing containing maximum security cells we converted to an ammo and explosives holding area as well as a place to keep our most sensitive documents. Each troop would also be given two cells each for their weapons storage. Within another wing, the squadrons would designate an area for each troop to keep anything else they wished. These bays were always kept very neatly and usually reflected the personality of the troop that used them. There were lockers and occasionally a refrigerator with the hand-printed sign: "The brew is 25¢. Please deposit your money in the cup." The troop bays, to my knowledge, never displayed pinups. More often you'd see a photograph clipped from a newspaper or magazine, which showed a recent terrorist incident.

The mess facility was excellent. The prisoners at Fort Bragg had obviously eaten well. Operations and Intelligence shared a wing which they quickly outgrew. Selection and Training had its own area. The Stockade's theater and chapel, with a little construction, were turned into a briefing or conference room and a classroom. The old admissions office was taken over by the headquarters staff, and it was in this area that Country and I had our offices.

I wanted the outside of the Stockade to be tidy and reflect some of the smartness I'd found years before in the SAS camp at Bradbury Lines. A royal blue canvas awning was eventually hung over the front entrance. Because I am very partial to roses, I saw to it that a large rose garden was planted on either side of the path that led from the fence gate to the Stockade's entrance. Roses of every color and variety would eventually grow there—French Lace, All-American, Seashell, Dainty

Bess, Lady X—and although it was the subject of some joking, the garden eventually earned the unit a lot of pin money. We cleaned up on Mother's Day.

It also surprised many of our first-time visitors. They would tell us, "Coming from Washington to Bragg we expected to see you snake eaters swinging from trees, but this garden . . ." General Meyer said on his first visit, "You're beginning to get there. The place looks nice."

Although Delta now had a headquarters it could call home, I continued to spend much of my time in the Pentagon. It was there that most of my work needed to be done and the people I had to see were located.

On one such day, typical in every respect—it was the middle of October 1977, work was unexpectedly interrupted. People began to talk about some place called Mogadishu. We looked it up. It was in Somalia. A German commercial airliner had been hijacked and flown there. The story came in slowly off the wire all day. Finally, a West German counterterrorist unit called GSG-9 (Grenzschutzgruppe 9) had stormed the plane, overwhelmed the terrorists, and released the passengers. In the Pentagon that day, the shit just hit the fan. I knew there was a meeting going on in "the tank" of the JCS (Joint Chiefs of Staff) and lots of people kept running back and forth. I was sitting in my office. Tom Owen, who worked for Snippens, rushed in, "What do you know about GSG-9? A lot of people are asking questions." I didn't know much. SAS, yes, but not that much about the West Germans. I thought they were a police unit and not military. Owen asked, "Do you know what a 'flash-bang' is?"

"Of course."

"Whew! I'm glad, because they asked and I said if anyone in the building would know it was Charlie Beckwith. He wants to see you."

"Who?"

"General Rogers."

I'd never even been inside his office. When I got there it was about what I expected from the Chief of Staff of the Army. It was so neat and tidy and clean that if a fly had dared enter and settled on the wall it would have fallen off and skinned its ass.

A flash-bang has certain concussive, nonlethal properties, which I described to General Rogers. I had first been introduced to them in England. As a matter of fact, the German assault force that had used them had gotten them from 22 SAS. When I finished, General Rogers told me of a note from the President. It had surfaced in the tank earlier in the day and asked, "Do we have the same capability as the West Germans?" Much discussion had ensued before it was decided we did not. One of the generals present had said, "Well, I'm not going over to the White House and tell them we don't." General Rogers then informed the Chairman of the Joint Chiefs of Staff of his earlier decision to activate an elite unit whose mission was to combat terrorism. General Rogers seemed very happy to be telling this story and further informed me that it had been decided that the Army would be the prime mover in this effort. The Joint Chiefs of Staff had felt that since the Army had been doing more in this area than any other service it should handle it.

"The ball is squarely in my court," said General Rogers. "Where are we?"

Delta's status was explained to him. He turned to General Meyer, who had just walked in, "Why are we so far behind on this? I approved that paper months ago." He didn't know about the "too hard" box. General Meyer replied, "We haven't really lost any time. Oh, the paper got held up a little bit. Charlie, we haven't lost any time have we?"

"We can make it up," I replied. "No problem."

Then General Rogers asked, "Do you really think we can do this?"

"We can," I replied, "but I'm going to need some help." I pointed out to General Rogers that what we really needed was help in locating good people, and if he could occasionally check in to this vital area we'd stay on track. He readily agreed to do so.

Afterward, General Meyer was euphoric. Not only did we

now have the CSA's blessing, but his active participation as well.

When I returned in December from a visit to Europe—which allowed me to look over GSG-9 and touch base again with the SAS—a trip on which I was accompanied by General Mackmull, I learned that there were some top secret messages awaiting me at the JFK Center. One of them was dated 19 November 1977, and was the authority to activate Delta. It outlined the unit's mission, its structure and its high-priority status. Much of the order's language was familiar, as it paraphrased an earlier activation order I had been asked to write.

Unfortunately, some of it was very unfamiliar: to my great discomfort, I learned Delta's command and control mechanism would fall under Forces Command (FORSCOM). This was a very poor arrangement indeed and if allowed to stand could kill the concept we had fought so hard to sell. In other words, there was Delta. Then immediately above it in the table of organization was JFK Center and General Mackmull; above them XVIII Airborne Corps and General Warner: above them FORSCOM and General Kroesen; above them Department of the Army and General Rogers. Laid out on a blackboard, it looked like the schematic for a Chinese fire drill.

If there was anything I had learned in my year with 22 SAS it was that the chain of command for this type of unit needed to be clean and direct. It tore me up. Terrorist situations come down hard and they come down suddenly. There is precious little time to wade through paperwork, or climb up a bureaucratic ladder.

I had been under the impression that Delta would be activated directly under Department of the Army. Now I read that General Kroesen would be responsible and I knew he would ask General Warner over at XVIII Airborne Corps to watch over Mackmull and me. A very fit general officer and a West Pointer, Volney Warner was, like General Meloy, a Sterling Silver Ranger. This could only mean trouble. I suspected he wasn't convinced that Delta was necessary, and I knew he wasn't one of our biggest fans. Warner appeared to me to be egotistical and selfish. Now he was going to be breathing down Delta's young neck.

I became very unhappy and couldn't figure out how to get out of the corner into which Delta had been painted. I shouldn't have worried, because it got worse.

General Jack Hennessey was a little bent out of shape. We shouldn't have had a problem with him, but we did. And the problem was serious. The order activating 1st Special Forces Operational Detachment–Delta had been sent to every major command that had a need to know, including REDCOM (Readiness Command), which has its headquarters in Tampa, Florida. Under a counterterrorist contingency plan, which had been formulated in 1976, REDCOM and its commander, General Hennessey, were responsible for testing and then moving counterterrorist forces from the continental United States to the various unified command areas located throughout the world. General Hennessey was upset because he had not been informed of the Army's plan for Delta, or the JCS meeting that had given Delta and General Rogers its blessing. It hadn't taken much time for General Hennessey, once he'd received Delta's activation orders, to call General Mackmull and ask him to come to Tampa and brief him.

Mackmull grabbed me and we flew down to present the same brief that had been given to General Rogers. After we had finished, General Hennessey looked squarely at me, "I want to make it very clear to you, Colonel, that if something of a terrorist nature goes down in my area of responsibility, and I'm directed to respond, I'm going to call you!"

"Well," I said, "that won't do you any good, because I don't have anybody at this time. We're just getting started, sir. It's going to take two years to build this force."

He didn't even pay attention. "You weren't listening, Colonel. If I have a problem, I'm going to call you!" He was dead serious.

On the airplane ride back to Bragg, General Mackmull was distressed. "Charlie, I've got to do something. In the event something goes down and I'm called, I've got to have a response." A few days later he was still concerned. "Look, Charlie, I'm very worried about this requirement of General Hennessey's. It could become real. Here's what I propose. Go through the 5th and 7th Special Forces groups and see if you can come up with a unit that can bridge the gap until Delta's ready. If you don't want to do this, or can't do it, I'll find someone else. I'll also talk to Bob Mountel." Colonel Mountel was the commander of the 5th Special Forces Group.

I discussed Mackmull's plan with my three majors, Odorizzi, Buckshot, and Hurst, and we agreed it was not a prudent course for me to follow. There just wasn't going to be enough time to run two units.

When I saw General Mackmull again, I told him we felt we couldn't do two things at once and do them well. This made Bob Mountel very happy. Mountel was never without a pipe, and his teeth were worn and discolored because of it. He was also in the habit of carrying gloves, which gave him the nickname "Black Gloves."

General Mackmull gave Colonel Mountel the task of creating a unit to breach the short-term gap that now existed. But Bob Mountel didn't see it that way. He wanted to prove that the Special Forces community could establish an antiterrorist force quicker, better, and cheaper than Department of the Army. Bob Mountel saw he had to work very, very hard—and he had to put Charlie Beckwith out of business.

★ NINETEEN ★

ASSESSING THE RIGHT people, then selecting and training them, was the key to success for Delta. If the financial and personnel sides of the business can be worked out, other things will normally fall into line.

Because the Army consists of so many people, personnel management is complicated. We were now going to ask the Army to manage Delta differently than in a normal unit. The norm is to put personnel records into a computer: who you are, where you are, where you've been, what you've done—everything, practically down to your shoe size. This wouldn't work for Delta. Because of the security that needed to be maintained, it was not a good idea to have Delta's personnel records so easily retrievable.

I went to see Maj. Gen. Charles K. Heiden at the personnel center (MILPERCEN) in Arlington, Virginia. We asked him how to limit access to Delta's personnel to only "need to know" people. He had some experience handling Army intelligence personnel under a different system and didn't see this as any problem. We would be taken care of not by computers but by three or four people who used stubby pencils. "We'll find a way to keep you out of sight. I understand how important it is. I've just finished reading *The Man Called Intrepid*," and he gave me a knowing wink.

One of my major fears, one I discussed with General Heiden, was being too far out of sight, especially at promotion time. I felt that if Delta's people were not in the computer, they might be overlooked! But I was assured that out of sight did not mean lost or ignored. General Heiden's people really got on board and helped. One important way was by finding a cover name for Delta that could be used when we did want to disappear. When Delta's people wrote checks, for example, there was no reason to see a Delta endorsement on them; or if one of the troops wanted to build a house and he needed a loan, when the bank did a credit check on him, they shouldn't come nosing around Delta.

Another way General Heiden helped was in ferreting out good people for us to look at. Everyone in the Army knows commanders who have good soldiers rathole them away. Any good officer will do this and so would I, and did many times. Poaching is never appreciated. General Heiden and his computers could help Delta locate these hidden caches of men.

I'm sure General Rogers, following through on his promise to check into personnel for us, did a lot of good. Still, I'm convinced that General Heiden and his staff, without any nudging from above, would have helped us any way they could.

At this juncture Lt. Col. Dick Potter joined Delta's staff as my deputy. Like Kingston, Dick had been an exchange officer with the British paras. A man who likes good food, he occasionally had trouble with his weight. Because of a severe leg wound he suffered in 'Nam, on cold damp days Dick would walk with a slight gimp. However, if there was someone important around, no matter how dank the weather, Dick would suck in the pain and walk perfectly. Along with having a fine combat record, he was a good detail man who knew how to wade into issues and come out with a workable solution. Moreover, he wasn't a "yes" man. Dick concerned himself with getting the job done and not with winning friends or playing politics.

One of the first things he did was attend and referee a meeting which tried to determine how we recruited people. Initially, we were prepared to look over the whole Army. Then someone said. "Why don't you recruit just out of the infantry?" We almost got pushed into that single area, but I knew the British SAS had found its people in the Guards Regiments, the Parachute Regiment, the Royal Horse Artillery, the Royal Highland Fusiliers, the Royal Engineers—anywhere, as a matter of fact, where good men were. That's what Delta needed to do. It didn't make any difference where the volunteer came from or what he did, as long as he was willing, fit, and trainable. He needed, in other words, to be special.

Meanwhile, Bob Mountel had selected forty or so men from the Special Forces community, dubbed his unit Blue Light, and was in business.

Pressure began to build for Delta to get a selection course underway. Rumors flew around Bragg. "Beckwith's putting together something along the SAS lines." It wasn't a long time before a number of volunteers had come over, "Charlie, how do we get here? What should we do?"

A letter was sent to General Mackmull requesting his permission to recruit people from the 5th and 7th Special Forces groups and from the 10th, which was up in Massachusetts at Fort Devens. "If I let you do that," he replied, "you'll decimate the groups."

I was looking for only thirty or thirty-five men to start with. From the people who'd come and volunteered we had collected a list of 150 or so. Many of them we knew from Vietnam. From this list we figured we could burp out thirty. We needed men who were trainable, because they would be the ones who'd run the selection courses and later do part of the assessing. Without an initial cadre to conduct the courses, Delta wouldn't have anything.

Mackmull finally relented and at first, before he realized the scope and magnitude of the recruitment plans, let us run through the first selection course thirty men from the Special Forces community.

Chuck Odorizzi and Buckshot helped me plan the course. Buckshot was especially helpful. He had returned from going through the SAS selection course, where he'd done well. So well that the SAS commander told me, "If you don't want this bloke, send him back."

The thirty volunteers were first required to successfully

complete a demanding physical training test. The test consisted of six events that had to be completed within a designated period. A minimum of sixty points for each event had to be scored for the recruit to progress to the next test.

The recruits were required to perform: a forty-yard inverted crawl in twenty-five seconds; thirty-seven sit-ups and thirty-three push-ups, each in a minute; a run-dodge-jump course traversed in twenty-four seconds; a two-mile run completed in not more than sixteen minutes and thirty seconds; and, finally, a 100-meter lake swim in which the recruits were to be fully dressed, including jump boots.

The PT test eliminated several candidates. An eighteen-mile speed march further reduced the group to half its original size. These survivors were then expected to pass a selection course—right out of the SAS Training Manual—which had been set up, near Troy, North Carolina, in the Uwharrie National Forest.

The course, which each man was expected to run alone, carrying a 55-pound rucksack, extended over dense hardwood-covered mountains, crisscrossed by streams and rivers. Using a map and compass, the volunteer was ordered to go from one location to another, fast as he could; the time required to make the marches was never revealed. The terrain the men were made to march over was thickly wooded and sharply contoured.

At each rendezvous (RV) the recruit was told to march to another location, again as rapidly as he was able. This continued both day and night for an extended period of time. If a recruit should not make an RV in a prescribed amount of time, he was removed from the course and eventually shipped back to his old unit.

Survivors of the Uwharrie selection course then underwent careful psychological scrutiny and evaluation. A board was established consisting of Major Odorizzi, Major Buckshot, Sergeant Major Country, and me. An interview ran nearly four hours. I asked the Army for a psychologist and they began a search to find us one. In the meantime, we did the job.

"On a mission, you run across two little girls . . ." Some of the questions that were asked had no right answers. The men were asked to reason and to think. We wanted to catch their values, find out what cranked their motors. We looked for loners, guys who could operate independently and in the absence of orders, men who had just half an ounce of paranoia.

They read Machiavelli and explained what they thought he was about. We asked them to expand on a story of three people who had fled on foot from Siberia and had eventually escaped into Tibet. "Comment on that adventure: what did the escapees do right, what did they do wrong, what would you have done?"

We drilled holes in these guys and it wasn't uncommon to have them break out in a sweat. Did we want this one or didn't we? What about this guy?

We asked him, "You've done very, very well. You're nearly through, most of your peers haven't made it, you're good. Now, tell us what you don't do well. What do you tend to screw up?" If a man answered, "I don't have any weaknesses," we didn't take him.

We asked the finalists what they thought of President Truman firing General MacArthur during the Korean War, "Was it right or wrong? Why? What is your opinion?" Some of these men didn't know what we were talking about. I was shocked to discover our soldiers weren't well read.

Finally, we asked about skills. Could they repair an elevator, read a blueprint, rewire a house, survey a city block, memorize the contents of a museum? The Brits knew a lot of people could run up and down mountains and hit RV points, but that isn't what made them unique.

"Sergeant Jones, why should I take you? You did very well in the selection course. You really burned up those mountains. You looked good and did well. But now, you convince me on why I should take you. What have you got to offer?"

"Sir, I'm a good soldier."

"Shit, I got a bunch of them. What do you do different? Do you drive an 18-wheeler?"

"No, sir."

"Do you know anything about dogs? Ever work with them?"

"Sir, I had a bird dog once."

"Aw, shit, I'm talking about real canine dogs."

"Ah, no, sir, no more than anybody else."

"See, Sergeant, you really haven't told me anything. Think a few minutes and tell me some of your unique skills."

PAUSE

"Sir, I'm pretty good with locks."

"You are? How good are you?"

"I can pick 'em. I'm pretty good at that."

"How good?"

"Call so-and-so and ask him."

"I will. You're dismissed. We'll call you back later."

We'd call his reference and find out if he was telling the truth. The board wasn't interested if he was not an expert. What we were looking for was flair. If the taxpayer's money was going to be spent sending some individual to school, he had to have an aptitude for that training. As a result of the first selection course, Delta kept seven people.

Along with this small cadre of potential instructors, we looked around for two civilians who could help us. Stability, knowledge, and institutional continuity was what the unit needed. The first civilian hired lived in Florida. Dick Meadows had recently retired after compiling a fine Special Forces record. He'd participated in the Son Tay raid. Dick had also been in the SAS exchange program and had married the daughter of an SAS sergeant major. When he agreed to come and help Delta, I felt we had plugged a big hole.

During this time Dick Potter continued to work on a recruitment profile. This profile was very complete and it really described the desired measurable characteristics of each recruit. As outlined by Potter, the volunteer had to meet the following prerequisites:

Besides being able to perform at top efficiency his MOS (Military Occupation Specialty), the recruit needed to be at least a Grade 5 on his second enlistment; have no limiting physical profile; be at least twenty-two years old and an American citizen; have a GT score of 110 or higher; be able to pass a background security check; be able to pass a Modified Special Forces Physical Training Test and a physical examination; be airborne-qualified or volunteer for airborne training; have no recurring disciplinary offenses on his record; have two years active service remaining after assignment; and pass a formal selection course.

Our recruiters visited Benning and Knox, Sill and Hood, Leonard Wood and Ord, Carson and Lewis, Pope, Jackson, Belvoir, Meade, Riley, Stewart, and Devens. Back and forth they went, hitting nearly every Army post, camp, and station in this country. They went to the European command twice. It was a tough job. Having identified an individual was just the beginning of the process. We were, after all, looking for good people, and good people in the Army usually have choice jobs. We couldn't promise them much except a chance to have their lives made a lot harder.

I went up to talk to the 10th Special Forces Group. Its commander, Othar Shalikashvilli, who had earlier recommended me to General DePuy, again couldn't have been more helpful. On a Saturday morning, he stood in front of his own officers and senior noncoms and said: "The job that Colonel Beckwith has to do is a lot more important than the job we have to do. I would encourage anyone who has the desire to try out for this unit." On the basis of this presentation and an old affiliation with the 10th that Country had, we got nearly sixty people signed up to run through our next selection course, which was scheduled for January 1978.

Because its terrain was more rugged and resembled more closely the SAS's Brecon Beacons, Delta eventually moved its selection course to Camp Dawson, tucked into the harsh mountains of West Virginia. Having not yet received permission to make this move, the second selection course was again run through the forested hills and valleys of Uwharrie. Out of the almost sixty volunteers who participated, Delta selected five recruits.

Everyone worked eighteen-hour days, seven-day weeks. The paperwork never ended. Everyone chipped in—Country,

Buckshot, Chuck Odorizzi, Curt Hurst, and Dick Potter. Every evening before bedtime I'd write memos and messages. There was a lot of justifying that needed to be done. Lots of letters replying to General Mackmull, and the various support divisions that were doing business with us needed to be written. We wanted 180 people from Special Forces to participate in our second selection process. These were people who'd rung our bell, met our qualifications, and volunteered—180. Mackmull blinked, coughed, and said, "No way!"

I tried to get Rangers to try out. I knew Joe Stringham; he'd previously run classes through the Ranger School. Initially, I wanted him to come to Delta as my deputy. When I learned he was being considered to command the 1st Ranger Battalion—no one wants to be someone's deputy if he has the opportunity to command—I immediately fell off. I was told that the generals at FORSCOM, particularly Kaplan, appreciated my taking the hook out of Joe, and it eased some of the tension we were having with the Rangers. However, General Meloy continued to monitor very closely both Ranger battalions. Consequently, absolutely no Rangers ran through the second selection course.

Meloy also contacted Mackmull, and some of their message traffic inadvertently found its way to our headquarters. It appeared to me both commanders felt that if they completely cooperated with Delta it would cause chaos in the Ranger and Special Forces communities. It was decided, therefore, that Delta could talk to a handful of potential volunteers, but only those who were on a list prepared by the Rangers and Special Forces. General Mackmull allowed Delta to talk only to people with certain skills—demolition and weapons, for example. Under no circumstances, though, could we talk to medics or noncoms skilled in communications, operations, or intelligence. Experience had taught that the demolition and weapons skills were the easiest to acquire. Conversely, the medical, communications, operations, and intelligence skills were the most difficult and took the most training. It was apparent then that if Delta's staff recruited only those soldiers who appeared on Mackmull's list, they would not necessarily be talking to the best men available. General Mackmull was not entirely responsible himself for this policy, as he was receiving advice from his staff and the two group commanders. In civilian business it would be called "restraint of trade." Delta was being hamstrung and it couldn't survive that way. We stated our dissatisfaction with the system time and time again. However, the Special Forces list continued to be our only access to potential Green Beret volunteers. On the other hand, no Rangers, whatsoever, showed up.

Mackmull's small group of men, incorporated into the second selection course, did very badly. Absolutely no one on the list got through. Mackmull could not understand this. "I'm not sure they really wanted to be there," I told him.

Water temperature at Bragg began getting warmer and warmer. People kept beating down my door. "Colonel, I can't get over here. My unit won't let me." It got to the point that during grievance periods they were going to General Mackmull directly to complain to him. When this didn't change the situation, some of the men wrote to Department of the Army.

General Mackmull began to get nervous, and I thought rightly so. I became more and more unpopular, not only with my boss, but with the rest of the Special Forces community. "He's one of us, but now he wants to go his own way."

General Mackmull earmarked a lieutenant colonel from his personnel section to work with Delta. His name was Whitey Blumfield. He prescreened applicants for us, but when our people went over for interviews they'd find men who didn't even meet the prerequisites. We wasted a lot of time working with a nonresponsive mechanism. The pressure continued to build: Mackmull got angry with Blumfield; Blumfield got angry with Delta; Delta got angry with Mackmull and Blumfield. Friction and bad blood were the order of the day. Life at the JFK became tough for everyone who had any dealings with Delta.

It was at this point that General Mackmull began to throw some weight Blue Light's way, began to give them everything he was capable of giving. Mountel had gained momentum. His line was, "Delta really belongs in Special Forces but Beckwith doesn't want it there. Blue Light is in the community. Come out and look at what we're doing." They had been training hard and were motivated. Mountel had one problem, though. Blue Light did not own its money. No funds had been allocated directly to it. Whatever it had, Mountel had to take out of the hide of 5th Special Forces Group; and since he also commanded this unit, he was caught between a rock and a hard place. If Mountel needed more money, he had to go to the JFK Center to see if they would cough it up. This meant, with only one pot to dip into, that in order to strengthen one unit Mackmull had to weaken another. This, as you can imagine, caused problems.

Momentum began slowly to work in Delta's direction. It was imperceptible at first. But movement was there. It was then a matter of continuing to roll forward and of staying in front.

★ TWENTY ★

OF ALL THE papers we wrote during this period, none was more important than the one we called "The Robert Redford Paper." It justified everything we wanted to do. A few weeks earlier, the Department of Defense (DOD) had gone over to Department of the Army: "You've told us about Delta Force, but what we can't figure out is why it's going to take so long to put together. What if something adverse happens to the U.S., some incident? We're concerned." They couldn't understand why it should take two years to select, train, and assess combat veterans who had received maximum ratings on their efficiency reports and who were already highly trained and in excellent physical condition. How come they needed two more years to be ready? General Rogers's office had called me in early February. They, too, were now concerned because Delta was also spending big bucks. The Army, pushed by DOD, had wanted to know if we could go faster.

Early on, when I returned to England to update my SAS experience, in late 1976. Brigadier John Watts had made it very clear to me that it was going to take eighteen months to build a squadron. Recruiting, assessing, selecting, running four or five courses to assure we received the best men, then individual training and unit training; it couldn't be done in less than a year and a half. "But, Charlie, don't tell anyone that," Watts warned. "Tell them it's going to take two years. If you do it earlier, then that's all to the good. But don't box yourself in. Build in some running room and whatever you do don't let anyone talk you out of this."

Now Delta had to respond to the Chief of Staff's office: we had to justify why it would take two years to build Delta. I didn't fall off. I got hold of Major Buckshot and he drafted what we called our "Robert Redford Paper."

In it he outlined why Delta's four-phase assessment/selection process was required to select operational personnel and why the reliance on past records, or on a less thorough assessment/selection process, was inadequate. Johnny Watts told me they didn't know why their selection process worked—only that it did and had for twenty-five years.

The paper articulated historical precedents for this kind of training. At the 1972 Olympics in Munich, at the moment the shooting—which ultimately led to the deaths of a number of Israeli athletes—began, two of the German sharpshooters on the scene, who had terrorists in their sights, failed to fire their weapons. Their marksmanship had been assessed. Their resolve had not. Five years later, in Somalia, when the Germans assaulted the hijacked airliner on the ground at Mogadishu, all four terrorists were taken down without the loss of a single hostage. Ulrich Wegener, the commander of GSG-9, had no question about the resolve of his men. They had been thoroughly assessed before being selected. I knew of another instance. In Vietnam, a five-man Australian SAS patrol tracked an enemy patrol for five days through enemy territory. They eventually attacked and destroyed a North Vietnamese command post. The SAS had not brought those men into the regiment because they were good trackers—the training came later. They were brought into the regiment because, through the SAS selection course, they had proven they were dedicated, resourceful, trainable.

Stress was patterned after that used by 22 SAS and was the most misunderstood. On the surface it appeared to be little more than a test of physical strength and stamina. The volunteers were asked to perform a series of individual, timed, land-navigation exercises that were conducted in the mountains. The length of each increased daily from ten kilometers to seventy-four kilometers, with equipment increasing in weight from fifty pounds to seventy pounds. By the time the seventy-four kilometer, or forty-mile, exercise began, the candidates had reached a common level of physical exhaustion. They were totally pooped. We'd used up their reserves. The endurance march revealed clearly those candidates who had character—real determination, self-discipline, and self-sacrifice—and those who did not. The seventy-four kilometer, independently executed march across rugged mountain terrain had to be completed in twenty hours. The man was given the coordinates of a rendezvous point some eight to twelve kilometers distant. He was not told on reaching the RV how many more remained, what route to take, or whether he was going too slow. He was not encouraged or discouraged, advised or harassed. Simply told, "Your next RV is map coordinate . . ." It was a matter of seeing what each individual could do. Around the twelfth hour, if the pace was sufficient to meet the requirement, the man would be, in the medical sense of the term, almost totally exhausted. He began to look for excuses to quit, to slow down, even to hope he would injure himself. Anything to allow him to stop. It was then, after the twelfth hour, that many men quit, or rested too long, or slowed to a pace that prohibited them from meeting the time requirement. A few others had the sense of purpose, the courage, the will, the guts to reach down inside themselves for that intangible trait that enabled them to carry on. Without that ability, the man did not succeed. This was, perhaps, a crude method of evaluation, but it was the one on which the British SAS had relied for twenty-five years.

Yes, it would take two years to find individuals who were unusually inquisitive, sensitive, resourceful, and imaginative. Two years to find people who could be at times extremely patient and at other times extremely aggressive; who could operate under unusually restrictive constraints at one moment and be audacious, freethinking individuals the next; operate with orders and operate without them; be able to lead and to follow; withstand prolonged physical and mental activity and endure extended monotony. It would take two years, our paper clearly and convincingly informed General Rogers. We were building a foundation that would pay off down the road. Department of the Army forwarded our "Robert Redford Paper" to the Office of the Secretary of Defense. Delta received no further pressure to push on faster than the time frame that had been proposed.

★ TWENTY-ONE ★

BLUE LIGHT, SUPPORTED by JFK center, was competing against us. Delta's training program had not been evaluated or blessed. But worst of all, our recruitment situation was not getting better. The next selection course—the third—was due to be kicked off any day. I wrote a letter. There was no other way I could go.

> Dear General Meyer:
>
> Our unit has made progress in the short period since activation on 19 November 1977. However, obstacles have arisen which become more critical with each passing day.
>
> The most critical problems encountered thus far have been:
> The recruitment of volunteer candidates, as specified by the Chief of Staff of the Army, has not been totally supported, and in one known case the instructions of the CSA have been disregarded. . . .
>
> The atmosphere of competition fostered between the 5th Special Forces Group—BLUE LIGHT and 1st SFOD—Delta for technical assistance, equipment, and other assets impacts adversely upon our plans and priorities. Additionally, the high priority assigned to Delta for equipment and training support has been misused in support of BLUE LIGHT.

The formation of U.S. Army Rangers, U.S. Army Special Forces (BLUE LIGHT), USN SEALS, Delta, among others overseas, has caused confusion within government agencies (CIA, FBI and Secret Service) as to who within the Department of Defense has responsibility for welding together a force to counter terrorists overseas.

The military intelligence community is not geared to support low visibility counterterror threat situations. There is an urgent need for access to the holdings of appropriate national level intelligence agencies in order to train and prepare Delta for its mission. . . .

Recommendations:

1. That the existing chain of command for Delta be streamlined with the unit remaining at Fort Bragg as a tenant unit and receive base operational support from Commander, FORSCOM. Delta must be under the direct supervision of the Chief of Staff of the Army. . . .
2. That the DOD or State Department, if it plans to employ Delta, be thoroughly cognizant of the unit's low visibility capabilities and its external support requirements.

Who dares, wins.

I had one of my officers deliver it directly to General Meyer's office. Paranoia? Yes, but I've got no business doing what I'm doing without a small case of it: "Call me when you see this letter delivered to General Meyer." I knew lots of things went to Washington and sometimes they lost their way. A very clever action officer could "misplace" a letter. I didn't just think this would happen. I knew it could happen.

The call came around 11:00 A.M., it was 8 March 1978, confirming the letter had been received. The day was dark and the weather had turned cold. Within an hour I took another call. Lt. Gen. Volney Warner said, "Charlie, General Rogers is coming here this afternoon and wants to see you. After I've shown him some training I'll bring him back to my office and you can see him here. Meet us at Pope Air Force Base around 1330." I said, "Whatever's fair, sir." It began raining like hell.

I immediately asked Majors Hurst and Buckshot to go through our files and pull out every memo we'd written painting our problems. If General Rogers wanted to come back to Delta's headquarters, we'd be ready.

By midafternoon the hard rain had turned to a cold drizzle.

At Pope, General Warner spoke to me and to Colonel Norton, who was acting on behalf of Mackmull, then in Korea on a visit. "After I've shown him what I have to, we'll come back to my office. Do y'all have any problems with this?" "No," I said, "but I don't think that's what General Rogers is going to want to do."

"And what's that, Colonel?"

"He's going to want to go over to the Stockade and I'm prepared to lead the way."

General Warner didn't see it that way. I knew he wanted to be perceived as a nice guy, but I knew he was making life very hard. Mackmull used to tell me, "Things are not real good, because General Warner breathes all over me, Charlie. You need to understand that. He thinks you're trying to become a free agent and he wants me to keep you in line." With Warner biting from the top and me pecking from the bottom, Mackmull was having a tough go of it.

Colonel Norton and I were about thirty feet from where Warner greeted General Rogers. They spoke for some time. It was cold and damp enough to see their breath. The Chief of Staff was dressed in his Class A Greens. Warner turned and waved me over. "Lead the way to the Stockade."

At the Stockade, General Rogers sat down at one end of our conference table. We were in Delta's little conference room. Nothing fancy here. No battle paintings and no elaborate podium. Just a work space with a scruffy table and folding chairs. Some of my staff were present. I remained standing. I said, "General Rogers, the concept to establish a unit along SAS lines in the United States Army, which you approved for implementation, is off track. We have very serious problems.

I've documented them and I want to share this material with you." I thought he was going to say, "Yeah, that's the reason I'm here . . ."

When he didn't interrupt I continued, "Some of the problems I have recommendations for solving, others are too large for me. One of my major problems is in command and control. As you will recall, on 19 November 1977, Delta was activated under HQ, FORSCOM, passed to XVIII Airborne Corps, and down to the commander JFK Center. This is a serious mistake and could jeopardize the entire concept of Delta." I was very calm and articulating my troubles carefully. "The German's GSG-9 has a very clean chain of command. No in-between bureaucracy. SAS operates the same way. I would, therefore, request that Delta be a Field Operating Agency working directly under DCSOPS. I would like you to read some of this documentation."

General Rogers began to work his way through the piles of paper. The rain, which had begun falling again, could be heard on the roof. Eventually, he stumbled on a memo outlining Mountel's use of Delta's ammunition. "What's Blue Light?" he asked. "I didn't authorize that. Why are they using your funds?" Norton didn't say a thing. Then, General Rogers read the next memo, describing how the Rangers had been fenced off from me. Attached to the memo were the two messages from Mackmull and Meloy I had acquired. Very quickly General Rogers went through all the paper. "You know," he said when he was finished, "there's a four-letter word in Kansas for this kind of mess." He became very upset, "We have to get this straightened out. Why haven't you kept me informed, Charlie?"

I explained I didn't have the authority to send a cable directly to him but had to go to my rating officer, Colonel Norton, for permission to send through the JFK Center. General Rogers turned to Norton, "Who in the hell are you? You're not Colonel Beckwith's rating officer, so why really are you even here? General Meyer is Colonel Beckwith's rating officer and I'm his endorsing officer. Charlie, you don't work for Colonel Norton!"

Norton didn't say a word. He just froze in his seat and stared straight ahead. I understood then that General Rogers hadn't any idea of the size of the bureaucracy that had been put over me. In fact, Colonel Norton was my rating officer and General Mackmull *was* my endorser. I knew if it stayed that way I was a dead man.

General Rogers said, "Charlie, you will keep me informed." This meant I had the authority to release teletype messages directly. I no longer had to go through my commanding general or any other general at Bragg to send these hard-copy messages. Lots of people in the Army write messages, but getting them released and put on the teletype is a different story.

The shit truly hit the fan. You have no idea how it hit. People stood with their mouths open. My deputy, Dick Potter, was so excited he could hardly stand himself.

I asked General Rogers, "Would you like now to go back and visit some of the troops?" "No," he said. "I want to talk to you in private." General Warner was left sitting in my little conference room. Mouths dropped open wider. The Army Chief of Staff and I went outside and stood by the rose garden. The rain was falling hard again. General Rogers was not only angry, he was hurt, disappointed. There was some distant thunder.

"This is just a mess, Charlie."

I said, "General Rogers, let me, if I can, sir, say one thing to you. If I fail in this job, then, goddamn it, you ought to fire me. I want to do this job, but I need some support. I'm not being supported out of the Special Forces community. I'm not being supported by the Rangers. I didn't realize that there would be people who stood around the periphery and wished me to fail—but that is the case. There are people who really want to see Delta fail. I want this job more than anything in this world."

General Rogers looked at me. There was a pause. The four silver stars on his new black rain coat gleamed in the rain. He said. "Let me make one thing clear to you, Charlie. If you fail you're not the only one who's going to be fired. Oh, yeah, I'll fire you, but I'm going to get fired, too. The President, Charlie, wants this unit. Delta is important. We cannot afford to mess this up."

We walked back inside. General Rogers said to everyone in the room. "What I'm going to do is get Shy down here and we're going to get this problem turned around." He turned to General Warner, "I've got to get back to Washington." And he left.

I suddenly realized, General Rogers had not seen General Meyer that day, let alone read my letter. He'd been visiting Fort Stewart and quite by accident had decided on his way home to stop off at Bragg to see Delta. It had been an accident. The homework had been done and we were ready, but it had been an accident. Delta, finally, had had some luck.

The thunder was closer now.

★ TWENTY-TWO ★

JUST BEFORE TWILIGHT, General Mackmull walked through the gate. He didn't say anything but I could tell he was still very angry. On the dot of 1700 hours, escorted by General Warner, and dressed in boots and fatigues, General Shy Meyer arrived. He was as affable as ever. He smiled and shook hands with everyone. There was no clue in his behavior, no tip on what he was about to do.

Three days earlier, after General Rogers had left for Washington, Norton had been furious. I had blown the whistle on everyone; and he so informed General Mackmull who, reportedly, cut a couple of days off his Korean trip and returned home immediately. I had then received a call telling me that General Meyer was coming to Bragg on Saturday, March 11th. After he looked over one of General Warner's exercises, he'd be over to sort out Delta's issues.

Early Saturday morning I had taken a different sort of call. "I'm coming over to see you!" All of Delta's officers and key noncoms—there weren't many of them—had been lined up when General Mackmull arrived. He was so angry I suggested we talk in Lieutenant Colonel Potter's office—larger than mine. It was neutral ground.

"What you told the Chief of Staff," he said, "is only how you perceive the situation. Not as it really exists."

I went back to square one—the briefing for the CSA on 2 June 1977—and reminded him how he hadn't paid any attention to our presentation and of his pessimistic view of Delta's future.

"Furthermore, General, you were handed this whole thing on a silver platter. Bob Kingston did all the work and now you don't know what the hell to do with it. That makes me angry. You have no difficulty supporting Blue Light, but you won't let me recruit men who want to volunteer for Delta. We've got a conflict I don't intend living with anymore."

"What you did the other day, Colonel, was an act of disloyalty. From the beginning you have shown a reluctance to work within the system."

"I am not in this business, General, to get my ticket punched."

This was not an argument. This was a shoot-out. I had boiled over. Mackmull's face was red. We began shouting.

"Well, Colonel, what's your game then?"

"My game is to get out of Dodge. I'm gonna get this unit moved out of Fort Bragg, North Carolina."

"Well, that's not going to happen."

"We'll see."

"This will get sorted out when General Meyer gets here. I'll be back." He turned, threw open the door, and stormed out.

I had not wanted this to happen, but I'd known things were coming to a head. That afternoon I'd either win or I'd get fired. My future and Delta's would be determined when General Meyer arrived.

As soon as General Meyer, General Warner, General Mackmull, and their accompanying staffs settled in, I asked Major Buckshot to brief everyone on the new proposed training course. When this business had been concluded, General Meyer, the father of the Delta concept, who, along with Kingston and DePuy, had carefully steered it through the war of the briefings, stood up. There wasn't a sound in the room. The lights had been turned on.

"I want everybody but the following people to leave: General Warner, General Mackmull, Charlie, Dick Potter, and my action officers, Colonels Owens and Stotser. Everyone else will leave." No longer was anyone smiling. He looked around.

The thing that hit my mind, and it's funny, was this: King Arthur was sitting at his round table. He's so damn clear. He knows precisely what he's getting ready to do. I wish I knew what it was.

General Meyer said, "I have the authority from the Chief of Staff of the Army to hire, to fire, and to transfer anyone in this room."

"Colonel Beckwith," he said, "I know you would like very much to be a Field Operating Agency directly under DCSOPS. I know you'd like that. And, if I had another deputy, another general officer working for me, I'd probably do that. But I don't. So, you'll have to stay where you are. I'm going to leave you under Jack Mackmull. Is that clear?"

I said, "Yes, it is." And I began to really get emotional.

"Charlie, you've got to realize something. I think about you and the guys down here every day. But, I'm a busy man. I don't have time, personally, on a day-to-day basis, to run this unit. You have to stay under Jack."

I raised my hand. "Can I say something?" I stood up. I was choked up a little bit. "How in the hell do you expect me to do my job and run this unit when that general right there told me this morning I was disloyal? How can I continue to work under that man?" General Meyer looked at me and said very calmly. "I'm not interested in hearing that, so sit down."

I thought, "I've lost the ball game." I wondered how long it would take me to submit retirement papers and clean out my desk.

General Meyer spoke next to General Mackmull. "Jack, I'm not sure in my own mind you have supported Charlie. But, I'll tell you one thing you're going to do on Monday morning; you're going to open the gates and allow anyone in the Special Forces who wants to try out for Delta to come on over. He's got to get this selection course off the ground or he's not going to make his schedule. The Rangers are going to do the same thing. There's to be no more bickering. Do you understand, Jack?" He didn't give General Mackmull any slack either, but he was nicer to General Mackmull than he'd been to me.

No one in the room seemed able to move or cough or even breathe.

Then, to General Warner, "Volney, you have nothing to do with this. You have no role in this at all. However, I expect you to support this project in any way you can."

I quickly understood what General Meyer had done. Generals Warner and Kroesen had been removed from the equation. Delta would go directly to the JFK Center, and the JFK Center, for Delta, would now go directly to Department of the Army. What General Meyer had also done was cause a real problem. Volney Warner was very angry. He's a little man. I believe he has a little man's complex. Now he didn't say anything, not one word.

Jack Mackmull also had a difficulty. He had been double-hatted. As Commander of Special Forces he worked for General Warner. He also supervised Delta, which now Warner had nothing to do with. General Mackmull didn't say a word either.

General Meyer returned to me. "Charlie, I want to ask you a question. Will you do this job? Tell me, yes or no?"

I hesitated. He asked me the question again. I said, "I'd like to." General Meyer interrupted me. "You didn't answer my question. Yes or no, will you do this job?"

I looked at him. I figured I'd stay in the Army one more year. I said, "Yes, sir. I'll do it."

General Meyer then walked over to an easel, and with a black Magic Marker he wrote DEPT OF ARMY. "This is the Chief of Staff and me."

Below that he drew a box. "This is the JFK Center for Military Assistance and General Mackmull."

He drew another box below that. "This is Delta and Charlie Beckwith."

Here was a simple table of organization—Department of the Army, JFK Center, Delta—three boxes joined by a straight line, one on top of the other.

He looked at me. "Now, what you have the authority to do"—and he swiftly drew a curved line which bypassed JFK Center and connected Delta to Department of the Army—"is come directly to me when you and Jack have an impasse."

I hoped I didn't show the astonishment I felt. You dumb country bumpkin, I said to myself. You've lost the battle but won the war. The pendulum had swung back again. On the butcher paper, General Meyer had put Delta Force under the operational control of Department of the Army.

General Meyer said, "I want to get this train on track and moving." That was it. The meeting ended at 1815. It had lasted one hour and fifteen minutes.

On Monday morning, the 13th, early, right after PT, General Mackmull called. "I'd like you to round up your staff. I'm coming over to talk to you."

We had all worked on Sunday. I was still stunned by Saturday's events. We'd carved out some history. Events in the Army just don't happen that way, where this type of audience gets together, discusses the conflict, and is given direction. Also, no one now doubted, if he had before, how vital Delta Force was to this nation.

General Mackmull did very well that Monday morning. "I want to put aside the problems we've had and I want us to get along." He wasn't humble and I'd have been disappointed if he had been. He never mentioned the approval I'd received to make a left-end run. But he wanted peace and he wanted to help us. I respected him for that. I still wasn't ready to trust the man, and he wasn't ready to trust me, but at least now we might be able to get off to a fresh start.

The third selection course was conducted with about seventy candidates. We got a lot of Green Berets to run through it and some—not many, but some—Rangers. Fourteen candidates were accepted from this course. It was decided then to compress the time period, and within a ten-day span we put through the selection course another class of volunteers. This was another very productive class; from it sixteen good men were selected.

By the middle of April 1978, Delta had conducted four selection courses and from the 185 volunteers who'd been asessed, fifty-three had been chosen for the first individual training course.

On April 28th, seventy-nine new recruits participated in the fifth selection course. Out of this group, twenty recruits were chosen for training.

With enough men now in hand to make up a squadron-sized unit, it was time for Delta to move to the next stage.

I began focusing on counterterrorist training requirements, trying to make some sense out of them. New ground was going to have to be broken. I suddenly realized, "Nobody in this whole bloody Army has any experience in this arena."

★ TWENTY-THREE ★

ONCE A VOLUNTEER passed the camp Dawson selection course, he entered at Fort Bragg an intensely demanding Operators Course that would, in nineteen weeks, teach him the skills required to handle any terrorist incident.

The new Delta operator was provided a unique curriculum, one he could not receive anywhere else.

During this nearly five-month-long Operators Course, each Delta operator had to demonstrate the ability to: hit a target; perform command and control functions; establish and maintain secure communications; move from position to position using appropriate techniques in support of assault operations; gain entry to a crisis point; manage hostages; stabilize an injured person for at least thirty minutes; properly employ and maintain optical equipment; operate selected machinery and wheeled and track vehicles; negotiate natural and man-made obstacles; navigate on the land from one point to another; protect hostages from the threat of explosive ordnance; perform selected airborne and airmobile techniques and tactics; conduct selected maritime techniques; disarm and disable a hostile opponent.

The training was mentally demanding, physically tough, complete, and unique. No one could afford to have a bad day. In an American college, if a student daydreams during an English Lit lecture he might receive a failing grade on the next exam. If one of Delta's students daydreamed during a lecture on assault operations it might cost him his life. Operators had

be able to cope with any terrorist situation, in any environ-
ent, at any time. Some of the subjects taught seemed ar-
ane—picking a pintumbler padlock, for example, or knowing
ow to drive an SSB1200 diesel locomotive—but each was
ecessary. Delta operators not only became jacks of all trades,
ut masters of them as well.

Climbing skills required each operator to perform various
dividual rappels; to climb and rapple from buildings, instal-
tions, and aircraft; to evacuate wounded personnel by means
f rapelling; to perform unassisted balance climbs; to perform
vo-man climbs; to place and use all traversing systems; to
lace and use a fixed rope.

Delta snipers had to hit 100 percent on targets at 600 yards
nd 90 percent on targets at 1,000 yards. In combat marks-
anship competition, which were conducted on an irregular
asis, Delta always finished first. In head-to-head matches only
e Secret Service ever beat Delta's snipers. Most of these
atches were fired with M14 7.62mm rifles using iron sights
n standard NRA targets up to 500 yards.

Shooting was, obviously, a large part of each operator's
aining. No matter what his specialty he was expected to shoot
ree to four hours a day, five days a week.

One of the first pieces of business to be tackled as soon as
elta had moved into the Stockade was the building of a
ooting house. This $90,000 complex was built directly be-
ind the Stockade. It became known as "the House of Hor-
rs." Each of the building's four rooms included sophisticated
rget systems that were portable and interchangeable. Shoot-
g was done nearly in the round. One of the systems utilized
ound stop-motion picture projection. Seen from the Delta op-
rator's point of view, the film showed a room full of hostages
nd the terrorists holding them captive. The operator had to
ecide who was who and shoot the terrorists. At the precise
stant he fired his weapon, the projector would freeze so the
hooter could see on the screen exactly what he had hit.

The first room in the House of Horrors was a warm-up room
here very simple shooting was done. As a switch was
ushed, eight silhouette targets, both good and bad guys,

would abruptly spring up. Training was geared to allow the shooter just seconds to enter the room, identify the targets, and fire.

The second room was used for this purpose: take the offense away from the terrorist. The principle is to put him on the defensive. As the door to the room explodes, in the split second that it takes for the terrorist to shift his attention from the hostage to the explosion, the good guys have to enter the room and kill the terrorist. Room clearing, as it is called, has to be done quickly and violently. Four men are the number you want to enter a room. They must each enter swiftly and go in different directions. The situation will dictate the weaponry. If it is a single room, with two or three terrorists, the 4-man team will attack with handguns; the last man could go in with a 12 gauge shotgun. If a large area with many interconnecting rooms is held by a sizable number of terrorists, a 6-man attacking team might be used and they'd carry submachine guns.

Delta operators were taught to put two head shots in each terrorist. And they must keep moving, never giving the opposition a chance to hit a stationary target. Training included clearing a jammed weapon on the run and while under fire.

The basis for formulating an assault plan is information from negotiators and from other people who have recently been in and around the crisis site. Knowing in detail what the team will face on the other side of a door will also push it confidence level up. Squatting outside, waiting for a door to be blown, it is important for the operator to feel acquainted with what he'll face in the next few seconds. Conversely, the risk of failing successfully to clear a room in which the fire team has no idea where anything or anyone is, is very high— the wrong people can be shot.

Targets in the shooting house's room-clearing space were usually pictures of known terrorists.

The third room in the complex was used for night shooting with the operators using night vision goggles, and for blowing various types of doors. We spent a lot of money in this room replacing the fluorescent bulbs, which would shatter along with the doors.

The fourth room contained a detailed aircraft cabin mockup.

Since aircraft hijacking has become fashionable, Delta spent a lot of time studying the subject. In the event a United States owned or operated commercial airliner was hijacked and flown out of the country, Delta would be called upon—as West Germany had called upon GSG-9 in Mogadishu—to safely recover the passengers and, if possible, the aircraft. It was an area in which we felt we had a large responsibility.

The Federal Aviation Agency proved to be helpful. One of the first things they did was provide Delta with a Boeing 727. The airlines, obviously because it was in their own best interests, also cooperated fully. Many nights were spent, for example, in a TWA hangar at Kennedy International Airport.

At first we made mistakes. In an early training exercise an assault team carefully crawled along a wing in order to gain access to an emergency door. After Delta had gained control of the aircraft, the hostage actors in the cabin admitted they had known something was afoot when the plane began to rock very gently back and forth. The lesson we learned that night was to find out how much fuel was stored in the wings. Obviously, the plane would rock more if the wing tanks were empty and lighter.

There was a lot to learn about taking down an aircraft. By spending vast amounts of time on the subject, two of Delta's operators became fountains of aircraft knowledge. They learned everything there was to know—how planes at O'Hare were refueled, how flight crews were changed at LaGuardia, how food was loaded at Dulles. They knew where each of the nine hatches on a stretch 727 was, whether a DC-9 could be entered through its wheel wells, which lights would blink on when certain hatches were opened on a wide-body DC-10. There was nothing that these two operators hadn't learned about airplanes and how they could be entered.

Of course, shooting skills are critical in an aircraft takeover. It's not unlike shooting fish in a barrel. The sharks have to be identified and separated from the guppies—the terrorists from passengers—and this art was practiced time and time again in the airplane cabin in the shooting house behind the Stockade.

* * *

When the shooting starts—and this was a large part of what Delta was expected to do—and people begin to die, no matter how many hours of training are involved, it comes down to the man who is pulling the trigger. In this area Delta was unique.

★ TWENTY-FOUR ★

IT WAS DURING the early selection courses that Delta began accepting some of the men who eventually shaped the unit's character, colored its personality, defined its style, and gave it class.

One was Edward Westfall, but that's like knowing the Lone Ranger's real name—it's unimportant. In Delta he was known as Fast Eddie. This was sometimes shortened to Fast. And he was.

He had been one of the seven recruits chosen from the very first selection course. It was during the psychological boards when we recognized that in Sergeant Westfall we had someone different. During the hours of grueling interrogation he went through, he always managed to answer our questions with candor, honesty, and sincerity.

An E-6 (staff sergeant), he was a big, very fit man who was topped off with a mop of wavy red hair. Fast wasn't the type to wear a three-piece suit. He'd have felt he should fasten all the buttons on the vest.

Fast owned a skill Delta prized—demolitions. Hardworking and creative, he was like all first-class demolition experts—he had a passion for disintegration done finely and he loved loud noises.

Because it wasn't unusual for him to get carried away, I always felt that someone should watch Fast Eddie. Fort Bragg has certain regulations on its ranges, limiting the size of the explosives that can be used. On one range, for example, you can't use a charge in excess of ten pounds, on another the limit is twenty. I sort of felt that Fast Eddie never really cared about those rules and didn't feel obligated to follow them.

One day he came in to see me. "Boss, I'd like to go up to the Navy shipyard in Norfolk and see if I can scrounge up some targets."

Being what I thought it to be, a reasonable request, I sent him on his way with my blessings.

It was during the time when we wanted to see what certain types of explosives would do to cars, trucks, steel doors, and the like.

A day or two after Fast had left, I received a phone call from some admiral asking me to confirm a Sergeant Westfall's credentials. I should have suspected then that Fast was living up to his name.

Within the week, six flatbed semis arrived at the Stockade's front gate, all piled high with Navy surplus. The point to be made is that some of this so-called "junk" looked to be in pretty good shape. In the shipment, Fast had managed to include several nearly new cars; a dock crane; a variety of 8-inch, 6-inch, and 5-inch naval gun barrels; a couple of perfectly good propeller shafts, and as the pièce de résistance, a mint D-8 bulldozer.

I got a little nervous, especially when I found I had to sign for all this stuff. All the objects, except the bulldozer, were taken out to the range where, during the next few weeks, they were blown up. The dozer was kept at the Stockade, hidden in the back, until we could think of something constructive to do with it.

Fast made several more trips to Norfolk to obtain targets. As fast as they arrived they were blown up. I remember during one of his interviews he wanted to be assured that Delta, once it got off the ground, would not relent on its selection or training requirements. This appeared to be very important to him. I learned how important it was several months later.

We had on board for a while an officer who was in Delta's communications division. One night, when he was duty officer, and Sergeant Westfall was the duty NCO, the officer accidentally discharged his side arm. The punishment for this mistake was simple and direct—instant dismissal—and warnings of the consequence were posted in two places within the Stockade. The next morning as I walked through the gate, Fast Eddie was waiting to see exactly how I would react. The choice was direct. I either sacked the officer or took down the signs. The officer was out of the unit in less than twenty-four hours. Fast Eddie returned to the range satisfied that Delta had lived up to its standards.

Another redhead was one of the most proficient operators Delta ever had. An E-8 (master sergeant), Allen (pseudonym) was a total professional in everything he did and he came from the old school. He was one of Delta's best shots, but then he did everything well. Unless you were watching carefully and knew what to look for, it could have been easy to overlook Allen. He was very quiet and a loner who verged on being an introvert.

This was a man who always gave more to the unit than he took. After an exercise had been run, he was the first to want to critique it, then improve it, then run it again. In 4-man patrol concepts he was constantly improving on the tactics and techniques used in taking down an aircraft or a building.

When Delta eventually grew in strength and was about to form a second squadron, I remember that its new commander, Logan Fitch, felt strongly about moving Allen over from A Squadron. There was never any argument about it. In the following months, to no one's surprise, Allen's troop became one of the best in either squadron.

Because I never remember Allen making a bad call, when he became angry with me in Egypt, after we'd returned from the Iranian desert, I took the time to reevaluate some of the things I'd said.

Ish really came to my attention for the first time when I took command of the Special Forces School. On my first day in the job, before I even learned where the washroom was and where I could hang my cap, I noticed a letter addressed to me sitting on the desk. I shoved it into one of my pockets and forgot about it until that evening when I rediscovered it. On my back porch I learned it had been written by the senior noncom representative to the School's operations and intelligence committee, who had just left Bragg to take up a new post somewhere else.

The five-page, well-written letter, which I carefully read, expressed the writer's thoughts about the School's curriculum and the committee he had sat upon. I realized this sergeant knew what he was talking about and that he had taken a lot of time to express his thoughts. The letter was signed. "Very respectfully, M/Sgt Wade Ishimoto."

The letter and its writer were soon forgotten in a flood of work. Sometime later, as Delta began to smoke, I talked to an old NCO friend, Forrest Foreman. I wanted him to come to Delta as my senior operations sergeant. I also asked him to keep a sharp lookout for other NCOs he knew of who were the right cuts of cloth for Delta.

At that time Forrest was out in El Paso, attending the Army's NCO Academy at Fort Bliss. As it so happened, enrolled at the same time was one of Sergeant Foreman's dearest friends, a master sergeant named Wade Ishimoto.

Soon, both sergeants began working for Delta, Forrest Foreman in Operations and Wade Ishimoto in Intelligence. They also both completed their schooling at Fort Bliss through the U.S. mail.

Wade was born in Hawaii. He worked very hard to put himself through the University of Hawaii. He was a hand-to-hand combat, judo fanatic who spent a lot of time taking various martial arts courses. I'm not sure how good he was, but he devoted a lot of time to it.

One day, several months after Sergeant Ishimoto had joined the unit, I was visiting the State Department, trying to get them to give us a communications link that would instantly notify Delta whenever terrorist incidents occurred anywhere in the world. While in the EOC (Emergency Operations Center) two high-ranking officials buttonholed me. "This Ishimoto you've got working for you, Charlie, is a very impressive guy. He's bright and does what he says he'll do. It's a damn shame he's only a sergeant. If he were an officer he'd walk through these halls with a lot more clout."

This started me thinking. I knew that Ishimoto held a reserve commission, and if this country ever went to war, the next day he would be commanding a battalion. In the afternoon I drove over to Arlington to vist my friends in Personnel.

"What's the possibility," I asked, "of making one of my senior NCOs an officer, of bringing him on active duty as a captain?"

Within two months the promotion came through and Captain Ishimoto became the number-two man in Delta's intelligence division.

The fence around the Stockade required strengthening, and a card-activated electrical gate needed to be installed. In these early days everyone did whatever was necessary, regardless of his military occupation specialty; and on this occasion I asked Wade Ishimoto to deal with the fence problem. An estimate to repair the gate and install an electrical locking system appeared on my desk shortly afterward. The figure was $18,000. There was no way Delta could cough up that kind of money. I scribbled a note back to Captain Ishimoto informing him of this and that he should find cheaper methods.

The next evening my door was slammed closed, and looking up I saw I had a very angry captain on my hands. "You know, Boss, I gotta talk to you. You don't understand. If we repair this fence it's going to cost money."

"Captain, what you don't understand is that you don't know what you're talking about. You guys haven't done your homework. Eighteen thousand dollars! Give me a break!"

At this point he dropped on my desk all the facts and figures, and how they had been arrived at. The work was thorough and the numbers didn't lie. He then advised me I was a nickel nose. Other miserly expletives, many of which I'd never heard before, filled the room.

We spent a half hour talking through the situation. He finally convinced me he had been right. I suggested that we might be able to hold the cost down somewhat if we did some of the work ourselves instead of contracting it out. It was the first time I ever saw him compromise, but he agreed that this might be done. Within several weeks the fence had been hardened and a new locking system put in place. It ended up costing $15,000.

In Delta a "yes" man would have felt ill at ease.

The Remington Arms Company was kind enough to build for Delta some 40XB sniper rifles. When they began arriving, one of the first ones was given to a sniper we'll call Boris. He had been born of Polish parents and he spoke Polish and a little Russian. A small man, probably 5' 6", weighing about 165 pounds, he had the build of a middleweight. Blond, with blue eyes, he exuded confidence. Our psychologist identified in him all the traits required of an outstanding sniper: poise, patience, concentration, stability, calmness, and meticulousness about details.

In June of '78, Delta ran an exercise in the desolate high country out beyond El Paso. The scenario called for a mountain cabin to be occupied by some terrorists and their hostages. One of the sniper's primary responsibilities is to get into position early and then gather all the information he can about the target.

It had gotten dark quickly, as it does in west Texas, and Boris had been in position close to the cabin for several hours, hidden in a rock fall. A terrorist role-player, unaware that a sniper team was in position, left the cabin and, walking over to where Boris lay hidden, urinated on him.

Any other sniper probably would have jumped up yelling, "Hey, man, what the hell do you think you're doing!" Boris was not *any* sniper. He never moved, and the role-player returned to the cabin unaware of what he had done. Later, after the target had been taken down, Boris let off some steam. When we learned of the incident, we were very proud of Boris's stoicism!

During the second selection course, which we were still running in the Uwharrie National Forest, Buckshot and I went up there in the evening so we could watch the recruits come into an RV the next morning. During the night the weather turned real bad and it began to snow heavily. Around 6:30, just as it was getting daylight, I saw Walt Shumate walk into the rendezvous to get his next set of instructions. I almost didn't recognize him. His beard, mustache, eyebrows, and cap were painted in ice. The rest of him was wringing wet from having, an hour earlier, stepped into a creek. He was cold and miserable. When he saw me he didn't smile. His endurance was being stretched, and his sense of humor had deserted him.

A few weeks earlier at Bragg, Sergeant Major Shumate had come over to see me and wanted to know, as an old friend, how he could join up. I told him. He said, "I'm not getting any younger, Colonel, and I'm not sure I'm fit enough to get through that selection course." "You better start working then," I'd said. Walter was about forty-four at that time. Anyway, he'd gotten in shape and had come over and volunteered to go through selection. It was in February.

The snow fell more heavily and Buckshot stomped around trying to keep warm.

Walter Shumate received his instructions for the next leg. He pulled out his compass, checked the map, and began walking, I realized, in the wrong direction. I moved down to the ice-coated figure.

"You know where you're going, Sergeant?"

"Oh, yes, sir. I've got my head down and my ass up."

"If I were you, Sergeant, I'd double-check it?"

He dug out his map and compass again. "Oh, Lord," he said. "I just had a dumb attack," and he shuffled off, this time in the proper direction. I finally lost sight of him in the blowing snow.

I first met Walt when he ran recon for Project DELTA in Vietnam in 1965–1966. I'd put him over on that island across from Nha Trang, where I asked him to design some immediate action drills for the unit. Walt had done a good job on this. I'd lost touch with him in the intervening years, until that day at Bragg, in early 1978, when he looked me up and asked how he could join Delta.

When Walt got through selection and had come on into Delta, I made him the senior NCO in charge of selection. He was a great fan of Gen. Douglas MacArthur. During the psychological boards, Walter would always ask the recruits what they thought of Harry Truman's decision to sack the General. For Walter there was only one right answer. Most important. Walt was good for me. Because we'd been together in the mud in Vietnam, I felt I could confide in him and could trust his judgment.

He was from West Virginia; and it wasn't unusual, after he'd gone home to the hills on leave, for him to come back and give me a fruit jar of good corn whiskey, the kind they call "White Lightning." Not a big man, probably 5' 11" and 175 pounds, he wore a magnificent waxed handlebar mustache.

Walter Shumate was a scuba expert. He had taken all of the courses, was fully trained, and very good at it. When Walt came over to volunteer for Delta, before he got to Uwharrie, he had to take the PT test. When he took the swim test, 100 meters with clothes on, he failed it. No one could believe it. He'd been swimming so long with masks, oxygen tanks, and flippers he'd forgotten how to do the dog paddle. We gave him a couple of days and he finally did very well in it. It was a long time, however, before he lived it down.

When people leave Special Forces and retire from the Army, they normally join the Special Forces Decade Club or the Special Operations Club, in which there's always a lot of gossip. I'd always send Walt to these conventions to find out what was being said about us. As I've said, Walter's very good with people.

Anybody who had been in Special Forces in the past fifteen years and had died, Walter Shumate would know about it. Periodically he'd come into the office and say, "Sir, remember that little Chicano sergeant who was in Project SIGMA back in '66?" I'd try to remember, "Yeah, I think so." Walt would say, "Well, day before yesterday he passed away." He liked to know who was coming and who was going.

★ TWENTY-FIVE ★

IN THE ARMY you learn to accept change. Sometimes it's good. Sometimes it's bad, but change is something you learn to live with.

General Snippens left his slot in DCSOPS and was replaced by Maj. Gen. Jack Faith. A brigadier's post, which had temporarily remained open under Snippens, was filled with Gen. Roderick D. Renick, Jr. But one other change probably affected Delta the most. Tom Owens, our chief liaison contact with the Pentagon, was supplanted by Lieutenant Colonel Whitman (pseudonym). We learned quickly that Whitman was flexible, unselfish, and supportive. He would work long hours on Delta's behalf, and was secure enough in his own skills to admit when he didn't know something.

A new team began working under General Meyer and looking out in the Pentagon for Delta's best interests. We started to live with each other. As someone pointed out, not one of our three new superiors in the chain of command to the top had Special Forces experience. Only Whitman had Ranger and airborne training. In two of the cases it would make no difference, but in the case of Rod Renick it would.

The Stockade in early summer: the initial individual training phase had successfully concluded and the first stages of unit training had begun. Delta's A Squadron, comprising two troops, was commanded by the enthusiastic Major Buckshot. The machinery was in place and working smoothly. A lot of hard work and sweat was generated that summer. Fort Bragg in July is a hot place to be.

Suddenly, unexpectedly, Delta was asked to ante up.

"You've spent some big dollars. Because of your situation reports, we know where you are and what you've been doing." This was Lieutenant Colonel Whitman calling from the Pentagon. "General Meyer believes it's time we evaluated Delta."

"Well, you know, my two years aren't up yet. Delta has only been in business about eight months. I think we ought to wait."

General Meyer disagreed. Whitman was understanding but firm. The message was clear: "You're going to hear more about this, Colonel, in a few weeks. I've been told General Warner will do the evaluation for the Army."

Oh, shit! I thought. Pentagon politics are unfathomable. Could General Warner have bypassed General Meyer and gone directly to General Rogers? I knew they were good friends, but I didn't know how close. The emotional pendulum began to swing again.

General Meyer told me, "I walk the halls of the Pentagon daily and people say to me. 'How is Delta doing?' I respond by saying. 'They're doing good.' Then I begin to think, 'How good is good?' "

Carefully considered, the reasons for the validation made sense and there were quite a few of them:

a. Determine Delta's status since its activation.
b. Develop a yardstick to measure the unit's performance. (Army Training Tests were available to all units in the Army in order to determine their performance, but there was no ATT written for Delta.)
c. Justify the amount of money spent to get the force under way.
d. Have a first-hand look at the established force.
e. Allow others to have a look, too, hopefully to clear up misconceptions they might have.

I understood the above rationale, but did not understand why FORSCOM was tasked to conduct the validation. My fears were well founded. I expected the worst when the news arrived that FORSCOM had selected the commander of XVIII Airborne Corps, Lieutenant General Warner, to conduct the validation. Warner's deputy for the validation was going to be my "old friend" Brig. Gen. "Sandy" Meloy.

The trouble was Warner and, of course, Meloy—who had crossed swords with General Kingston over the philosophy—appeared to me to be totally unsupportive of Delta. I believed that both officers felt Delta's mission should be entrusted to the two Army Ranger battalions. Furthermore, because neither Generals Warner nor Meloy had ever observed Delta's training activities, they remained ignorant of the unit's unique strengths and skills.

There being no alternative, however, to having the validation supervised by FORSCOM, it was imperative for Delta to be evaluated against the standard the unit had trained to. No sense testing a violinist on a trombone. It became important, therefore, for the unit to frame a paper that would clearly reflect its various training activities (shooting, physical fitness, explosive, hand-to hand combat, as well as intelligence and operations skills as they applied to combating terrorism). A letter detailing all this information was provided to Lieutenant Colonel Whitman in Washington and to Major General Mackmull at the JFK Center.

The letters notwithstanding, I saw the validation as a sandbag job. The pressure was really on. If Delta failed this test, there was a chance the unit would be deactivated, and either Blue Light or the Rangers would pick up its counterterrorist assignment. And the foxes were going to protect the hen house.

A validation group, consisting of Generals Warner and Meloy, Colonels Thomas and Spinks, Lieutenant Colonel Redman, two or three field grade officers from XVIII Airborne Corps and the Ranger battalions, and ten to twelve noncommissioned officers from within the Special Forces Groups at Bragg, framed a test by which Delta would be graded. The validation would be broken into two parts—individual skills and team skills.

It surprised no one. Delta didn't do well in the shooting stations. Warner's evaluators had us shooting at distances and targets that were unrealistic. They were too long and too small. We'd been doing room clearing, very close quarters shooting; dash into a room and take people out very, very quickly. We hadn't been, as the expression goes in the Army, punching paper. In other words, Delta didn't worry about the black in a bull's-eye. We'd been shooting at silhouettes. The techniques Delta had adopted were patterned after the British 22 SAS and not along U.S. military or police lines.

The sniping station was unrealistic. It was done at night and because of the optics involved very few snipers after dark are fail-safe. The scenario was just Buck Rogers-ized. With scopes, a shooter cannot tell at night whether a target is wearing a red shirt or a blue shirt. All he sees is gray. Obviously, the wrong person can easily be shot. It became apparent to everyone on the Delta side that the validation group had little, if any, knowledge or experience with terrorist tactics and techniques. And yet, one handgun station using multiple targets gave the shooters ideas on how they could improve their combat shooting techniques. It was well designed and very stimulating.

Everyone knew Delta operators could land navigate very well. It was no surprise to see a rigorous land navigation course put in over in Uwharrie. The lanes were put through some typically rough terrain. The three guys tested made it easily. They said, "Sir, it was a waste of time. It didn't measure the skills that we measure." It was just a flog, a march from one point to another.

Delta was evaluated on hand-to-hand combat. We'd spent very little time on throwing people around. An instructor in the martial arts from the Special Forces was brought over, he was Sgt. Willie Chong. I was asked to cough up a couple of people who would go in with him. Delta had one inexperienced man and he was put in second. After a few minutes on the mats, Chong was taken to the base hospital. We were told later he suffered a brain concussion. No other evaluators had been lined up, so Delta received 100 percent on hand-to-hand combat.

It was time to test the unit skills. This second leg of the validation was designed to test all of Delta's intelligence, operations, and command and control procedures, as well as the squadron's tactical proficiency. A large-scale field exercise was prepared, which required that Delta take down, simultaneously, two targets—a hijacked airplane and a terrorist-held building. Obviously, this scenario was the linchpin of the evaluation.

No question that it was a difficult assignment. Buckshot would need to divide his squadron. He decided that First Troop would take down the aircraft and that Second Troop would take down the building. The exercise was going to be evaluated in both planning and execution.

Planning required accurate information. Delta was prepared with an excellent crisis checklist. The SAS had helped us design a detailed list of tasks to be accomplished at the site of the crisis, and Ishimoto and the other personnel in the intelligence shop had improved on it.

The first thing Delta's operations and intelligence staff did, therefore, was ask the evaluators the questions that appeared on the checklist. "How many people are on board the aircraft and in the building?" They didn't know. They'd have to go and find out. "What type and model aircraft is being held? When did it last refuel? How much fuel remains? How much baggage is on board? How much of it is carryon luggage?" The questions were real-world and would be asked in any straightforward crisis situation. The evaluators were caught at a distinct disadvantage. They hadn't been prepared for this type of response and didn't know what to do. Delta was relentless. Curt Hurst, Wade Ishimoto, and Forrest Foreman of the ops and intel staff had the evaluators by the tail. "What are the physical characteristics of the pilot? Of the crew? Who are the passengers? Where are they coming from and going to? What group is holding the targets? Find us a similar plane we can rehearse on."

General Mackmull came over to me. He was grinning, "Where did you get that checklist? You've got the evaluators confused and it's great." As the Delta staff continued down the checklist, his smile went from ear to ear.

"What kind of building is being held? How many stories does it have? Is it attached to anything? Is anyone inside sick? Do any of the hostages have unique characteristics? How are the terrorists armed?" The answers Hurst, Ishimoto, and Foreman received were often, "We don't know" and "No, you can't do that." That was the easiest way. The questioning went on for some time.

"Who's handling the negotiations?"

"We don't know."

"Please find out. When can Delta coordinate with the negotiating team?"

"We don't know."

"Find out."

"Can we survey the targets?"

"We'll get back to you."

Eventually we were able to look over the targets, and I went out to see what I could. An umpire prevented me from getting too close to the occupied building.

Thirty-two miles west of Fort Bragg, out by Big Muddy Lake, the validation group had chosen a recreational building at Camp Mackall. Used during World War II as a training site for the 82nd and other airborne units, the area was generally controlled by the Special Forces School. Many of us knew it well and that was a break. I was more worried about the aircraft. This was an old National Guard AC-121 parked on an improved strip about 1,000 meters west of the barricaded building. Delta had been training on modern jet passenger aircraft procured through the generosity of various U.S airlines and the good offices of the FAA. Evidently, the evaluation group hadn't known how to obtain a 727, or an L-1011, which in the real world stood a better chance of being hijacked than an antique AC-121.

When Delta knew everything there was to know about both

targets, Major Buckshot moved A Squadron to a nearby assembly area, and at dusk divided the unit into its two elements. General Warner accompanied First Troop and General Meloy followed Second Troop.

On the aircraft side Delta had a Sergeant Franklin, whom the men called "No Lips." He was a very fit senior noncommissioned officer. In the darkness, his movement toward the plane was a model. He simply became part of the environment. Unless you watched him closely you wouldn't know he was moving at all. Because there were no windows in the aircraft's tail, the remaining operators of First Troop stealthily approached it from that direction. Padded ladders were softly laid on the fuselage. Two hatches had been selected. In the time it takes to suck in your breath, both doors were blown and the plane was taken. Even I was impressed.

Second Troop, over near the building, contained a very hard man. He was, as they say, as tough as woodpecker lips. His name was Jacks (pseudonym). He'd studied the target, particularly the wooden window frames. Delta had trained on taking out windows by violently running a steel pipe around their inside rims. When the order was given, Sergeant Jacks and his pipe, along with several other operators, very professionally, very decisively and very violently dismounted all the building's windows. The assault force leaped through them. Within seven seconds the terrorists had been taken out and the hostages freed.

Later I learned the cost of repairing the building was nearly $5,000. I don't think General Meloy realized what was going to happen or he might have stopped it.

The action had been sudden and swift. Most of the role-playing terrorists had been frozen by the violent manner in which Second Troop had entered the building. One role-player never had had a chance to move off a bed and another fell victim to one of the operators who in springing through a window landed on his back.

Both targets had gone down around 0400 hours. By the time we returned to the exercise headquarters, the sun was just lighting the eastern sky. The critique began shortly afterward.

The conference room was packed. Maybe seventy or eighty people stood or sat wherever they could. Delta officers and senior NCOs were still in their combat gear and carrying their weapons. There had been no opportunity, either, to wash the camouflage off their faces. In addition to these familiar painted faces, I noticed a lot of what I call straphangers. The room was filled with cigarette smoke and the rich odor of sweat. General Meyer, who'd flown down the night before to observe the aircraft assault, sat nearly inconspicuous amongst the troops.

General Warner began. "That was the most professional cross-country movement I have ever seen. Never heard a person say a word. Had the targets been real, I believe Delta Force would have been successful." Standing in a corner, General Meloy watched and said nothing. He used his colonels, particularly G. G. Thomas, to castigate us.

In the shooting phase of the validation, some of the guys had done well, but others hadn't. General Warner remarked. "Work on this, Colonel. You don't want to be known as the unit that can't shoot straight." Finally there was nothing more to say and General Warner announced that Delta had passed the evaluation. Looking at me, he asked, "Do you have anything you want to add?" "Yes sir," I said, "I do!"

I stood up and looked around the crowded room. "I hadn't realized the Army had so many experts in what I do. You know, there's not a single one of you, except for General Mackmull, who ever attended a day of my training. So, I don't know what makes you think you know so much about this business. I consider this whole thing a setup, and I don't appreciate your comments." I spoke my mind. I said my piece. "Some of the shooting stations were totally unrealistic. If you had read our paper you would have known what we could do."

I was really emotional by then. I had good reason to be angry. To get to the plane we'd had to march through a swamp, carrying aluminum ladders. Realistically, that wouldn't have happened, instead they would have arrived in small vehicles. We were, I thought, being evaluated the way a Ranger battalion would be. We were better, more sophisticated than the Rangers. Dragging long aluminum ladders through a swamp . . . We'd done it very, very professionally, but it was stupid and all so rudimentary. We were so far past that type of action. It gave me a chance to blow off some steam.

Colonel Thomas spoke up, "I'm sorry now I gave Delta Force as many points as I did. I wish I hadn't." Colonel Spinks also spoke up. Some strong words were exchanged.

It was then up to General Meyer to wrap up the proceedings. He thanked General Warner and extended his appreciation to everyone in the room who helped make the evaluation run as smoothly as it had.

The meeting broke up, people talked in groups, there was some laughter across the room, some handshakes, and congratulations were passed on. I heard someone say. "You know, we're not making cornflakes here." Bright morning sunlight filled the room. I found myself in a cluster of generals. General Meyer said to me, "Charlie, I'd like to see you in private."

In one of the many metal prefab buildings that are found all over the Fort Bragg reservation, we found an empty room. The day was going to be another scorcher.

General Meyer sat back. "O.K. What's on your mind?" A few days before the evaluation I'd sent him a message asking to talk to him. I answered, "I sort of sensed Delta would come out of this the way we did. But I need to do some more blocking and tackling. I need more time. I need the rest of my two years." He understood that. "Charlie, you've got to understand, it's only fair to check you out periodically. We need to see if you've kept on the right track. Everyone has to be checked every now and then, even me. What's next?"

"Do I have the authority to send people overseas to see an actual incident if one should occur? I gotta be able to see for myself. I gotta talk to people. There's only so much I can do at Bragg."

"I don't know," he said, "but I'll check."

He was writing all this down. I asked him some more questions and he told me to see his deputy, General Faith, about them.

Blue Light seemed now, after our evaluation, to be redundant. Delta Force had filled the gap and we could be put on alert. If anything went down, we were ready to handle it. "There's really no more need for Blue Light, sir." General Meyer agreed. Mountel left Fort Bragg shortly after that. Went to India, I think.

Then General Meyer said, "Let's just talk for a few minutes, Charlie. How are you doing? How's your family? You look tired." He made me feel good. Put me at ease and gave me a lot of confidence. He knew how to do that well. This only took a few minutes. He stood up. "I'll see you later." And he slapped me on the back.

A few days after the evaluation I received a phone call from one of General Warner's aides. Could the general, he wanted to know, some morning take PT and run with Delta? I explained to the aide that for security reasons Delta never conducted its PT program in a formation—as did other units on the post. We never ran as a body. Physical fitness. I explained, was an individual responsibility in Delta, and the men ran at various times of the day and probably not more than two at a time. I was told that General Warner was angry when his aide gave him the message.

★ TWENTY-SIX ★

MONTHS BEFORE, WHILE we were working in the pentagon trying to get Delta's TO&E finished and pushed through TRADOC before it was turned over to Department of the Army for further massaging, a staff officer had asked the big question: "Who's gonna command this here Delta?" I had picked up the phone and called General Mackmull. "Who's going to command Delta?" He'd laughed, sort of. "You are. That's what I think." Hanging up the phone I'd gone up to where the staff officers were putting the final touches on the TO&E. "Put in there 'Colonel Charlie Beckwith' where it asks for the commander."

You can see how unique this was. MILPERCEN had meetings to decide who would and who would not be put on the command list. Then from this list another board decided who got command of battalions, brigades, and so forth. My name hadn't been on any command list. A lot of people used to kid me, saying once I learned the Army didn't have a unit for me to command I went out and built my own.

But it would be wrong to suggest I did this building on my own, that I received no advice, that no one helped this poor ol' boy out. The fact is I received help and guidance from several people.

On one of the nights I couldn't sleep, one in which all my troubles kept surfacing, I decided to go over and see Gen. Sam Wilson, who was to be the Special Forces School guest speaker the following morning and who was staying on post at the Normandy House. A retired lieutenant general, General Sam had a reputation for being one of the best intelligence officers the Army ever had. In Burma where he'd served as a young lieutenant during World War II, he commanded an intelligence and reconnaissance platoon with Merrill's Marauders. I woke him up.

"Sir, I really apologize for bothering you, but I need to talk. I need to talk to someone." General Sam invited me in. "You're not bothering me. Sit down, and let's talk." He knew of me, and I had heard him speak several times and was impressed with what he'd said. General Sam realized the importance of units like Merrill's; small free-ranging units unhampered by fixed ties with their bases. I told him I needed someone to talk to about my command and control arrangements and about the problems I was then having with the JFK Center. We decided to meet the next day when I would lay out the whole story.

Sam Wilson proved to be a good listener whose advice was always carefully thought through and laced with wisdom. For the cost of a tank of gas, which he used whenever he drove from his farm in Virginia to advise Delta Force, we got a blue chip consultant. The arrangement had nothing to do with anything I'd checked out beforehand with the Army or General Mackmull. It was simply between General Sam and me.

I also had three other people I went to. Bob Kingston was sorely missed; General Meyer was way up in the stratosphere, and my subordinates were too close to the issues to be objective. So I contacted Art Simons, who had led the Son Tay Raid, and asked him to come up from Florida and help us with our sniper program. He spent several days. It was good for us, and it was good for him. Colonel Simons helped Delta develop the precise loads and projectiles on which snipers depend. Additionally, he helped set up our loading room where we loaded our own ammunition. I learned to confide in him. His advice was always realistic. "Be careful, Charlie, how you fight the bureaucracy. You're in a no-win situation. Colonels doing business with generals . . . They'll throw you to the wolves and not think twice about it. Continue to do your homework before you act." Another time, he said, "What you're doing, Charlie, is so important it would be stupid to stumble because you acted too emotionally. Rather than always sharpening your sword and charging into battle, sit back sometimes and say, 'It's not worth worrying about.' " Art Simons was someone I learned I could go to.

Another was Butch Kendrick, Col. R. C. Kendrick, an old boss of mine at CINCPAC I have a great deal of respect for. When he retired from the military he went and ran a bank. He knew me, he knew my emotions, my dynamics, and he always gave me sound counsel and pointed me in the right direction.

On some weekends Buzz Miley—who had picked me out of the gutter my first week back at Fort Bragg after I'd returned from England—and I would go bass fishing. He knew the Special Forces community, and I shared many of my problems with him. He did a lot of interpreting for me and offered suggestions on how issues could be handled.

Because they were too far away from the problems and the pace which had to be maintained, I didn't always take their advice. But knowing they were there and having their support and encouragement made me feel more secure.

Of course, they were very concerned with the recent validation and how it had gone. As godfathers they shared a lot of my emotions during that period. They, too, were elated with the results.

It was another unreal hot and soggy summer, and August brought with it some additional heavy weather.

After the validation, Delta had gone back to its scrimmaging.

Then Lieutenant Colonel Whitman called.

"We're going down to Corps tomorrow. FORSCOM is going to make one more pitch to grab you."

"Oh, shit, not again. What a waste of time."

"Yeah, I think you're right, Colonel, but the boss has gotta go through the ritual."

"See you tomorrow."

This was August 7, 1978.

The briefing room was up at XVIII Airborne Corps. General Warner's large office was filled with stars. It was like a Delta class reunion. General Meyer was there, along with General Warner, General Mackmull, and General Haldane. Haldane, I remembered, had presided over the Delta brief at FORSCOM where General Meloy and General Kingston had gotten into a battle royal over the subject.

I found a seat to one side of General Meyer, and Lieutenant Colonel Whitman found one on the other side of him. Across from us sat Generals Haldane and Warner. General Meyer chided General Haldane, asking him if he still had the action officer who had screwed up a previous brief. General Haldane smiled. When this particular major walked in, Meyer said, "Yes. I see you still have him."

After the major found a seat and the laughter had died down, General Haldane began the briefing.

"What we've done, General Meyer, is taken a good look at the situation and want to present our position. We believe we can help Delta Force. We can help them in personnel, intelligence, operations, and logistics." That was the whole ball of wax. "We have carefully analyzed each area and now want to show you how our support can help Delta be a dynamic, viable force within the United States Army."

The FORSCOM action officer cleared his throat, it wasn't every day someone briefed the Deputy Chief of Staff of the Army. "General Meyer, after close scrutiny it is FORSCOM's belief that Delta would be a stronger entity if we became involved in their personnel selections." He didn't get any further. General Meyer came back immediately. "Come on, how in the hell can FORSCOM help Delta when they are being serviced directly by General Heiden and MILPERCEN? There's no way you can do the job better than those people. Why do you want to get in their system? Delta has Department of the Army looking out for it in the people business. Really, I'm not interested in this. It's no help. Let's go to the next point."

I peeked a look at General Haldane. Surely he had to be feeling, "Hey, I'm in a no-win situation here. FORSCOM's really got nothing to offer. Who in the blazes sandbagged me into doing this?" General Warner sat staring straight ahead. Yet he must have been uncomfortable. Surely he wanted to cross or uncross his legs, or fidget just the smallest amount.

The briefing continued. "This is how we can help Delta Force in gathering and interpreting intelligence." General Meyer spoke up again. "What are you talking about. All the intelligence FORSCOM handles is for training. Delta receives its intelligence directly from the appropriate intelligence agencies in Washington. I'm sorry. This will not wash." There was now an edge to his voice. "What's next?"

General Warner was becoming less stoic and more and more frustrated. Obviously he was one of the framers and backers of the planned takeover.

The staff briefer, before he even began the logistics presentation, was stopped by General Meyer. "There's no way FORSCOM can help Delta in the logistical business. Theirs works very well. What else have you got to offer?"

No one spoke.

"O.K.," General Meyer said, "there are some areas in here where you can really help. One is flagging airplanes and making arrangements for Delta to get their air hours in."

That's the way the briefing went. Shy Meyer stopped the takeover cold. But he was wise. He recognized General Warner was a senior field commander, had XVIII Airborne Corps, so he treated him like one. "What I really need, Volney, is for someone to do what you did on the evaluation. Go over to Delta every now and then and look over Charlie's shoulder. See if he has any problems and try to help him."

I spoke up. "I don't really need any help from Forces Command, and I don't need any help from Corps."

That really made General Warner mad. "I agree with Colonel Beckwith," he said, "and I don't want to go to Delta, nor do I want to be involved." If General Meyer had been angry with me, he would have said, "Shut up, Charlie," but he didn't.

The briefing broke up and I left with Lieutenant Colonel Whitman.

Turning around I saw Haldane, Warner, Mackmull, and General Meyer still sitting around the table. The door closed behind me. Whitman was grinning. This didn't make sense.

"What the hell are they talking about now?"

"You. Remember when you were not selected for permanent colonel?"

"Yeah, I remember. So what. The money's the same, so's the command. All I gotta do as a temporary colonel is leave the Army after twenty-eight years. Hell, I don't even know if I'll be alive by then."

"You don't understand, Colonel. This has come to the old man's attention. There are some people who are pissed about it, so he's in there getting things straightened out."

"In other words, someone's afraid they're going to be embarrassed and the word's gonna get out that a passed-over temporary colonel down here's running a shit-hot unit."

"You got it, Colonel. Now the boss wants to tidy up the battlefield. He thinks you've earned it, too."

★ TWENTY-SEVEN ★

FALL OF '78 and on into the winter and the next year, Delta went back to basics. We reexamined our shooting program in view of improving it. We'd made mistakes, but we'd gotten smarter and we were profiting from them. Delta used a lot of ammunition—perhaps 30,000 rounds of .45 ammunition a week. The guys used handguns on the range in the morning and submachine guns in the afternoon. Our shooting improved.

The snipers began to concentrate on skills. We broke down the skill, tore it apart, and reassembled it. The snipers began to handload their own rounds. This took each man three hours a day. They became a little more careful about how many rounds they threw down range and more prudent about where they put them. Proficiency increased.

Our hardware had been upgraded when we began equipping our shooters with those 40XB heavy-barreled sniper rifles Remington was building especially for Delta. These rifles would shoot less than half a minute of angle at 100 yards. That's almost like putting bullet holes on top of bullet holes.

One day I was out on the range with Boris's sniper team. He was shooting one of the new rifles mounted with a 12x Redfield scope, and his scores were very high. He rolled over to look up at me. He was smiling.

"Boss, you've taken away all my excuses. I've got the best rifle, the best scope, I'm loading my own ammunition. I've got no more crutches to lean on. The ball's in my court. The only thing I gotta do now is work harder."

That was the kind of attitude you found in Delta. The troops were talking to each other and to their officers.

Innovation became commonplace. We developed small powerful lights which could be affixed to submachine guns for use at night to spot targets. Body armor was identified and improved on. Morale was very high even if the average workday was long. People came in at first light and left long after the sun had gone down.

Counterterrorism was at this time low on the public's recognition scale in the United States. Our country was not directly threatened, so terrorism didn't hold a high priority in the thinking of our intelligence community. The Army attaché in Nigeria, let's say, had as his number-one priority Communist activities in the country. His second priority was probably analyzing the capabilities of the Nigerian Army and the political affiliations of its key officers. And, so it would go, with an interest in terrorist activities somewhere down around sixth or seventh on his list. The CIA and the State Department began to try to change those priorities. Intelligence sources were crucial to Delta's role in combating terrorism.

Delta's communications division was putting together a state-of-the-art package. Several million dollars were spent on it. It had to be lightweight, portable, durable, secure, and cover a wide spectrum. Plans were made to patch into ships and relay through them. The thrust of the package was small, man-portable satellite communications. For a small unit Delta had a sophisticated and well-tailored package.

Earlier in Delta's development we had gone to the FBI, the CIA, and the Secret Service to ask advice and gather knowledge. Now, some of them were coming to us. Joint Staff officers, mostly colonels and lieutenant colonels, began coming down to the Stockade to look over the unit's capabilities. One officer told me, "Many people in Washington believe that with Delta General Meyer has his very own Tinker Toy. Each morning he winds it up and watches it run around the room." Jealousy was nothing new, and it certainly wasn't going away. In a way, Delta was flattered by it.

With nothing but training and more training there was the

fear that Delta could end up being a firehouse unit—damn good at sliding down the pole and jumping onto the truck with no fires to fight. When a fire would come no one could guess. But that it would come someday no one doubted. In the meantime, Delta had to get its operators on the street, out doing things. Some of them needed to be given a free hand, to get out of the country and observe how the rest of the world lived. They needed opportunities to make mistakes. For example, how did an operator go by train from Bonn to Munich; or in France, on a bus, how did he get from Clermont-Ferrand to Nantes by way of Limoges and LaRoche-sur-Yon?

We asked the State Department if we could carry the diplomatic mail for a while, which would give us a chance to look over a number of our embassy buildings and determine their hardness. Some folks in the Army and State got cold feet. "Oh, my God, Beckwith's going to get us involved in international intrigue." The fact I carried a Colt .45 made General Renick, who worked under General Meyer, uncomfortable. He volunteered to interface with State or DOD for us. I didn't want him speaking for me. "I'm not speaking for you," he replied, "I'm speaking for the Army." Renick saw me as an unguided missile.

Eventually, after the first of the year, 1979, Delta began to do some advanced training activities in Europe. An operator would land in West Germany and be met by a contact who had been arranged for from the 10th Special Forces Group. Receiving instructions to proceed to London, he would be tasked to collect all the information he could about the British Museum where, in this scenario, terrorists were holding several American tourists hostage. The operator would be expected to complete his mission in a prescribed amount of time, but this was never enough to completely succeed in doing everything he had been ordered to do. Performing under this kind of stress we had a better idea of what an operator could or could not do. Back at Bragg, the operator would be debriefed and his actions critiqued.

Delta began an exchange program with the SAS. From a sergeant they sent, we learned quite a bit about booby traps.

He'd spent time in Belfast. Then, too, GSG-9 looked us over and we them. So too, the French Groupe d'Intervention de la Gendarmerie Nationale (GIGN), and the Israelis. Delta became a part of the free world's counterterrorist community. We learned and we taught. Over and over we discussed new ideas and skills for the three basic terrorist situations—barricade, open air, airplane takeover. Tactics for breaking into planes, buses, cars, trains, subway trains, elevator shafts, office and apartment buildings, rooms of every size, shape and location were discussed, rehearsed, critiqued, rehearsed again.

Delta had a think-tank session in the Stockade once a week. Ideas flowed from the group. My door was open to anyone who wanted to talk to me. All I asked was that they put their idea on paper first. That cleaned out a lot of the bullshit. Many good ideas also came in this way. Sometimes the men asked to change a certain policy. Writing didn't mean it would happen, but their idea was considered. Everybody knew they could be heard. And they were motivated.

Major Buckshot would sometimes come up to me late in the day, maybe around 1700 hours, and say something like, "Boss, we got this new guy and he's all shot in the ass with your ideas briefing. He's got a list a mile long and there ain't one of them that's worth a damn. But, I don't want to turn him off. I've got some of the guys working with him. So, if he screws up and stops you in the hall and tells you about his ideas, keep it alive and stroke him. We might get something from him yet."

Delta was moving and, like the speakers in a stereo system, we vibrated. There were good ideas, there were poor ideas, some were insupportable, unrealistic, others were brilliant.

"Hey, Boss, got a good idea. I want to go out and check out this driving school on the West Coast."

"You know, sir, we got all these civilian radios here. They cost a lot of money. I hate to ask, because I don't know how to do it, but we gotta get a guy to school to learn how to maintain them ourselves. How do I get to the manufacturer and ask them for help?"

Fast Eddie would want to go back to Norfolk. "Time I went back to the Navy, Boss, and got more targets." "I'm afraid to send you, Sergeant. You're liable to come back with a cruiser."

We made mistakes. People came back saying, "Sir, that was a dry hole. It isn't worth farting with anymore."

We constantly tried to improve our breaching technique. Explosives will take a door down, but depending on the technician they will also blow out your eardrums. What we wanted to do was get into a room without drawing blood from our ears. Logan Fitch said, "I've been researching explosives, done all my homework. I think I've found a civilian vendor on the West Coast who makes a lead sheath type of explosive. It looks good. I'd like to go out there and get some to test."

"Don't let the door hit you in the ass."

He and Fast Eddie went to the vendor, got all the specs, bought some of the sheaths and had them shipped back to Bragg. We found in our tests that the device was extraordinarily efficient for what we wanted it to do. Delta wouldn't have found it if one officer hadn't been interested enough in the problem to spend his time solving it. Our foreign friends visited and saw its effectiveness. They came back and bought American.

As contemplated earlier, A Squadron was divided into two smaller Squadrons—A and B. Buckshot gave up his job as CO of A Squadron and spent his whole time on the vitally important task of developing and coordinating all selection activities and training courses. The new A Squadron was given to a former armor officer, Major Coyote (pseudonym), and B Squadron went to an ex-infantry officer, Major Fitch. Each squadron acquired a separate personality reflecting that of its commander. One unit tended to act methodically, the other more quickly.

Squadron strengths grew and new faces appeared throughout Delta. Personalities emerged from the ranks and were recognized and nurtured. No one wanted to drive a square peg into a round hole. Someone asked one of the operators,

"What's the difference about being in Delta as opposed to your old unit?"

"Sir," he replied, "in the 82nd Airborne I was better than any guy in my company. Over here I gotta hustle just to keep up."

★ TWENTY-EIGHT ★

HERMAN THE GERMAN showed the Delta troop commander a telegram ordering the unit to fly immediately to Quebec: "Whether Delta will actually be used has yet to be ascertained, but you are to proceed, pre-position, and prepare your troop for any eventuality. An aircraft is waiting for you at Leesburg. Weapons, flak vests, ammunition, individual kits have been sent up from Bragg and are being loaded. Move out." A guy's adrenaline had to begin to pump. At the airport, Major Coyote received a thorough briefing.

"American hostages have been taken in Canada by a band of terrorists. The Royal Canadian Mounted Police SWAT is en route and available, but the government in Ottawa has asked the American government for assistance. An American hostage has been shot and killed. Please load your unit on board as quickly as possible. You are needed at once."

In Leesburg, when the Delta troop boarded the waiting aircraft, they found on board Canadian-made candy wrappers and magazines. It was late in the afternoon. The aircraft immediately took off and headed north.

What Delta had wanted to do was find out, in a real situation, whether its operators would really pull a trigger. It's a difficult thing to do. Will a man kill another man? At the moment they could have taken out, at the Munich airport, the Black September terrorists who were moving the Israeli Olympic athletes, the German snipers froze. The opportunity was there, but they froze. Was it buck fever? Or something else?

One must say to oneself, "If I'm really going to be a professional in this business and I have to pull a trigger, how sure am I that I will?" Selected personnel had worked out a scenario that we believed would reveal that moment. Major Altman (pseudonym), who we called Herman the German, was very good on scenario development. He'd run exercises all over the southeastern United States. The scenarios were complicated, and designed to test the men's resolve, ingenuity, patience, and daring. But Herman the German's scenarios could not tell us if a man would, when necessary, kill. We had struggled with this for a long time.

Approaching New York, the air controller traffic was piped into the plane's cabin.

"Mac three three five nine-er seven, New York Center. We show you clear to Quebec via direct Hancock, direct Plattsburg. Highlevel five sixty. Company requests you do not contact Montreal Center for security reasons." The unbelievers in the troop became believers. "Jesus Christ, we're going!"

In late summer of '79 we had finally hit upon a scheme we thought could work. Major Coyote and First Troop, fifteen or sixteen operators, had been sent on one of Herman's stock scenarios—Charlotte to Raleigh to Richmond to Washington, D.C. It had been a typical mission, one the men had been on before—tasks to be performed without sufficient time, RVs to be made, information gathered, sketches drawn. All of it had been normal, and in Washington First Troop had rendezvoused before returning to Bragg—end of scenario. "Got time to have a beer, sir?"

After Herman the German had broken the news about the hostages, maps were distributed to First Troop, and a plan to take the farmhouse where the hostages were being held was discussed. Busy in the plane's cabin, at last light, the Delta unit did not notice the imperceptible change in course that took the plane south, not north. Its destination, of course, was not Quebec, Canada, but a rural part of North Carolina which we called Camp Smokey. Months earlier, in an out-of-the-way area, on some government land, a small farmhouse had been located and prepared for the scenario. Hidden in a hardwood forest—that happened to resemble the woods of northern Quebec—the house was totally rebuilt. A basement had been dug, the building reinforced by sandbags, rigging hung to support life-size mannequins, remote-controlled television cameras installed. Few within Delta knew of this exercise. My daddy had told me the way to keep a secret is don't tell nobody. Dick Potter used to get mad as hell at me when I'd go off and he couldn't find me.

When the plane landed near midnight at a small airport, the men were met by role-players. They were taken by a van bearing Quebec license plates to a nearby building. Inside they were briefed by people who had been carefully rehearsed in their roles. There was a Mountie captain, a political representative from the Government in Ottawa, an assistant attaché representing the U.S. Embassy, a senior law enforcement officer of the Province, and some other officials. All these men spoke with Canadian accents; you know the way the Canadians make the "aou" sound for o. Nothing had been overlooked. Delta's First Troop, for all it knew, was in Canada.

The briefing explained there were three terrorists, two males and a female, who had taken hostages, of whom two, at least, were American. The Canadians were not sure they could handle this operation. Telephones rang, some people carrying papers chased after other people, doors opened and closed, everyone was jumping around. There was a sense of excitement and expectation. First Troop was asked to formulate a plan to rescue the hostages.

On closed circuit television, from another building, I monitored the entire performance. In the background I could see some of our operators whispering to each other, "Are they shitting us? The fucker's real."

Major Coyote asked his questions, and Delta got on with it. For them, in their minds, this was real. The months of training were over. "Stop asking so many damn questions. Please get on with your plans! We're running out of time." "Why isn't Colonel Beckwith here?" "He's en route."

It was really good. This drama went on for nearly three hours. The house was reconnoitered, the terrorists were seen moving around outside the house, intelligence was gathered, and the Delta plan came together: Negotiations have failed; the terrorists already have killed a hostage; no alternative is left. The house must be taken by force of arms. A message arrived from the American Embassy giving Delta authority to take the building down. The Canadians were anxious that it be done quickly and effectively. The message traffic looked very official. The troop was taken to the vicinity of the house.

Two terrorist actors who were standing on the porch of the farmhouse, before the Delta snipers could get in position, turned and went into the house. Once inside they climbed down to a prepared dugout basement, locked the trap door, and were replaced upstairs by moving mannequins.

The grainy television pictures I was looking at showed the farmhouse.

Major Coyote deployed his operators through the woods, the snipers got on station. A deer surprised by one operator crashed off through the dense scrub. The men began loading their weapons. A final authority was given. First Troop rushed the house. There was firing. It was all over in eight seconds.

The evaluators were interested in how many bullet holes there were in the terrorist and hostage mannequins. We isolated First Troop afterward for three days to allow them to come off this traumatic high and to allow them to sort out their emotions and the events leading to the attack. Back at Bragg we debriefed them. At that time it was explained—the artifice we had used and why we had done it. Eventually they accepted our reasoning, but at first they were very upset. They'd done something none of them had ever done before. When it happened, in their minds they were shooting for real. People were dying. One of the men said, "Boss, don't you ever play with my mind like that again."

The terrorists all had bullet holes in them. There were no bullet holes in any of the hostages.

★ TWENTY-NINE ★

THE MEETING WAS held at 0900 hours. As I went into the conference room, General Warner, who was standing waiting on General Rogers, repeated that the Chief of Staff of the Army had no plans to visit Delta.

Department of the Army had announced earlier that General Rogers would replace Gen. Alexander Haig in Europe. Before leaving Washington he had scheduled a farewell meeting of all the commanders at Fort Bragg. I had asked General Mackmull if General Rogers had any plans to look in on the Stockade. When he'd called General Warner's headquarters to find out, he had been told that no visit to Delta had been considered. I'd said to myself, if General Rogers comes to Bragg he will come to Delta. The staff had gotten ready, just in case.

General Rogers went around the room asking the senior commanders to give him a progress report of their commands and ideas they had that could contribute to his new assignment as NATO Commander. The exchange was open and some good recommendations came out of it. He then discussed his new role and what it would mean to everyone. It turned into a long meeting. As it began to wind down General Rogers scanned the back of the room till he found me, "As soon as I leave here I'm going down to see you." "In that case, sir, I'd like permission to leave." General Warner shrugged his shoulders, indicating this was the first he'd heard of it.

I jumped into my car and raced to the Stockade to follow up on our preparations.

Five minutes later, accompanied by Generals Warner an
Mackmull, General Rogers stepped through the door. He aske
what kind of shape we were in. "Sir, we're not the best coun
terterrorist force in the world, but there's nobody any better.
I then took the opportunity—he'd asked at the earlier meet
ing—to tell him I believed Special Ops in NATO had prob
lems, particularly the viability of Special Ops plans in th
event of a war. I also volunteered my services to help him.

Perhaps two months earlier I had heard a rumor that Moses
too, was going to be reassigned to Europe. Everyone in Delt
called General Meyer "Moses." He'd saved us so often he wa
always referred to by this biblical name. I wanted to learn fron
him if what I'd heard on the street was true, and if so, ho
this would impact on Delta. I made an appointment and the
went up to the Pentagon to see him.

General Meyer told me he didn't really know if he wa
going to be reassigned when General Rogers left, but in an
case Delta would continue with business as usual.

General Meyer had then shifted gears. He'd said, "You nee
to develop Task, Conditions, and Standards for Delta." Thi
meant, at its simplest: Task—fire your weapon; Condition–
darkness; Standard—at 100 yards hit the bull's-eye with thre
rounds. Of course, Delta's would be far more difficult.

"Damn, General, that will take me a year."

"No it won't. You'll do it in the next few months. Yo
can't command Delta forever, Charlie. Its next CO will nee
a yardstick to measure Delta's status and progress. Otherwis
he could reinvent the wheel and in so doing destroy the unit.

I totally understood what General Meyer had meant, be
cause I'd seen so many commanders come into the Speci
Forces and do just that—reinvent the wheel. Task, Conditions
and Standards would be a useful tool for any new incomin
commander.

A lot of work was done on preparing this document. Whe
completed it filled a large spiral notebook nicknamed "th
Black Book," and it covered all of Delta's skills. It spelled ou
what each individual had to be able to do, then what eac
patrol, troop, and squadron had to be able to do. About sixt

individual skills were listed, then probably twenty-five patrol skills, eight or ten troop skills, and three squadron skills. This last section was the shortest, simplest to name, and most difficult to accomplish: Take down three situations—barricade, open air, aircraft.

In April I took "the Black Book" to Moses for his blessing. He carefully read, then approved, the document. Because of the reassignment rumors I'd heard, I asked him to initial the cover page. "Charlie, that isn't necessary." However, I was afraid if Moses left, Delta would be surgically whittled up and the pieces fed to the wolves.

Over beers, the Delta staff used to chew on this predicament. Someone once said, "Wouldn't it be a miracle if when Rogers leaves they made Moses Chief of Staff." Which, of course, is exactly what happened in June of '79. Delta felt a wise and prudent decision had been made.

No matter how the changes at Department of the Army would affect Delta, the unit had to continue honing its skills. This included participating in two theater exercises—one with CINCPAC, the other with REDCOM. In the exercise with REDCOM at Key West, Florida, in February, we learned that Delta and the Rangers could interface smoothly and be a great deal of help to each other.

In the summer of 1979, the unit tried to get its oar in the water at the VIII Pan-American Games, which were being held in San Juan, Puerto Rico. Delta was not welcome. There was the FBI. The SAC (Special Agent in Charge), who was responsible for the Games' security, was an old Army Ranger. His point of view, "If I need any tanks or .50-caliber machine guns, I'll call on you." After we finally got the chance to brief him, he reversed himself. He said he'd be stupid not to have us there. The Army and certain action officers in the JCS wanted us to pre-position a squadron on the island in the event of an incident. On the other hand, there were some Joint Staff officers—the same ones who perceived that General Meyer wound us up each morning and watched us run around his office—who got in the act and confused the issue. In any event, we lost the mission. Three of us, however, did get to observe the Games' security arrangements and work with the FBI in their command center.

To be perfectly frank, during that summer (the last one I thought I would have as Delta's commander), I felt the unit had plateaued out. I'd be dishonest if I didn't say that. For one thing, we weren't shooting as much. The ammo sergeant could measure brass from what was left in the boxes. There was also a certain feel about the Stockade, the feel said, "flat." To pick up the pace, get guys' adrenaline pumping, Delta ran some unannounced alerts; mostly in the early morning or late in the evening. A clock was put on these alerts in order to make the men work against something. The clock was never set to give anyone sufficient time to get everything done.

★ THIRTY ★

EVENTS THEN BEGAN to pick up speed. General Rogers wrote from Europe to the new Army Chief of Staff, General Meyer. "The American side of NATO Special Operations is in bad shape. Beckwith has had Delta a long time. What would you think about sending him over?"

General Meyer told me, "You will take command of SOTFE [Special Operations Task Force Europe]. You can really help the Army there. Let's begin, Charlie, to look around for someone to replace you in Delta, and we'll make provision to send you to Germany around late October or early November. First we'll get Delta evaluated, then we'll send you off."

A year had passed since Delta's last evaluation. The unit then was young and newly trained. Now there would be no reason for it not to excel. Delta had had its two years. It would never be in better shape. If any complacency had crept in during a slow summer, it was certainly dispelled when I announced that we would again be validated. The men of Delta tightened their belts and got down to business.

The Black Book was taken out of a file drawer and dusted off. In it were the standards the unit would be tested against. The operations people prepared an additional paper asking for a system of tests that excluded nurtured suspicions, latent resentments, and political maneuverings. The paper was straightforward and honest and explained how the unit could be tested to its ultimate capabilities. The unit needed to be tested, not in a duel of paper tigers, but in a viable, real-world scenario.

An offer was made, which was accepted, to place two of Delta's officers and a senior noncom on the evaluation team to help it construct solid tests that would truly reveal Delta's skill levels. This was the best time to show all the government agencies, which had so kindly given their advice and support, the quality the unit had achieved, and to receive back from them the recognition of Delta's status as a national asset.

An Exercise Directorate was established. It included Ambassador Anthony Quainton from the State Department's Office for Combating Terrorism, General Sam Wilson, representatives from the CIA, FBI, Department of Energy, FAA, the Secret Service, the Treasury and Justice Departments and selected Special Forces people who were made available by General Mackmull. Some of these men knew Delta Force, knew what the individual and organizational skills were, and could insure that the unit would be fairly judged on them. During the critique we were looking for insight, not hindsight. After it was over, Delta wanted to say, "It was a damn good test." If it couldn't, then it made little difference whether it passed or failed.

The SAS sent an observer. The West German GSG-9 chief, Ulrich Wegener, came himself, and so did the French GIGN's Christian Prouteau. General Meyer was represented by his new DCSOPS, Lieutenant General Glenn K. Otis.

Delta submitted a shopping list of scenarios. We suggested, because taking down a 727 is different from taking down an L-1011, three aircraft scenarios, several open-air situations, and a few barricade assaults. All, of course, included hostages.

The first phase of the evaluation tested individual skills. The evaluators, not Delta, selected the men to be tested. I don't remember what my feelings or emotions were until the first day had ended. Then I felt wonderful. The hardest part was yet to come, but the first day had gone as expected. The shooters had performed well under stress, and the scenarios were tough and realistic. It was a day punctuated with the oooh's and aaah's of the evaluators. They'd never seen anything like it before.

Another day and night of individual skill testing proved to be a duplicate of the first.

The following morning Delta was alerted that it should be ready to move with all of its equipment.

The scenario, when it was finally revealed, explained that a terrorist incident had occurred overseas. The country, of course, was bogus. My role was to survey the incident and advance a recommendation on how Delta should proceed.

Shortly afterward, I, along with a radio operator and his communications package, were flown to Savannah. There we were told to wait in a nearby motel for several hours. This was the time that, if the crisis had been real, it would have taken us to fly to the actual location. Eight hours later we were moved to Fort Stewart, Georgia, where I was briefed on the situation. It was going to be very tough: two targets had to be taken down simultaneously. Command and control would be difficult enough, let alone the nature of both targets. There was just no way for the plane to be approached without the attackers being seen. The barricade situation was tougher yet. Hostage-holding terrorists were in two connected buildings and they had the flexibility to move from one building to the other. This scenario was so sophisticated and devious, it might as well have been real.

Since there was no way of knowing when the terrorists might begin killing hostages, the first task was to design an emergency plan. It was a straightforward assault I hoped would never have to be used, because the risks involved were high and the probability of success not very good. Once this plan was in place, work began in earnest on the primary maneuver.

At this time Delta Force was transported from Fort Bragg to Maxwell AFB in southern Alabama, where it staged for the move to Fort Stewart. Buckshot and the two squadron commanders joined me at the site. Because these operations are fast-moving, dynamic, and go down with a great deal of impact. Delta always did its own reconnaissance work and planning. It was at this time that many questions were answered: what size force, type and amount of equipment, time of attack, communications needed, ruses to be used, further intelligence required, terrorists identified, hostages counted, support called in. These were critical tasks and on their being answered accurately, and wisely, rested the success of the mission.

The squadron commander responsible for the airplane, Major Coyote, had a problem. Its location. "I gotta get that 727 moved." How? A problem with the APU (auxiliary power unit) that was feeding electricity to the plane was induced and, after long and very realistic negotiations with the terrorists, the plane was moved fifty feet to the location of another unit. Delta operators, dressed as maintenance people, did the moving, and while doing so made some important observations.

At dusk, on the 3rd of November—the evening promised to be balmy—Delta Force presented its plan in the event a force option was needed. Close questioning followed. Any politician who doesn't ask, "How many casualties will we take, What are the risks and what is the probability of success?" is obtuse. The planning group was put to the task for nearly two hours.

The decision to use force at any terrorist-controlled crisis site is always a political decision; it's not, nor should it be, a military one. Many times in this situation, the planners had to get clarification and then authority to do certain things. They were often frustrated by the "host" country, who had sovereignty, when certain prerequisites weren't granted. The original plan had to, therefore, be modified. It was further adjusted as the intelligence base grew.

Suddenly, a hostage was "killed." The use of a force option seemed to be the only solution. Negotiations with the terrorists broke off. The snipers had been in position for several hours, and they continued to observe the two targets. The 727, after it had been moved, became manageable. The buildings remained difficult. However, this flexible target, through on-site intelligence gathering, slowly began being cut down to size.

Once the assault plan had been approved, a rehearsal was run on the Fort Stewart reservation, on buildings found to be similar to the ones being held by the role-playing terrorists.

A sliver of moon kept the night dark.

The warning came, "Delta should prepare itself to take down both targets." A and B Squadrons slid into position.

"Take them down!"

Because the approach to the buildings proved more difficult than the approach to the 727, the plane went down about forty-five seconds before the buildings. A Squadron's assault on the plane was straightforward. Several entrances were simultaneously breached. The terrorists became rattled, and their concentration and resolve broke.

Delta inundated them!

Because of some very substantial barricades put up inside the buildings, it was decided by Fast Eddie and others that, to breach them successfully, high explosives would be required. When this was explained to the Directorate, in order to protect the role-players, the scenario was modified. Window frames were reamed out, doors were blown open, and from three directions Major Fitch's B Squadron stormed the buildings. Through corridors and into rooms the operators raced, clearing everything in their way. A complex and critical assignment; take down terrorists, save hostages. There's no more than seven seconds between entering a room and clearing it before the situation can go sour. It moves very fast. The drills for this, so meticulously worked on in the shooting house behind the Stockade, paid dividends here. All the hostages were released unhurt. The terrorists were taken down.

A few minutes before midnight the exercise ended. The medical people had gone in and taken care of all the simulated injuries. On the aircraft there was one actual serious injury. One of the female role-players refused to surrender and a Delta operator fired a blank .45 round near her face. She suffered bad powder burns. Delta's burn specialist went into action; as a result of his action the role-player suffered no permanent damage or scars.

A thorough debriefing followed the exercise, and representatives from all the key agencies gave their critiques. The quality of their response was impressive. Then the Exercise Directorate outlined the mission's objectives and voiced their opinions. Delta received the highest marks. Ambassador Quainton, who had seen all the counterterrorist capabilities in the free world, was particularly complimentary. Finally, the foreign representatives were asked to state their opinions. The SAS response was classic. "You know, we play these games, too. Just like you chaps, the military, the Ministry of Defence, and the Foreign Office all participate. But, I must tell you, when we play, Maggie plays. We are very serious about it." The way he said this and the way he looked around the room gave the impression he didn't think we were serious enough. Representatives, he implied, no matter how exalted, are no substitutes for the principal players who will, in a real national crisis, make the vital decisions. A lot of time was spent discussing the issue. It became crystal clear that some general, whether he wore one star or five, should not make the crucial decisions involving a terrorist incident. The military had built the tool, but the decision to use it would be politically based, and the authority would come from the Commander-in-Chief, the President. I wasn't sure in my own mind that some of the military types who sat in this briefing room understood this principle, but Ambassador Quainton made it very clear.

After midnight—it was now the 4th of November 1979—we went over to General Sam's motel room to talk over the events of the past few days. Sam Wilson, who occasionally enjoys a little squeezing from the vine, acted as host to my officers and others who were close friends of Delta.

Major Fitch, B Squadron's commander and the one responsible for taking down the barricaded buildings, thought I had not sent him in early enough. "If you had," he said, "both squadrons would have acted in perfect accord." This was a lick on me, and I agreed with his assessment. I learned something.

There were some pretty happy and tired people in this room. Some of us were relieved as well. Our technique worked; our principles were sound.

About 2:30 we went over to an all-night restaurant and ordered big breakfasts. Thoughts began running to getting back home and the party broke up. A few people worried about their transportation, which had to be secured in the morning. I looked forward to several hours of solid sleep. It had been many days since I laid my head down on a pillow. Delta Force was already asleep in their billets at Fort Stewart.

I was awakened by the news around 7:00 A.M. One of my officers called, "Thought you'd like to know, Boss. The American Embassy in Iran has gone down. The entire staff is being held hostage."

★ THIRTY-ONE ★

THIS WAS SUNDAY, 4 November 1979. Delta Force had already closed back into Fort Bragg by the time I drove in at 1500 hours.

The drive north was without incident. Occasional patches of dark color showed through the leafless trees lining the interstate. The morning sun had still held a little warmth. Around Marion, South Carolina, I'd stopped and called the Duty Officer at the Stockade to determine if there were any messages waiting. In North Carolina it was a day on which to play football—crisp and cloudless.

A and B Squadrons were unpacking and cleaning their gear as I read the AP and Reuters wire service reports of the takeover. Through the headquarters there floated a sense that Delta would somehow have a role in this.

Late in the afternoon, when nothing official had arrived, the troops were sent home.

The first telephone call came in early Monday morning; it was from Major Shaw in the Army's Special Ops Division, asking Delta to send a liaison officer to Washington to work with the staff officers of the JCS. Buckshot and Major Watson (pseudonym) of Delta were selected to go. Buckshot was outranked by Watson, but as he had a better understanding of the Joint Chiefs arena he was placed in charge and authorized to speak for Delta. Major Watson was not real comfortable with this arrangement, but indicated he could live with it.

A couple of days later Dick Meadows was also dispatched

to Washington. Everyone in the Pentagon knows how this game is played. If Delta had sent one man to the JCS, the action officers there would have said, "Beckwith doesn't really think much of this or he would have sent more men." One man could be thought to be opinionated and therefore ignored. Two men might be outvoted, but three men acting together would be heard. I didn't want to learn that some notion or plan had been put in concrete without Delta having had an opportunity to have its comments heard clearly, accurately, and forcefully.

Buckshot called on a secure phone line each day. "The planners are still looking at various alternatives, but I don't really think they have any role for us yet. It seems they are compiling a list of viable options that can be used against Iran."

Dr. Zbigniew Brzezinski, the President's National Security Advisor, had gone over to the Pentagon and his visit had instilled in the planners a feeling of urgency. The Special Ops Division, Buckshot reported, just hummed with activity.

I had not at all begun to assess the problems of mounting a rescue mission, beyond realizing what any military man would know—logistically speaking it would be a bear. There were the vast distances, nearly 1,000 miles, of Iranian wasteland that had to be crossed, then the assault itself, against a heavily guarded building complex stuck in the middle of a city of 4,000,000 hostile folks. This was not going to be any Entebbe or Mogadishu. Nothing could be more difficult. If our government does elect to use force, I thought, obviously Delta, the country's door-busters, will be used; but they'll never get to that point. Too many other diplomatic options remain unexplored. Negotiations and compromise are the tools this administration will use. Delta might get to an alert status, but this administration really doesn't have enough grit to do anything more. My opinion of President Carter was very low. I had not voted for him and I was bitterly disappointed when he gave amnesty to those Americans who had gone to Canada to avoid the draft during the Vietnam War. I was also concerned with the way the administration was forcing some of the most experienced operators out of the CIA. In any event, I knew I'd have nothing to do with any rescue mission—real or hypothetical.

My household goods had all been shipped and my family and I were preparing for a permanent change of station to West Germany. Teheran was a long way away. Then, things changed almost immediately. Buckshot called just at dusk on the 10th. "I'm coming in, Boss, and we gotta talk. They're flying me down in a T-39." Normally anyone traveling back and forth from Bragg to the capital went on a Piedmont 737. Occasionally the Army coughed up a small prop aircraft, but a T-39 was more expensive than flying a commercial airline. If they're using it to whip Buckshot down here tonight, I thought, it has to be important. T-39 Sabre-liners are used to fly generals around, not majors.

We met outside Base Operations at Pope Air Force Base. Buckshot was very serious. "Everybody in the JCS is leaning forward, but in some cases they're grasping for straws. I've heard some idiotic concepts and some of them include Delta. Some guy today thought we could parachute into the outskirts of Teheran and just like tourists ride up to the embassy in a motorcade. Before they commit us to something stupid, Boss, you need to go up to the JCS and shoot down some of these concepts. The trouble is that Meadows has a tendency to go along with some of those ideas. Maybe he'd be put to better use back here."

I drove Buckshot to Bragg and we sat in the car talking in front of his quarters.

"I have informal approval for Delta to relocate to a secure training site in the northern part of the state. You'll be receiving more information on this from Washington either tonight or tomorrow morning," Buckshot said.

Before he got out of the car, he told me that a decision had been made to appoint Major General Vaught commander of the rescue task force. General Kingston and Mackmull had also been considered for this command, but moving either of them out of their respective command positions at this time would have telegraphed to other countries our rescue intentions. General Vaught, an officer with Airborne/Ranger experience and a distinguished career who was already assigned to the Pentagon, seemed an appropriate choice.

I began to examine the news Buckshot had brought me. If they direct Delta to move to what was called Camp Smokey—the secure training site—someone was getting serious about this. After dinner I began to work out the necessary logistics required to move A Squadron and a handful of support personnel out of Bragg and to the new location. During a sleepless night I pondered whether B Squadron should be recalled from its ski training in Colorado.

Moses called on secure first thing Sunday morning. It was a miserable day; cold and rainy. November at its worst. He wanted my opinion on relocating to Camp Smokey and whether it could be done without drawing unwanted attention to ourselves. Operations security, he emphasized, was paramount. He would call General Mackmull. I told him I'd call him within the hour.

The Delta staff was collected and we discussed our ability at Fort Bragg to tailor Delta for a rescue operation. It is the home of the Special Forces and the 82nd Airborne Division, and is the target of hostile intelligence services. The Russians and Cubans listen to message traffic through their commercial flights, which are rigged with electronic monitoring gear. Although their flight patterns keep them over the Atlantic, they are still within range of Bragg. It, therefore, became very clear that if any reasonable degree of operations security was to be obtained, Fort Bragg was out. Furthermore, it was decided the move from Bragg to Smokey could be made that evening—the post is usually quiet on Sundays—without attracting unnecessary attention. Torrents of slanting rain continued to pour down from the darkened sky. Lights were turned on early in all the offices.

I called Moses back and received his blessing for the relocation that evening. After I hung up the secure phone, I recalled that months earlier we had worked on a proposal with Keith Gwynn at the State Department about assessing several of the American embassies and trying to harden them where necessary. The Army was willing to pay the temporary duty expenses for two or three Delta operators to travel to embassies, but some State Department people couldn't come up with their share of the money. The trip was canceled. Embassy security had a very low priority. The embassy in Teheran was one of the facilities scheduled to be appraised before it was called off. It was sickening.

The November chill seeped through the halls of the Stockade.

Over several cups of coffee, Delta's staff finalized the plans for moving A Squadron to the piedmont country of northern North Carolina. The actual location of Camp Smokey was no problem as it had been the area of the Quebec terrorist training exercise.

Our plan called for small groups of men to travel in rented cars. The support people made calls all Sunday afternoon to a number of car rental agencies throughout the area—Raleigh, Durham, Greensboro. To have rented a bus or asked for a plane would have alerted anyone who was watching Delta.

Wade Ishimoto and No Lips were ordered to go on ahead, and in a small motel north of Raleigh they set up an office where the operators would stop to receive directions on how to get to their final destination. The drivers were given the motel's address, a room number, and a time when they were expected to check in with Ish and No Lips.

In the motel, because there was some time before the first Delta car arrived, Ish decided to go out and get something to eat. No Lips, who is a very fit type of individual, was not inclined. He was more concerned with doing his exercises. But Ish pulled rank and the two went to dinner.

Buckshot and I left Bragg earlier than the troops, to make sure their arrival at Camp Smokey would go smoothly. Unfortunately, I had to leave Katherine in our quarters with a flooded basement.

Around midnight Buckshot called the motel to tell Ish we would be coming in shortly and that we'd be taking him with us when we left.

Once Ishimoto was picked up, No Lips was left alone in the motel room. Over the next four days he would give final directions to the Delta drivers who checked in with him. Because only the drivers knew when they would arrive at the motel, No Lips could never leave the room. The maids became suspicious. Who was this man who never went outdoors?

At first the messages I received, as the early cars drove into Smokey, were that No Lips was getting awfully lonesome. By the end of the second day, the messages said he was getting awfully hungry. Toward the end of the third day the drivers reported that No Lips had resorted to bribery. He would not give them their instructions until they either went and got him a Big Mac or they let him go and get one.

During those long four days, No Lips continued to do his thousand push-ups and thousand sit-ups. The last car through picked him up and he arrived at Smokey fit and famished.

I had one problem that caused me a lot of worry during this period. What if one of the cars had an accident on a back country road and a local deputy sheriff found the ammunition and machine guns packed in the trunk? Each of the drivers carried a card with an Alcohol, Tobacco and Firearms 800 emergency telephone number. A call would clear up any situation, but it would be awkward and not what Moses had in mind. It was a great relief to watch the last one drive into Camp Smokey.

Monday morning, not long after the sun had come up and begun to dry out the ground and barracks, intelligence community personnel installed a secure telephone-teletype line from the new headquarters at Smokey to the Pentagon. Nothing works that fast in the Army unless it has a very high priority. At the same time a secure teletype line to the Stockade was installed.

Much needed to be done at the new camp, so much that it was decided that Major Buckshot would not return to Washington but stay at Camp Smokey to help settle Delta into its temporary home. I grabbed him. Captain Ishimoto, and a packet of 3" × 5" cards and began to make notes on a rescue scheme.

What was needed most was intelligence. Where in the embassy compound were the hostages being held? How many hostages were being held? At this time, many figures were being used and issued to the press—all in an attempt to keep the Iranians from deducing that in fact six Americans were hiding in the Canadian Embassy. Delta needed to know the *true* figure. What did the embassy look like? Were the hostages being held in a group or had they been separated? Who was holding them? Were they students, militia, or regular army? Were there any Palestinians involved in seizing the embassy? In guarding the hostages? Precisely how many guards were there and how were they armed? What were their routines, especially during night hours? Where were they posted? Where were the walking guards and where were the stationary ones? What kind of reinforcements could they summon? To whom could we go for information about Iran and its geography? It is a long way from the green hills of North Carolina to the gray stony deserts of Iran.

From the nature of the calls I was receiving, it was obvious that Department of the Army had chopped Delta to the control of the Joint Chiefs of Staff. It became even more evident, when I was told to report to the River Entrance of the Pentagon. The River Entrance is the JCS entrance.

I flew up on Monday afternoon. On this bright, early winter's afternoon an Army car was waiting at Davison Army Airfield at Fort Belvoir to take me directly to the River Entrance.

Inside the Pentagon, after showing a military ID. I turned right on the E-ring and walked a short distance down a busy corridor. The portraits of American military immortals—Sheridan and Stuart, Halsey and Spruance, Ridgway and Stilwell—looked out from the walls.

Shortly after passing the offices of the Chairman of the Joint Chiefs of Staff, I hung a left onto corridor 8. If you miss this junction you will end up sometime later at the Mall Entrance. These rings and corridors wind around for seventeen miles and it's easy to get lost in them. I had learned this the hard way a few years earlier when I was getting Delta off the drawing board.

A little way down the corridor, past portraits of former

Chairmen—Admirals Radford and Moorer, Air Force Generals Twining and Brown, Army Generals Bradley, Lemnitzer, Taylor, and Wheeler—there is a closed door which opens into the Special Operations Division of the JCS.

On entering this large room I noticed six times as many people and more activity than I'd ever seen before. A lot of paper was moving around. I heard typewriters, telephone bells, and the murmur-murmur of a dozen conversations. Small groups of action officers huddled together and I began to hear, like a siren above city traffic, the word "Delta."

"We can infiltrate Delta by foot . . ."

"Delta can be dropped in . . ."

People I'd never seen before were talking about Delta the way they talked about the Washington Redskins. Buckshot was correct. There was a lot of activity being generated in this division. I saw a lot of new faces. The key, of course, was to identify who amongst them were credible and who weren't.

I worked my way into the office of the Director of Special Operations, Col. Larry Stearns.

"Come in, Charlie, and shut the door." That was General Meyer. I looked around and saw two other general officers standing there. Gen. Glenn Otis was one of them. He was General Meyer's DCSOPS. The other one, Maj. Gen. James Vaught. He had visited Delta at an earlier time and, because of the slow way he had of speaking and the way he chewed on his words, some of the troops called him "The Neanderthal Man." I knew him fairly well. I was going to get to know him much better.

General Vaught, whose radio call sign was Hammer, perceives himself as a soldier's soldier. He'd served in combat and was very quick to tell you he'd served in three wars: World War II, Korea, and Vietnam. He is an airborne general. I saw him as having a large ego matched only by his ambition. I knew of him when he had been Chief of Staff for the XVIII Airborne Corps and met him when he commanded Fort Stewart and controlled the 1st Ranger Battalion. We had spoken during one of my recruitment drives and I felt he was in favor of Delta. A few of his soldiers from the 24th Infantry Division at Fort Stewart had even volunteered to come up and run our selection course. General Vaught wanted everyone to know he was, first, a general officer and, second, that he was in control. He would have told you his first name was General. I never once called him Jim, yet I was comfortable with him. The planning phase of the mission he now commanded was to eventually be dubbed, for operations security purposes, Rice Bowl.

General Meyer asked my opinion about a rescue attempt. I told him we had real problems with the distances we'd have to travel. After I'd dropped Buckshot off, the night he'd flown down to Bragg in the T-39, I'd gone home and looked at a big *National Geographic* atlas. With Afghanistan and Pakistan to the east, the Persian Gulf and Gulf of Oman to the south, Iraq and Turkey to the west, the Caspian Sea and the Russian steppes of central Asia to the north, Iran is a long damn way from Fort Bragg, North Carolina. Teheran, the capital, is buried deep in the Iranian interior, surrounded and protected by mountains and deserts. I wasn't telling General Meyer anything he didn't already know. What kind of airplanes would be used? Where would they take off? Where would they land?

When I finished asking all the questions I had written on those 3" × 5" cards, he said, "Charlie, you need to clearly understand that the people you saw on the other side of this wall will not do your planning. You will develop the ground tactical plan—how many operators are required, the nature of the equipment you'll need, and whether you're ready to go. If you cannot answer this last question positively, the President will be so informed." I appreciated Moses talking like this. It was reassuring, especially after overhearing some of the ideas I'd heard in the outer office area. I also appreciated that General Vaught had heard all of this and now knew what my charter was in the newly formed joint Task Force (JTF).

I restated the concerns I was having about getting into and out of Teheran. "Charlie," General Meyer said, "that's really the responsibility of the air people. They're the ones who have to fly you there. Let them worry about that particular problem. I don't object to your sticking your nose into it, but it would appear to me that you have a full plate designing the ground tactical plan."

After this business had been settled and our meeting adjourned, I spent some time with a nucleus of planners I was introduced to. Air Force Gen. David Jones, who was then Chairman of the Joint Chiefs of Staff, had begun to pull together officers from his own staff. Requests were also pending for recruits from the different services and commands—the European Command, Military Airlift Command, Tactical Air Command, the Navy, others.

Some of the operations planners were responsible for coming up with ideas for the rescue. They told me, "Some of the ideas you'll hear are weird, but we'd like to drive them by you anyway." I then heard ideas for using parachutes, fixed-wing aircraft, helicopters, trucks, buses, and automobiles.

One of the planners said, "What we ought to do is get on helicopters and crash land them in the embassy."

"Well," I said, "if you crash land them, how will we get out?"

"Oh."

He hadn't thought that part out yet.

Delta had been given a mission: Assault the American Embassy in Teheran; take out the guards; free the hostages and get everyone safely out of Iran. That part was simple. All we needed to do now was come up with a plan. But without sufficient intelligence, nothing they said made any sense. We needed three things: information, information, and information.

I was concerned with one piece of news I'd heard earlier in the evening. It was hard to believe. I'd been nosing around the intelligence planners in an attempt to learn the status of their effort; and I'd been introduced to the CIA liaison officer who recently had been assigned to the Joint Task Force to support and assist in its planning. He knew the Iranian situation well, having previously been assigned to Teheran. I'd said to him and others standing by, "What we gotta do is get in touch with the stay-behind assets in country and task them with our intelligence requirements." (In English, get in touch with our agents in Teheran and have them answer the mail.) He led me to a quiet corner and whispered the astonishing news, "We don't have any."

All the news wasn't that grim. The intelligence section of special ops at the JCS had done a lot of spade work. Besides acquiring detailed maps, they were having built a large-scale model of the embassy's buildings and grounds. There were no people in this section who hadn't read past *Ned-The-First-Reader*. They were optimistic, busy, and professional. An Air Force lieutenant colonel whom I'll call Ron Killeen spent a lot of time filling me in with what he knew.

Before departing the Pentagon that evening, I asked General Vaught if he had any guidance for me. He said, "I've just been called back from London and don't know any more than you do. I've got to play catch-up ball, then get this task force in gear. As soon as I can, I'll be down to see you."

During the flight back to Camp Smokey that evening, conflicting and confusing images ran through my mind. There were just too many questions and too few answers. Not much useful would come out of what was then known.

It was well past midnight by the time I arrived back in Camp Smokey.

★ THIRTY-TWO ★

THE NEXT MORNING the KW-7, which linked Camp Smokey to the Pentagon, began to clatter with incoming message traffic. Most of it was information that was passing from CIA to the JCS. Some of the information was of course useful, but some of it worthless.

At this time Delta had only two intelligence analysts available to sort through the reams and reams of material being transmitted. What was acute was to figure out the various rating systems on how reliable information was considered to be. Nearly every agency that sent us material used a different system. A report would come in stating that the source was "untested." The intelligence guys needed more than that. Was the source reliable on any basis? Another report might read. "An untested source received through an unofficial contact . . ." What does "unofficial contact" mean? Was the contact reliable or unreliable in the past?

Some people in intelligence became highly indignant when we complained about the reports. An official came down to point out that well over 200 reports had been furnished Delta. Wade Ishimoto explained, very nicely but firmly, that most of the information we received and laboriously read dealt with material having nothing to do with the hostages. A report he pulled out listed fourteen items that had come from travelers who'd just returned from Iran. The fourteen items covered everything from the Turkish border area down to Baluchestan va Sistan in the south. Not one of these was even remotely related to the hostages.

Eventually, messages coming into Smokey that related directly to our needs were slugged with a code name for easy identification.

Major Coyote's "A" Squadron had settled into Camp Smokey and was becoming acquainted with its new surroundings. The support people we had left behind in Bragg were having a far more difficult time. Lieutenant Colonel Potter and Captain Smith (Delta's adjutant) were responsible for putting up the appearance that Delta was still at Bragg and doing business as usual. This involved all the administrative support personnel—clerks, supply haulers, and communications personnel—who had stayed behind. They had to go down to the range and bust caps, drive specific vehicles assigned to Delta around the post, receive all incoming phone calls and carefully provide a reasonable response to each caller. Among the many incoming calls the Stockade received were several to me from General Renick at Department of the Army. I was informed of these calls, but remembering General Meyer's warning not to speak to anyone about the Joint Task Force, I chose not to return them, which of course made Renick furious. He called often and when I could not be reached for the sixth or seventh time, he began to berate the officers at the Stockade. Finally, I asked General Vaught to get General Renick off my back. The calls suddenly stopped. Dick Potter and Smitty were most appreciative.

While in Washington I had obtained permission to transport B Squadron's forty-five men back from Colorado via a 727 charter aircraft. In Bragg they collected their operational gear and made their way to Camp Smokey in the same manner as had A Squadron. Major Fitch's B Squadron closed into Camp Smokey and there were many smiling faces. Training now had a specific purpose attached to it.

One advantage Smokey had over Bragg was that the whitetail deer population near the camp was high. Periodically, the troops would go out and poach two or three of them. You wouldn't believe what the taste of roast venison cooked over a wood fire could do for morale.

During the entire time Delta stayed at Smokey it received truly magnificent support from the camp's commander, someone we called "Big Ed." The difficult tasks we gave him he solved immediately, the impossible ones took a little longer—24 hours.

In a few days General Vaught visited Delta. We had just completed an emergency assault plan. There was no way of knowing when or if the Iranians would begin killing the hostages. General Vaught was briefed on the plan. It was straightforward—and suicidal.

Delta would move by aircraft to the vicinity of Teheran. There, east of the city, it would parachute in, then commandeer vehicles and find its way through the city to the embassy compound, then free the hostages, then fight its way across the city to the Mehrabad International Airport and take and hold it until American aircraft could come in and airlift everyone out. In the event the weather turned sour, Delta and the freed hostages were equipped with small Evade and Escape kits. Each kit contained a Silva compass, a 1978 Sahab Geographic and Drafting Institute plasticized map, U.S. dollars and Iranian rials, air panels, strobe lights, pills for water purification, antibiotics, and a Farsi phrase list (Don't move—Ta kan na khor, Where am I—Man koja has tam, Which way is north—Rahe kojast shomal, We are brothers—Ma baradar has team). With these kits, Delta and the released hostages would attempt to escape overland.

"What's the risk, Colonel Beckwith?"

"Oh, about 99.9 percent."

"What's the probability of success?"

"Zero."

"Well, we can't do it."

"You're right, Boss."

"I've got to buy time from the JCS."

General Vaught then philosophized about other options and how they might be received in the political arena. We talked for an extended period of time. Vaught, a South Carolinean, speaks slowly and clearly. I understood what he said. One, he wanted it plainly understood he was the Task Force Commander. Two, he wanted to work very closely with Delta. Eventually the conversation bent its way back to the problem of getting to and from Teheran. Every conversation began and ended with this critical problem. We had a tiger by the tail.

Without "stay-behind assets," intelligence agents, information gathering was slow and tedious. That's where America was in November 1979—without anyone in Teheran working for it. The Central Intelligence Agency was working to locate someone in the area, but that process would take some time. Hell, it takes five to seven years just to train and emplace an agent. He or she has to be spotted, recruited, trained, assessed, and introduced into country. Then he or she can become productive only after they've lived their cover for a reasonable period of time.

The Carter administration had made a serious mistake. When retired Admiral Stansfield Turner went into the CIA, a lot of the old whores—guys with lots of street sense and experience—left the Agency. They had been replaced with younger, less experienced people or, worse, not replaced at all. Why this happened I don't know. But I do know that in Iran on 12 November 1979 there were no American agents on the ground. Nothing could be verified. Delta was proceeding thus far without accurate and timely intelligence.

It had always been assumed, in establishing a counterterrorist unit, that when Delta was needed overseas, the country in which it would operate would be friendly or at least neutral. When the target was taken down, Delta's backside would be protected. Ish seemed to sum up the situation in hostile Iran perfectly. "The difference between this and the Alamo is that Davy Crockett didn't have to fight his way in."

We had to accommodate this new situation. Delta continued to be the only available team for the job, but it must now adjust. Snipers were converted to machine gunners. Delta's room-clearers selected as their weapon the Heckler and Koch MP5 9mm parabellum submachine gun. Both the Brits and the Germans use it. It feels good in your hand. It is smaller and lighter than a Thompson, and it can be used with a silencer. It was ideal for Iran. Other operators used the CAR15 and a few carried .45 grease guns (M3A1s) or M16s.

Additionally, two light machine guns, the M60 and the HK21, both 7.62mm. were used in Camp Smokey. Their hammering could be heard on the range every day. The American M60 can fire 550 rounds a minute and its air-cooled barrel can be replaced in seconds. The West German HK21 is a Rolls-Royce. It fires full automatic or single shot, has an effective range of 1,200 meters, a cyclic rate of 900 rounds per minute and can fire drums, link belts, or box magazines. And, unlike the M60, which is a two-man gun, the HK21 requires only one operator. Light, flexible, and accurate, for the tasks we had to perform, it's one hell of a good weapon.

Selected personnel were trained to use the M203 and M79 handheld grenade launchers. The M203 fires a variety of 40mm projectiles and is a single-shot, breech-loading, pump-action weapon that can be attached to the M16 rifle. A percussion-type, single-shot grenade launcher which breaks in the middle like a shotgun, the M79 fires its high explosive round as far as 400 meters. Both were easy to handle and, because of the extra punch they offered, became great favorites in Delta.

Of course, the standard sidearm was an accurized M-1911A1 .45 ACP (Automatic Caliber Pistol). It is dependable and has great stopping power. The ones Delta use had come out of the Anniston (Alabama) Army Depot and had been accurized by our gunsmith, Ron Waananen. When he was through working on the slides, receivers, barrels, and barrel bushings, they no longer shook, rattled, or rolled. Triggers were either National Match or standard Colt and adjusted for each operator. Bo-Mar adjustable sights were removed and replaced by a specially made rear fixed sight.

A lot of people argue that a .45 is not the best sidearm available. In Delta there was no argument. I'd seen what its big, heavy 230-grain bullet could do. It'll knock a man slap down. Plus, a .45 ACP slug travels very slowly. Whereas a 9mm projectile will run between 1,100 and 1,200 feet per second, the .45 moves at approximately 850 feet per second—standing behind it you can actually see it moving. In an airplane cabin, a 9mm bullet fired from an HK P7, because of its muzzle velocity, will likely go through a terrorist, through a seat, and end up in an innocent bystander. A .45 slug, on the other hand, will penetrate but may not exit the target.

Based on what intelligence we did have, tactics and techniques that appeared to be necessary were developed and sharpened. Because the embassy compound was circled by a nine-foot wall, climbing skills emphasizing quickness and silence were stressed.

We rehearsed with C4 plastic high explosive charges, both ribbon and linear types, necessary to cut heavy steel doors and knock down sections of wall or other obstacles. Fast Eddie spent hundreds of hours determining how much C4 would be necessary. Dozens and dozens of doors and walls were built and blown down. Fast Eddie walked around each day with a smile on his face.

Most of this was conducted at night. Speed became an essential part of the training process. Every operator had to understand the roles he would perform and those of his mates. A lot of time and effort went into developing the most efficient method of carrying extra ammunition, flashlights, evasion and escape kits, maps, and other special equipment. Instilled in every operator's mind were the principles—surprise, speed, success.

We were helped by the arrival of the large-scale model of the embassy compound and surrounding streets. The model, which was eight feet wide and twelve feet long, showed an enormous amount of detail. Based on new incoming intelligence reports and photographs, the model was frequently updated. Separate scale models of each building located in the compound were also constructed. The roofs could be lifted off each and individual floor plans could be studied all the way down to the basement.

The model of the compound answered one of the intelligence planners' biggest questions. How big would the problem be once Delta got to Teheran? Now they knew. The embassy compound, which from above resembled a backward block letter L, consisted of fourteen separate buildings situated on twenty-seven acres of walled-in real estate. In other words, the compound was the size of a small American college campus. Of the sixty-six Americans originally taken hostage—the Iranians released thirteen later in November, on the 18th and 20th—what we believed then were fifty-three were to remain captive somewhere in this complex of heavily wooded areas and widely distributed buildings. All Delta had to do was learn precisely where they were being held and design a tactical plan to rescue them. The model, indeed, answered a big question—but the answer was not encouraging.

In late November, when the thirteen released hostages returned home, we learned that three Americans were being confined outside the embassy. On the day of the takeover the Chargé d'Affaires, L. Bruce Laingen, the Political Officer, Victor Tomseth, and a security officer, Michael Howland, were doing business in the Iranian Foreign Ministry building. They were still there, being held captive on the third floor. Therefore, as Delta would have its hands full with the fifty hostages held in the embassy compound, another force would have to be found to attack that second location.

In the evenings, we watched all the network television coverage. The Iranian segments were taped, and screened over and over. They carried much valuable information: how the gates were secured (the motor pool gate, for example, was chained and padlocked); types of weapons (the Pasdaran revolutionary guards outside carried G3 rifles, while the militants inside carried a variety of handguns, Uzi submachine guns, M3 carbines, and G3 rifles). We watched to find out if the guards handled their weapons like well-trained professionals, or like amateurs—we decided the latter. Were grenades or extra bandoliers of ammunition in evidence? (Grenades were never seen, but there were instances when more than one magazine to a guard was visible.) The amount of business going on in the streets (streets were usually crowded) indicated the Pasdaran's unwillingness or inability to control the situation outside the walls. The nature of the buildings facing the wall was important. The compound, obviously, was in a commercial district; and many of the surrounding buildings were high enough to look into the embassy grounds, particularly a nearby twenty-story building and a fourteen-story building west of the main gate. We checked from the broadcasts whether there were obstacles placed in the roads to control crowds during demonstrations. The width of streets and alleys (the two main avenues, Roosevelt and Takht-E-Jamshid, were four lanes and the alleys two lanes) was measured. We checked where covering fire could be placed (machine guns at any intersection would control access in either direction). We guessed at the number of people who lived in the area. It was low to medium density except to the north on Roosevelt Avenue, which showed upper-middle-class apartment buildings.

Television made everything real. There, for example, was Roosevelt Avenue, not lines on a map or fuzzy dots on an old black and white file photo; rather, in living color, just the way it had actually been several hours before when filmed.

Between the model, the television network pictures, and discussions with people who had recently returned from an assignment in the embassy or to Teheran, the planners began to color in the black and white sketch they had carried in their mind's eye.

In Washington, where I had flown to attend another brainstorming session, I was introduced to Air Force Col. James Kyle. General Vaught had added him to the Joint Task Force (JTF) staff as his deputy to supervise the planners responsible for getting Delta in and out. Jim Kyle impressed everyone. As a former air commando, he obviously knew his business.

When Kyle left his permanent duty station, which was in Hawaii, to join the JTF, having no idea how long it would be necessary for him to stay, he arrived with one change of clothes and the blue blazer he wore on his back. Months later, still in Washington, he continued to wear the same blazer. The lining, through numerous dry cleanings, became frayed and hung below the bottom of the coat. It was sort of a joke. Eventually, Buckshot loaned him another jacket and some ties.

Our mission flushed a covey of would-be helpers out of the offices of the JCS. There were some people who began to stick their noses into our business, trying to find out what was going on. Rubberneckers, all very interested and very official, continued to run in and out of the meetings. Some officers tried to get more involved than they needed to. They showed more curiosity than expertise. There was a lot of I-wish-I-was-more-involved-itis going around. The strap-hangers never seriously interfered with Rice Bowl, but at briefings they ate up a lot of time. There was also the problem of security. The more people involved, the more critical the problem. It was a matter of trying to determine who truly had a "need to know." General Vaught tried to deal with it, but he never really found a way to make it go away.

One officer who was never a problem was Air Force Maj. Gen. Philip C. Gast. He had been in Iran several months earlier as the senior military advisor. General Gast became an important part of the team. He said, "I know nothing about Special Operations, but I do know something about Iran and I can help there." He came down to Camp Smokey where the intelligence types like Wade Ishimoto picked his brain. He identified people who had recently worked in the embassy. He also knew which people worked in what office and in what building. These people, when tracked down through the Department of Defense, were brought on board and began answering some basic questions. General Gast also made every effort to take some of the load off General Vaught, whom, incidentally, he outranked by seniority.

★ THIRTY-THREE ★

FOR DELTA FORCE a typical day at Camp Smokey in lat November 1979 would begin with the lights coming on in th headquarters area occupied by the intelligence shop.

Wade Ishimoto would be up at 7:00 A.M. in order to watc the early morning network news programs. Messages that ha come in during the four hours he had been asleep would als need to be read.

Around 9:00 o'clock, Ish or one of the other staffers woul call the Pentagon to talk to Ron Killeen about the most re cently received situation reports and intelligence estimates.

With the aid of an Air Force officer, Maj, Harry Johnsor who had recently been the assistant air attaché in Teheran, Is tried to figure out how all the doors in the chancellery workec which way they opened, how they were constructed, what kin of locks closed them, where were the keys or—in the case o electronic locks—the controls. Which doors could be breache without high explosives and which ones would require it?

That was the little picture. The big picture also needed t be attended to. For example, where were the Iranians posi tioning their Russian-built ZSU-23-4s? Those mechanized gu mounts posed a threat to any planes or helicopters Delta migh use. They also threatened Delta on the ground. Capable o firing 6,000 rounds a minute, they could eat a wall whole Nobody knew in late November where they were and muc time was put in at Camp Smokey trying to figure this out.

Sometime during the morning Ishimoto would get up fror

he stacks of paper he had on his desk and give an updated ituation brief to the two squadron commanders.

In mid-November squadron commanders believed the staff night do something without telling them about it. They would, herefore, come and go at their convenience, playing the good l' boy game, asking questions and interrupting the systems nd schedules the intelligence staff were trying to establish. Iaving to stop to answer questions all day long ate into the ours the staff needed to analyze the reams of data coming to he headquarters. There was just no way Ishimoto or the other nembers of the overworked intel staff could answer each quadron or troop commander.

Buckshot and I clearly saw this as a problem and on at least hree different occasions Buckshot pissed the troops off by rdering them to get the hell out of the office and leave Ishmoto alone. The problem was solved by giving the squadron ommanders, and others who needed to know, daily scheduled riefings where, once the dump of raw information had been orted through and interpreted, it was presented in a clear and oncise manner.

One of the two big intel dumps that came in each day would rrive before lunch.

In the afternoon Ishimoto and the others would go through he tedious process of reading each report and studying each hotograph, trying to decide what could be directly used, what vas peripheral, and what was no use at all. In this last category vould be a report, say, that came from a Swiss businessman vho, while visiting Kerman five days earlier, had noticed ougher travel restrictions. Kerman was a long way south of Teheran. But then, a West German who had recently gone hrough Mehrabad International Airport had noticed arrival rocedures, and his information was carefully filed.

At this stage, options for Delta going into and out of Teeran were still open. Every means was studied—everything rom parachutes to trucks, buses to commercial airplanes—everything but submarines coming through the Caspian Sea. There were dozens of workbooks, filled with information conerning possible drop zones and landing zones, road condi-

tions in and around Teheran, the roads and checkpoin
coming from Turkey, Iraq, and Pakistan, conditions at Meh
abad affecting arrivals and departures of international fligh
the kinds of delays being encountered by these flights and th
nature of the delays, whether custom checks were being han
dled by the tough Pasdaran or the easier gendarmerie, the pre
ence of barricades on any of the runways and which runway
were being used and which ones were closed down?

Even with the scheduled briefing in the morning, Ish woul
be interrupted probably ten to twenty times during the afte
noon. Logan Fitch, whose squadron was running an exercis
that night, needed more precise information. "Hey, Ish, what
the distance between the DCM [Deputy Chief of Mission] re
idence and [the warehouse called] 'the Mushroom'?" Is
would stop what he was doing, go over to another workboo
the one dealing with the physical properties of the compoun
and dig out that piece of information.

The workbooks were bibles. From early afternoon to 190
hours, when dinner was served, Ish read, studied, filed, ana
lyzed, and was interrupted. He could never catch up with th
new material, which was unending.

After dinner he'd corner me and begin bitching about th
lack of time he had. He'd get emotional. "Boss, I couldn't g
my workbooks finished today. I got interrupted 900 time
Fitch needed to know something I think I'd already given him
That visitor from the JTF took some more time. Vaught too
a half hour wanting to be briefed about the doors in the chan
cellery. God, I hope nothing comes in tonight."

Around 11:00 P.M. the teletypes would begin hammerin
away and the second large dump of IRs (intelligence report
would come pouring in. Ish and the other staffers would por
over it until 3:00 A.M., when they went to bed and tried to ge
some sleep. The network newscasts were scheduled to begi
in four hours.

My days were never the same. Too many fires needed t
be put out. A big problem was to keep as many people as
could away from the intel shop. Because the tactical plan t
assault the compound depended largely on what they knew,

was important that those analysts have as much time as possible.

There were the visitors who flowed into Delta as regularly as the Potomac flows into Chesapeake Bay. Trips had to be made to Washington. And the problems surfacing at Fort Bragg were communicated to me by Dick Potter.

Every day wasn't that way. Just most. There were those days when things would quiet down, particularly those days after a big meeting like the one after Thanksgiving. Then maybe the next day I could play catch-up. But normally it was a fast train. I spent most days in late November fighting fires, overseeing the training schedules, smoothing frayed tempers—and most important, trying to keep everything in perspective.

On a normal day I'd go down after breakfast to where the squadrons were billeted, which was about a mile from headquarters. Buckshot and I tried to do this often because the troops, not just our men but any men who are under stress, are curious about the larger picture. "What's the Old Man doing up there? He had a lot of visitors from Washington with him yesterday. I wonder what they wanted? Do we have a go ahead yet? I wonder . . ." No sooner had a plane landed than one of the squadron commanders would magically appear, "Hey, Boss, who's here?"

In combat there's never a rifle squad that doesn't want to know what its platoon is doing, or a platoon that doesn't want to know what its company is doing. When men are going to risk their lives in combat they're going to be curious about the circumstances that might cost them their lives. Fact is better than rumor. I tried to keep the squadrons in the picture.

Visitors were a constant problem. Ish wanted to know about the doors in the chancellery. He'd call Washington. Up there they would bust their butts finding people who knew about these doors. I'd get a message a day or so later. "We found Smith and Jones who were in the embassy three months ago. They know all about the doors. We're sending them down."

Early afternoon a plane arrives and Smith and Jones ditty-bop in. They're curious about everything and they rubberneck and ask questions. You stop whatever you're doing and talk to them. After all, they're here trying to help. Sometimes Smith and Jones are helpful—they did know how the doors work, so you don't mind spending time with them. Other times Smith and Jones contradict themselves on every detail and to be perfectly frank about it, are no fucking help at all.

Jim Kyle, wearing his blue blazer, would come down to Smokey. He had the job of getting Delta in and out of Iran. So we've got time for Kyle. He asks, "How are we going to get in?" He's dead serious. The workbooks fall further behind. I have a memo I must send to General Vaught about a training exercise. All is delayed because of the question: how will we come in, and go out?

I often received calls from General Vaught. A normal call for this time: The JTF has an exercise they want Delta to participate in. In seven days they want the squadrons to fly west and do some desert training, and they want our recommendation on how we see this going.

Buckshot says, "They don't know how to do a damn thing. We're going to have to send somebody out there to make sure that sonovabitch gets set up correctly. They don't even know how to get approval to use the exercise land."

It wasn't that the JTF planners were stupid. Rather, it was they had never done anything like this before. Special Ops is a rare and exotic bird.

I'd get back on the telephone with General Vaught, "Look, sir. Why don't you let us set this thing up? It will save time. We know who we have to contact." "Fine, Charlie. You do it. I'll send a guy with you."

The squadrons had a more straightforward day. Their routine was more structured—whether developing better ways to carry all their equipment or rehearsing soundless wall climbing—and a little simpler than, say, Ishimoto's. The skills they were required to master, however, were very sophisticated.

They'd take a weapons system and make sure everyone was qualified on it. The M79 grenade launcher, for example. Both squadrons would go out to the range and they'd fire the M79 all day. The air would be heavy with POPs as the launchers were fired and KARUMPs as the missiles landed. That night they'd go back and shoot at more sophisticated targets in more realistic settings. The next two days they'd get checked out on the other launcher, the M203.

Logan Fitch, B Squadron's CO, would give Allen, one of his troop sergeants, an assignment. "Your troop is responsible for locating hostages in, and clearing, the Ambassador's residence."

Allen would then take his morning and go up to the headquarters and begin to study the model of the compound and the model of the Ambassador's residence. "Ish, the leaded door which leads into the safe. Can we get it open if we have to or will we need to blow it?"

From his observations and the responses to his queries he would design tasks and exercises for his troop. Then, with his answers and with blueprints, the model and maps, Allen will coordinate his tasks with other troop commanders in B Squadron and begin to solve the riddle of how he will storm the residence and free the hostages. It wouldn't do to blow a door when another troop has at that moment to move past this area. Create and coordinate. Allen is kept very busy. *And* he must also qualify on all weapons systems and climb as swiftly and silently as his mates.

Fast Eddie has another kind of trouble. The embassy compound's wall. He was given the task in mid-November of designing a charge that will slice the wall in two.

Fast comes bouncing in on Ish, "Hey, partner, what's the thickness of the wall between the DCM's residence and the Ambassador's home?" Without this data he can't begin to work on his explosion formula. A workbook produces the correct information and Fast is off.

He first has to find somewhere in Smokey where he can build a wall of the same height and thickness as the one surrounding the compound between the DCM's and Ambassador's residences. Then he has to blow it down without knocking out every window in the camp. He will do it until he does it perfectly. He'll do all the scrounging and building himself, including finding a cement mixer to mix the mortar which goes between the bricks.

His attitude is, "I'm the only man here who has a mission. Everyone, out of my way. No one's job is more important than mine." He'll interrupt everyone, in good conscience, so he can get his job done. And, he'll eventually blow that wall down as well as anyone since Joshua at Jericho.

Boris has fallen in love. He is no longer a sniper. In Teheran he will be a machine gunner and he has been smitten by the HK21. For hours and hours he has familiarized himself with every nuance of the weapon. He's changed barrels, he's changed ammunition, he's changed feed systems. He can take its roller-locked delayed blowback system apart and reassemble it blindfolded in a matter of seconds. He makes the HK21 sing on the range. The problems he is solving in late November revolve around his weapon—how much ammo should he carry and how will he carry it, will it be more efficient to carry and fire drums, belts, or magazines?

Besides his weapon, Boris has backup responsibilities to learn and perfect. He must teach the man who will back him up everything he has learned about the HK21 and about his job of covering the southern sector of Roosevelt Avenue. It will be his job to prevent reinforcements from coming toward the compound from that direction. How well Boris does it might determine the success or failure of the entire mission.

When you meet Walter Shumate you might say he isn't the smartest guy you've ever seen. You'll be wrong. A senior NCO, he took it upon himself to act as liaison between the troops and the headquarters staff. A difficult job and one Walter did with aplomb.

The troops wanted to know: "Are we going or aren't we?" "How long are we going to stay here in Smokey?" "Can I call my wife? It's our anniversary." "My kid's sick. What can I do?" Walt had to be the man who solved these problems. He's got to come up to headquarters and say to me or Buckshot or Country, "Hey, look, we got cut a little short on chow yesterday. Can you make it up tomorrow?" "Chow arrived on the range late and cold today. What can we do to prevent this from happening again?" "We got a laundry problem." "The mail is slow coming in." These all seem like unimportant complaints. I can assure you they aren't, when you have to keep morale high so that troops will be ready to go at any instant. It was like a football coach trying to prepare his team for the Super Bowl without knowing when he'd have to play it.

On a day in late November at Camp Smokey, probably around chow time in the evening, while everyone on the headquarters staff was watching the network newscasts, Walter would sashay in. He wouldn't rattle anything. He'd just glide through the door. Before you knew it you'd look up and there would be Walter, at peace with the world, calmly watching Cronkite or Chancellor. He knew he shouldn't be there, but he also knew as a good friend of mine and a man I respected he wouldn't be asked to leave. He wanted to be able to go back and tell the troops that everything was O.K. with the Old Man. He'd talk some to Ish, trying to read my mood. After chow he'd saunter up to me, "What d'you think, Boss? How's it going? You need more rest. You look tired." Then Walt would float away and no one would remember seeing him leave.

Back with the troops he'd draw a crowd for his report. "Boss looked good tonight. Everyone was up." Or, "Boss is real preoccupied. Got a big meeting with the Neanderthal Man tomorrow. Something big's about to happen." Then he'd tell everyone a war story, "I remember once going in ahead of an operation around Long Thanh. The Boss asked me to do a quick bomb damage assessment, the problem was all the VC weren't dead."

Later in the evening, before the second big intel dump would come in, Country, Delta's sergeant major and my right arm, would come up to me, "Boss, don't talk to these guys that come in here. Let me take care of that." That's fine, but I didn't want to be rude and just tell the visitors to get out. That would cause sparks and no one wanted that. We came close several times, but nothing that couldn't be smoothed out.

It would be fair to say that Buckshot is moody. On idle days, when time hangs heavily on your hands, when there's too much time and not enough to do, Buckshot will not fit in very well. He'll either piss somebody off in Washington on the phone or he'll go down to the squadrons and have a disagreement with one of the commanders. If it's a fast-moving day with lots of activity or stress, a day in which there is too much to do and not enough time to do it in, Buckshot's happy.

In late November Buckshot was very happy.

He'd normally get up a little after Ish and a little before me. Once breakfast was out of the way, he and I would go in to see Ish and try to very quickly get a rundown on what, if anything, had happened while we were sleeping. Ish, depending on the day he'd had yesterday, or the day he was about to have, was either cordial or brusque. "Nothing came in we need to worry about," or, "Jesus Christ, guys, we're real busy right now. Can you come back later? Please!" More often than not Buckshot and I would hear, "Something important came in. You might want to read it. It's on top of the pile over there. By the way, Boss, you gotta call Vaught. He's called already."

This would be Buckshot's cue to leave. "I'm going down to the range. The squadrons are working on the M79 and I want to see how it's going." He was not one for sitting around waiting for the phone to ring. He'd rather go out to find work.

Around noon he'd return from the range and it would be either real good or real bad—never middle of the road. "Things are really screwed up down there. The range is pure shit." Or, "The guys are doing great. They love that M79. It's one hell of a weapon." Whatever, Buckshot's going to be honest.

At the range, Fast Eddie had talked to him, and Buckshot would want my opinion. "Boss, Fast has got these three areas staked out," and he'd point them out on a map that hung on the wall of the office. "What d'you think? He's gonna make a lot of noise and he's gonna blow up something big. Why not move him here to this corner, where he can't hurt nothing."

He'd come back from the squadron billets all charged up about the troops. "How come the men haven't received their mail yet, Country? Two of the guys got some problems back at Bragg. They owe some money but can't pay until they get their bank statements. Also, so-in-so's little boy just had an ppendectomy. The next time you call Potter ask him if he can find out how the little fella's doing. His Dad's worried."

Buckshot always handled visitors. Usually they'd come down toward evening. General Vaught would arrive and might have the CIA's representative to the JTF in tow. Buckshot would meet and greet them at the airport and on the way back to Smokey pull out of them whether something heavy was about to come down. At headquarters he'd either give me a wink or get me aside and tell me what he'd found had been bothering Hammer.

Buckshot would stroke the visitors. Whether he had to give a brief or take General Vaught on an exercise, it would be done with poise and self-assurance.

Once General Vaught had left, Buckshot and I would go back to the intel shop and get briefed on the events of that day in Teheran. We read message traffic and IRs until we couldn't keep our eyes open any longer. Then we'd go to bed.

Ishimoto would still be up, looking to add information to his workbooks.

★ THIRTY-FOUR ★

ON DECEMBER 2ND, the Sunday following Thanksgiving Vaught came down to Camp Smokey accompanied by Gast Kyle, and many of the JTF staff officers.

The purpose of this meeting was to determine the best way to infiltrate and exfiltrate Delta. There were various option open to us. One not open, but nonetheless suggested by an Ai Force brigadier, was that Delta, after landing by helicopter ride through the streets of Teheran on bicycles. "Nobody'l bother you." This individual frightened me. He had been in Iran. I don't know; he either had some very good information or I didn't understand it.

Another option, once Delta had parachuted in the vicinity of the city and freed the hostages, was to have the entire party evade and escape overland. I couldn't see myself carrying a hostage around Iran for six months, two years, or for howeve long it took to get back to this country.

These ideas now sound ludicrous, but they were perhaps the fevered results of the excitement generated by the media. On television, each and every night, Americans were told they were being held hostage. People were driven to the point of saying, "We gotta get these hostages out of the hands of those Iranians. When and what are we going to do? Try anything but *do* something." Bicycles and E and E tactics weren't the solution, but we had to proceed this way. "Describe the options and accept or discard them on their merit, no matter how crazy they at first seem."

At this Sunday meeting on December 2nd the parachute option was carefully analyzed. At first blush it seemed reasonable. But the more it was discussed the more impractical it became. Experience since World War II revealed that if 100 paratroopers were dropped in rough terrain, about seven of them would become casualties. Some would be hit by small arms fire. Others would suffer twisted backs, sprained ankles, broken legs. Seven percent casualties. Now at Normandy or Arnhem that wasn't bad. But what's Charlie Beckwith going to do with a man on a drop zone in Iran who's got a broken leg? He doesn't want to leave him and he doesn't want to carry him either. Although it wasn't the perfect solution, the parachute option was favored by some of the planners. It continued to be one of the acceptable choices.

Another possible solution to the problem: why not enter Iran from across the Turkish border in trucks? It sounds like a real good way to get in and get out, because a large number of trucks cross into Iran each week. They move from West Germany to Pakistan and back again. At the border these trucks are carefully checked by customs officials. If the paperwork is not perfect, the trucks would be stopped and searched. The Agency had begun checking on this documentation at each border crossing in the event the truck option proved viable. The trouble was, if there were any slipups on the Iranian side of the border, if the Pasdaran opened a refrigerator truck and found it full of Delta operators and not frozen beef, what the hell were we going to do?

There was also the problem that trucks would take a long time to drive across Iran and this would increase the time in which Delta could be discovered. The terrain in northern Iran requires vehicles to stay on the few roads that cross the region. Furthermore, no one could come up with a foolproof plot for clearing all the Iranian Army, police, and IRG (Iranian Revolutionary Guard, the paramilitary group also known as Pasdaran) checkpoints and roadblocks that might be encountered.

In the long run, if you could really figure out all the logistics, the trucks were probably a pretty good way to go at it, but the truck concept allowed no other option if something went wrong.

Furthermore, I learned our country had decided for security or political reasons that Turkey would not, or could not, play any role in our rescue plans. In the long haul, this proved very unfortunate.

The conference table was soon covered with papers, maps, charts, overflowing ashtrays, and Styrofoam coffee cups. After much discussion, the only way which argued for any degree of success was the use of helicopters. Everyone who served in Vietnam carried no illusions about them. They could, at times, be undependable, but if properly backed up they would get the job done. On this Sunday, in the view of the air planners, the helicopters' strengths outweighed their weaknesses and on this testimony the choppers began to win the day.

There was no question that the choppers offered a vast improvement over the contingency plan Delta had worked out in the first few days of the crisis. General Vaught eventually decided for planning purposes to propose the helo option to the Chairman of the Joint Chiefs of Staff, Gen. David Jones.

In the event helicopters were used, several major questions and problems emerged and were discussed at length. Which series of helicopter would meet all the load and range requirements? There were several options: CH-47 Chinooks or CH-46 Sea Knights, HH-53s or RH-53s. It became apparent, when all the specifications were laid out, that the 53 series met most of the requirements. Additionally, the Navy RH-53D, known as the Sea Stallion, had both foldable tail boom and rotor blades, which permitted them to be carried on aircraft carriers. These choppers were designed for mine-sweeping missions and their presence on board a carrier would not cause any surprises, thereby strengthening security considerations.

The RH-53D is the largest helicopter in the military's inventory. With a full load of fuel they'll generally carry thirty people. As fuel burns off while it's flying, the chopper becomes lighter and its carrying capacity increases. At the next stop, therefore, depending on how much fuel it has consumed, the chopper might be able to load forty or fifty people.

Although the Sea Stallions had heavy lift and long-range erry capabilities, they did not have the range to fly from the Gulf of Oman to Teheran without refueling somewhere in the 900 miles between. How, then, would they refuel and where? Would it be somewhere in the Iranian desert or, as someone uggested, at a lightly manned or abandoned airfield in the vicinity of a small Iranian city. This site made little sense to ne. It meant people would be killed. Killing wasn't the problem—that was one of Delta's jobs—but to kill people unnecessarily would be stupid. Also a firefight increased the risk of discovery. The option to seize an airfield lay on the table like n old balloon. The desert? Not if MC-130s, configured to carry fuel, were to be used. The desert, it was believed, would never support their weight. Assuming, however, this problem could be solved, how would Delta, after they freed the hostages, leave Iran? The choppers would face the same problem departing as they had entering. Fuel. Where would they refuel on the way out? Looking at a large map of the area, it was obvious they could not double back the way they'd come. It was just too far and the refueling point, if the same one was o be used, stood a chance of being discovered. Someone suggested that the helos could lift Delta and the freed hostages to a location where fixed wing aircraft could land and from there fly everyone out. But where would the rendezvous take place?

One by one the problems began to assume manageable proportions. Everyone was by now in shirt sleeves, collars open. Empty coffee cups were stacked on top of each other. How many days would the mission require to accomplish its objective? One? Two? Surely, one day was preferable to two, but t became obvious as the meeting wore on that there was going o be too much to do for it all to be accomplished in one day. It would probably take two. Three was out of the question. On the first night, Delta would be moved to Iran and located outside of Teheran; on the second night the assault would take place and Delta and the freed hostages would be lifted out of Iran. This left the day between the two nights—a period of time when the assault force and helos would have to remain hidden. Obviously this hide-site, or hide-sites, would require

isolation, but it would also require access to a road whe
Delta would travel by motor vehicles to Teheran. Anothe
problem for the planners. Find Delta and the Sea Stallions
place to hunker down, someplace where they could remai
undercover and undetected for twelve hours.

A staff officer turned to me. "Colonel, how many of you
men will be required to handle the mission?" In an earlie
meeting, one of the sessions held at the Pentagon, I ha
laughed when it was suggested that forty of them be used.
hell of a lot more than that would be needed! I answered tha
seventy was a good number. General Vaught looked uncom
fortable and sat up. "Goddamn, Charlie, that's too many." Th
problem was carefully explained. There was simply too muc
to do. Delta couldn't assault the large compound, seize an
clear fourteen buildings, secure and hold adjoining Roosevel
Avenue, organize, protect, and move fifty-three hostages—
couldn't do all that with fewer than seventy operators. Jus
like taking a ham sandwich to a banquet, it couldn't be done
Economy of force is a basic principle of combat. Accuratel
assessing the number of men to constitute the force is the trick
Delta had been asked to come up with a realistic number fo
the mission. The staff had spent days carefully working ou
all the eventualities and arrived at the number I submitted
Most of the planners accepted seventy as viable. Genera
Vaught returned to Washington with it.

In the days following the meeting at Camp Smokey, Genera
Vaught wisely recommended to General Jones that six RH
53D Sea Stallion helicopters be delegated to the Joint Tas
Force. Based on experience, judgment of the routes, distances
loads, and temperature, the staff planners at first determine
six helos would be needed to support the mission. Four, I wa
told, would be sufficient to carry the necessary personnel—
fact which had come out of the Sunday meeting—and the
other two would act as backup. Accordingly, in early Decem
ber, six Sea Stallions from Helicopter Mine Countermeasure
Squadron 16 were placed aboard USS *Kitty Hawk* (CV 63)
which at the time was on station somewhere in the Indian
Ocean.

These Navy/Sikorsky RH-53Ds were drawn from a fleet of hirty minesweeping helicopters that had been built for the Javy between June '73 and December '75. Modifications for he mission included removing from the helos their mine-weeping gear and adding fuel tanks, which increased their ange by more than 200 nautical miles.

Much had been decided on December 2nd, but so much nore still needed to be determined. The normal Navy crews vho trained on the 53s had no experience in the type of mis-ion we envisioned. In fact, there were no pilots in any of the ervices who had been trained to fly in the conditions this nission required. Where would they come from?

Also, and closer to home, Delta still lacked sufficient intel-igence necessary to weld together a viable, deliberate assault plan. With the great distance from the Gulf of Oman to Te-eran, the planners knew they had to locate and fabricate a efueling site. Beyond that, the assault plan was sketchy. Its hances for success were very slender indeed.

The basic scenario looked very complicated. It also revealed hat at this time the Armed Forces of the United States had either the present resources nor the present capabilities to pull t off. Training was needed to accomplish unique and de-nanding tasks.

The puzzle had been described. It seemed a gargantuan task or everyone involved to solve all its problems and make each omponent part fit together. But at least a beginning had been nade.

★ THIRTY-FIVE ★

A LARGE PART of the puzzle fell into place shortly afterwar
General Vaught called with the news. His staff had found
place from which Delta and the freed hostages could be picke
up once the choppers had flown them out of Teheran. Th
puzzle piece, thirty-minutes flying time from the capital, lo
cated between Teheran and the holy city of Qom, was calle
Manzariyeh. There, an asphalt-paved airstrip lay. Part of a
unoccupied former bombing range, the strip assured the Ai
Force they could use C-130s, which were designated for th
pickup. An Iranian Army engineer unit was known to be i
the area, but it was not considered a serious threat. After a
hell broke loose in Teheran, the airfield at Manzariyeh woul
have to be taken, secured, and held. A company-size Range
contingent would undertake this mission.

General Vaught's news was well received at Cam
Smokey's headquarters. At least now Delta had a plan to ge
out of Iran. There remained the issue of infiltration, getting ir
and, for Delta, the larger task of taking down the embass
compound.

Another bit of news that was forwarded made Ishimoto'
day. It was learned that photos of the compound would b
made available. The photos began to come in at once and i
gave the intel people a chance to compare movement withi
the compound with photos taken the day before, or the wee
before. If there were changes the analysts could arrive at som
deductions. One photograph showed twenty automobile

arked around the compound. If on the next day fifty were arked in the same area then something was happening and ıe message traffic might reveal what it was. If the analysts adn't been alerted to the change by the photos they might ot have spotted it in the cables.

One thing the photos pointed out was the existence of poles. laving assumed any American rescue attempt would use hel-:opters, either the IRG (Iranian Revolutionary Guards) or the ıilitants had begun to place poles at all likely landing zones 'ithin the compound. Without the photographs, the intel shop 'ould not have picked up this construction.

The photos, by themselves, were not going to take us to eaven. It was just one more element. What was truly needed /as confirmation from a source on the scene.

The backup arrived at the end of December, a Christmas resent for the planners, when the CIA managed to introduce n agent into the Iranian capital. Given the code name Bob, e was brought out of retirement for this mission. I was intro-uced to him. His mannerisms, the deliberate way he spoke, ven his appearance, reminded me of Anthony Quinn playing 'orba the Greek. He was a very professional individual, and /as prepared to do the job. He accepted all the risks and was onfident he would succeed. I have since read that Bob and I /ere bitter enemies. I can't believe that. If we were, I didn't now it.

Between Christmas and the first of the year, based on Bob's nswering the mail, Delta was able to get through enough ıformation for the planners to frame a detailed assault plan. t was determined that the hostages were being held in not ıore than six buildings, maybe four, and these were identified. t first, based on the information gathered from the release of he thirteen hostages in November, we'd learned virtually all f the embassy's buildings might be used to house prisoners. ater in November, then in December, the analysts began to liminate the number of buildings.

The analysts assumed the student militants who were hold-ng the hostages were receiving assistance from the Palesti-

nians or the SAVAMA, which is the secret poli
organization. From the thirteen American hostages who we
released it was learned that whenever they were moved th
were blindfolded. They would also be shifted around into di
ferent groups, deliberately no doubt, so no patterns could l
picked up. The militants could not be underestimated.

The process then became one of reasoning from a know
to an unknown, from the general to the specific. Fifty-thr
prisoners needed to be housed and fed. With the help of ps
chiatrists provided by intelligence officers, the analysts fe
that the student militants deep down inside did not want
hurt their hostages if they could avoid doing so. Therefor
what kinds of facilities existed within the compound to allo
the hostages to be looked after?

Using deductive logic, two of the fourteen buildings we
almost immediately eliminated from contention. Because the
were no cooking facilities and the heating systems weren't th
best, the motor pool and the general administration buildi
were eliminated. Also, these two buildings were observab
from a nearby fourteen-story building, and they abutted th
compound wall which faced America Alley. The militan
would not feel secure holding people in this area.

The intelligence people continuously used two words: prob
ably, which meant better than a 50 percent chance, and po
sibly, which meant less than a 50 percent chance.

The old consulate building proved at first to be very co
fusing to the analysts. It was known that early in the takeov
hostages were being held in there and continued to be he
there until the thirteen were released. But again, it was dete
mined it probably no longer held hostages. Not only did
border upon America Alley but Arak as well. Also, it did n
have sleeping facilities. Lastly, the building was semihard, ar
the militants had continuing problems trying to open the ele
trically operated doors.

The four staff cottages were altogether another matte
These were bungalows intended to house either families,
two or three people who would come to the embassy on
temporary duty basis. There were no consistent reports fro

sources being debriefed that there were hostages kept here. In any event, the staff cottages became a highly probable location for hostages.

Another building eliminated ran along the wall that abutted Kheradmand Alleyway. The alley dead ends at Arak on the south and runs north along the rest of the western side of the compound. This was an old structure whose north end contained the embassy's power plant, with the south end having previously been used by guards who had worked for the embassy. Again, because the building abutted an alleyway and was without cooking facilities and other amenities, it was eliminated.

It was hoped that the chancellery could be eliminated, but the wish proved ill-founded. A long, rectangular, three-story brick building, it ran east to west, or parallel to Takht-E-Jamshid Avenue. Located near the center of the south wall and in close proximity to the compound's main gate, it contained about ninety rooms. Although it did not include a kitchen, it certainly had enough secure rooms for the guards to house many of the hostages and at the same time keep them isolated from each other. The chancellery made the highly probable list. This was unfortunate, because it was a hardened building. There were security bars on all the lower-level windows and some upper-story windows contained shutters. It would be a damn hard building to get into. But to scope down from fourteen buildings to six or seven was a giant step. Specific tasks could be assigned and the number of operators actually needed for the job could now be realistically projected.

The vital importance of good, sound intelligence cannot be stressed enough. Without it there is nothing, with it there is something. It's the difference between failure and success, between humiliation and pride, between losing lives and saving them. Intelligence is to special operations as numbers are to a mathematician.

A telegram arrived at the Stockade. Dick Potter retransmitted it to me at Smokey. It was from Ulrich Wegener, the commander of GSG-9. "Charlie, am prepared to put in Teheran German TV crew. STOP. Would you like your people on it?

STOP." I informed General Vaught of Ulrich's message an recommended we pursue the offer. Somewhere in the Penta gon the idea died.

"Hey, this German's my friend. He's figured out what' going on and has offered us his help."

"This is too sensitive," General Vaught was told to tell me "We can't work with a foreign government on this."

"But you don't understand. He's my friend. He know Delta; he's visited with us. He knows how we operate an what we need. He'll help us."

"You don't understand."

Delta's intel section hoped the clergymen, when they re turned from their Christmas visit to the hostages, were thor oughly debriefed. They might have been, but Delta neve received any specific information it could be sure came di rectly from this source.

Even without hard specific facts, certain decisions involvin the assault on the compound were made. How to get from th hide-site to the embassy on the second night? The helicopter could not fly the unit directly into Teheran. They were to noisy and voided any chance the mission would have of se crecy and surprise. The answer was obvious. Delta would b driven from the hideout through the capital in covered trucks Someone within Teheran would have to make these arrange ments. Bob was the natural choice.

Helicopter pilot training began as soon as possible. Severa Sea Stallions were flown into Camp Smokey and they wer followed by seven Navy crews.

These particular helicopters are peculiar looking birds. The look more like huge hunchbacked hot dogs. Their main roto assembly has blades that measure more than seventy-two fee across and remind you of oversized electric fans. I don't lik them. I think all helicopters are ugly.

General Vaught and I flew with the Navy pilots their firs time up. They had obviously been doing a lot of straightfor ward flying. They were very careful in everything they did Their experience was in minesweeping operations and suc skills did not lend themselves to those which would be re uired for the rescue mission. When we landed, General Vaught looked at me and I smiled and shook my head. "I agree," he said.

We were looking for aces, daredevils, barnstormers, guys who flew by the seats of their pants, hot rodders, pilots who could pick it up, turn it around on a dime and put it back down with a flair. These Navy pilots didn't believe in taking the risks we knew were required of the pilots flying into an enemy-held city.

General Vaught thought the pilots should be given more time. Doc Bender, Delta's psychologist, carefully looked these chaps over. After the second day he came into the office. "You know, we got some guys here who are really shaky. They're beginning to understand what kind of mission you want them to fly. Sure, one or two might make it, but for the rest . . ." He shrugged.

Doc was proved right. During the following days it became apparent that these pilots were unable to fly in what is called "flight regime," which is the tight formation pilots use to navigate without landmarks and to land in darkness.

One of them actually quit a few days into the training. He flat out refused to fly anymore. Scared. He admitted it. I understood that. But quitting. That was something else. He'd lost his motivation, his objectivity, and his desire. He'd also lost his balls. I recommended he be court-martialed. He was restricted to the area; after all, he knew about the effort to mount a rescue operation. Eventually he was taken away and isolated somewhere else. None of us wanted a quitter walking the streets knowing what he knew. One pilot was kept on for further training. Reportedly, the rest were sworn to secrecy and returned from whence they came.

General Vaught then took up the problem of the pilots with General Jones. The J-3 in the JCS at the time was a Marine lieutenant general named Phillip Shutler. Not surprising, therefore, a Marine unit of helicopter pilots was flown down to Camp Smokey for training. Six of these pilots and their crews came from the New River Air Station near Jacksonville, North Carolina, and two others arrived from a West Coast

Marine base. Many of us in Delta questioned the wisdom behind this decision.

Were these pilots the best-qualified men in Department of Defense? There was some suspicion at the time that there were those in the JCS who wanted to make sure *each of the services had a piece of the action.* Up till this point there had been no role for the Marines to play. General Vaught told me these pilots had all been thoroughly screened and had come from a unit with a good record. Also, a Marine Corps officer, Col. Chuck Pittman, took over the training of the pilots. He understood helicopter operations. Pittman was an experienced pilot who got to know the pilots well. Like any good officer he was strong-minded and it was obvious that he was respected by those who knew him. He got along well with Jim Kyle and seemed to be a good addition to the team.

How to use the choppers best? Now, with Pittman on board some answers began to emerge. These RH-53Ds could not fly from the Gulf of Oman to Teheran without refueling. How should it be done? "Could the helos be carried in on C-130s?" "No, they are too big." "Could they be disassembled and then reassembled?" "Not within the mission's time frame." The riddle would not go away. The answer that finally emerged, at least until its practicability could be tested, was to drop the fuel in the desert and let the helos fly to it. The fuel would be loaded in huge 500-pound rubber blivets and parachuted in. The bigger question remained—where? But, at least if the blivets proved workable, the Sea Stallions could refuel in the desert and the landing field which the EC-130 tankers would have required, could be discarded. And so another piece of the puzzle was laid down on the board.

Life's lighter side began to emerge from the tedium of everyday training. Once Coyote was rehearsing his people in room clearing, trying to get everyone synchronized. "This thing has got to be like a ballet," he said. "We've got to have this choreographed just right, got to know what steps you're taking, and those of your buddy. We've got to do this in concert." That night, on the blackboard in A Squadron's hootch there appeared a wonderful cartoon of Delta operators armed with MP5s and wearing tutus, toe dancing into the embassy.

The operators often invented ingenious ways of getting into the embassy safely. After one lecture about Moslem customs and taboos, someone had the idea of parachuting a battalion of pigs into the compound. The only discussion was whether No Lips should dress up in a pig costume and be sent in ahead of everyone else.

Life was not without its small problems, too. I received a letter from Stuttgart, Germany, informing me in very complicated Army prose that the U.S. Army Europe was continuing to store my furniture in a warehouse, but they would not do so much longer without an official pronouncement about my duties with SOTFE (Special Operations Task Force Europe). I asked General Vaught to help me, and as he had done after the December 2nd meeting at Camp Smokey, he had my command of Delta extended. Poor Katherine remained in our quarters at Fort Bragg, sitting on folding chairs and eating off paper plates.

The Marine pilots who had been doing some flying around Camp Smokey and Newport News were commanded by a straightforward Marine lieutenant colonel by the name of Edward Seiffert. He was a no-nonsense, humorless, some felt rigid, officer who wanted to get on with the job. Some of the Delta operators felt he was aloof and hard to read.

It was decided by General Vaught that Seiffert's unit should go out to the southwest and do some night desert flying without lights. General Gast accompanied them to Yuma, Arizona, to oversee the training. A week later, it was shortly after the Thanksgiving weekend meeting, Delta loaded on C-130s and joined them.

At this time Delta had ninety-two operators at Camp Smokey, and I decided that all of them would go out west. The staff and each squadron commander believed the assault force should be increased from the seventy-two, which had been agreed to on December 2nd, to ninety-two. As the plan had grown, so had the need for more men. So much more was known now than was known earlier in November. As each day passed and as problems were uncovered, it became apparent that a force of seventy-two would not wash. If the intelligence analysts, for example, were correct in deducing that many of the hostages were being held in the chancellery then that building alone might require the better part of an entire squadron to assault and secure it.

To facilitate all the tasks that needed to be accomplished in the 27-acre compound, it was necessary to reconfigure slightly Delta's basic organization. Accordingly, the two squadrons were broken down into what were called Red Element, White Element, and Blue Element.

Red was basically A Squadron. Its mission was to free any hostages from the compound's southwest quarter, which included the commissary and four staff cottages, and taking down the guards at the motor pool and power plant. As an area it was a mess. There were alleyways and lanes, and the buildings contained a lot of square footage, much of it filled with equipment and supplies. If Major Coyote's Red Element was going to do its job without getting a lot of people killed, then they'd have to go through each of the buildings room by room, floor by floor. With two guard posts in the vicinity, there was also the potential of a very nasty little firefight breaking out there.

Blue Element, which by and large was B squadron, commanded by Major Fitch, had the task of clearing and releasing the hostages found in the two residences, a warehouse known as the Mushroom, and the chancellery.

Thirteen operators, taken from the Selection and Training element and from the headquarters section, made up the White Element. They would be responsible for supporting the assault force and securing and holding the streets around the compound.

From everything I knew about the mission, from working with the model and reading the intelligence data and Bob's reports, I didn't see how Delta was going to do the job without *all* of its operating personnel. I'm not sure that at this time General Vaught was convinced of this. But hoping he could be convinced, I sent Red, White, and Blue Elements, all ninety-two operators, into Yuma.

Delta based out of a large prefab building located in the desert. The weather was great; the bright sunny days, not too hot, the nights, very cold. The food consisted of one hot meal a day and C Rations. Small cooking fires were laid and hot sauce and jalapeño peppers were added to the C rations. Outsiders, if they could have seen us, would have thought Delta was a construction crew waiting to undertake a building project. We trained at night and slept in the daytime.

The Marines lived in billets at the Yuma Army Airfield. Delta infrequently trucked to those quarters to use the hot showers.

Most of the flying was done at night. It was obvious the Marine pilots had a lot of work to do. They knew it, too. The task they had been given was unusually hard. It was one that called for an altered mind-set. The transition from flying one helicopter to another, a Chinook to a Sea Stallion, for example, was handled very smoothly. That wasn't the problem. The real difficulty was in acquiring—and then developing and polishing—new, more complicated mission skills. These leathernecks were being asked to do something extraordinary. Before this time, flying a helicopter at night was unusual. When it was done, it was always in ideal conditions. Now these pilots were being asked to fly right off the deck through rough canyon country, not at 1,500 feet, but down in the canyons where radar couldn't detect them, and do it without lights!

It sure as hell scared me to death flying out there. I admit it. I'd been shot down three times in helicopters in Vietnam. I've taken dead troops out of crashed choppers. Flying helicopters is not a thing I enjoy doing.

The pilots wore PVS5s, night vision goggles. The glasses could only be worn for thirty minutes at a time. Then the copilot, who'd been reading the map and the instruments because they couldn't be seen with the goggles on, would switch with the pilot and he'd wear them. It was tough. Seiffert and his pilots flew various routes each night to improve their proficiency.

Knowing what I now know, I would have proposed providing General Gast with some help at Yuma. I considered it, but I didn't do it. Delta had at least a dozen people who had been deeply involved in helicopter operations in Vietnam. They knew how to plan and execute them; they knew when an operation was a good one and when it was a bad one. Master Sergeant Franklin (No Lips), for example, had a tremendous amount of experience in helicopters. I should have left two of these men out with General Gast.

Gast was no fool and he was a quick learner. He knew all there was to know about navigational systems, but he didn't know how to fly a helicopter. He'd been a jet jockey. I could have left two of my best men in Yuma to help and assist him. I didn't want to give up those two guys, though. They had critical parts to play in the take-down of the embassy, and I felt I needed them. I may have made a mistake. Maybe I was selfish. Maybe I was. I don't know. Hindsight is hard to live with.

★ THIRTY-SIX ★

WHILE IN YUMA I took part in the first fuel blivet parachute drop.

Those huge round rubber containers, along with their hoses and pumps, had the capacity of carrying 500 gallons of fuel each. They could be rolled along the ground by eight or ten men, or pulled by small wheeled gas-powered tugs called Mules. At 2000 hours, General Gast and I, along with staff officers, prepared ourselves for the first run-through of the proposed refueling operation. The desert night was cool and fully illuminated by a large white moon. The choppers were lined up in a row, neat as pins. General Gast, who knew nothing about parachute operations, was feeling uncomfortable with what was about to happen. His instincts were correct. I took one look at the row of parked RH-53Ds and the map showing the path the C-130 aircraft were taking and knew we had trouble. I asked General Gast if he'd let me be responsible for the drop, a request he happily acceded to. With a grin he said, "If this gets screwed up, you and I are going to Mexico." If the C-130s maintained their original track, they'd fly on an axis directly over the parked choppers. Any malfunction in the drop and the blivets from the aircraft would wipe out one or all of the Sea Stallions.

The approach lane was changed by radio and the C-130s banked in a half circle and came in at a ninety-degree angle to the helos. It proved to be a fortunate change of plan. Twelve blivets were shoved out of the C-130s, but only two parachute canopies opened. What a mess. These huge blivets burst on impact like ripe pumpkins dropped from a twenty-story building. It was like striking oil. And it was a disaster. An investigation showed the Army parachute riggers had improperly loaded the blivets. There was enough embarrassment to go around for everyone to share. A lot of experimentation followed. The next rehearsal ran smoothly and the blivets landed softly and intact. Once on the ground, these enormous rubber gas tanks posed new problems. First, they weren't as easy to move as we had thought, particularly if they landed in depressions or on rocky ground. Secondly, and worse, pumping the fuel from them to the helicopters took a very long time—time, in Iran, the mission would not have. The door was left open to explore other possibilities.

The approach of Christmas surfaced another problem, one on which General Jones and I did not agree. Delta left Yuma on December 20th and returned to Fort Bragg where everybody stood down for the holidays. I thought this was a mistake and that we should have returned to the isolation of Camp Smokey. I couldn't see how we were going to maintain operations security if the troops went home. There were now a heck of a lot of people involved in this effort—Marine pilots, helicopter crews, Air Force pilots, maintenance and mechanical people, Pentagon staff officers, Rangers' command staff, Delta. There was no way of knowing what someone would say when he was in the sack with Mama or out at a party with a couple of glasses of eggnog keeping him festive.

I recommended to General Vaught that Delta base at Camp Smokey and that the pilots stay out west. Most of my people were angry with me. They claimed they would keep their mouths shut. General Jones overrode my recommendation. Delta came back to the Stockade. A contingency plan was welded together to get everyone back at short notice. Delta trained half a day during the Christmas holiday period. I do not know what the other units did.

Because in Washington it was thought more convenient, Delta did not return to Camp Smokey after the holidays, but instead remained at its Stockade location in Fort Bragg.

Right after New Year's, on Friday and Saturday, the 4th and 5th of January 1980, a crucial meeting of the Joint Task Force commanders was held in Fort Bragg. In attendance were General Vaught, General Gast, the CIA liaison officer, Colonel Pittman, Lieutenant Colonel Seiffert, some of the helo pilots, the Ranger Battalion's CO and key staff, Delta's commanders and staff, planners representing intelligence, operations, communications, weather, logistics, and administration for the Task Force.

On Friday Chuck Pittman and I got off to the side and discussed the number of helicopters necessary to accomplish the mission. We readdressed the number of Delta operators and support personnel such as drivers and Farsi translators and considered the new figure of nearly 120 men and how their body weight and equipment could be distributed. With this figure and in view of start-up problems, maintenance, fuel requirements, and loads, Colonel Pittman thought the mission could not leave from the desert refueling site, which was now being called Desert One, with fewer than six flyable helicopters. He pointed out that if you needed two helicopters, because of their undependability, you actually had to have three.

This was one of the key lessons the military learned in Vietnam. Helicopters are unreliable and backups must always be included in plans which use them. The RH-53D helicopter doesn't start up by simply turning a key and having a battery kick the motor over. These monsters crank hydraulically. In Iran, at the hide-site, there would be an additional twist. Normally, when it's parked on a carrier or airfield, an RH-53D is started by an auxiliary power unit. It connects to the helicopter and gives power until the engine catches. In Iran, however, there would be no APUs available. Instead, each Sea Stallion would carry two canisters of compressed air, which would do the same job as the APU, that is, crank the turbines which drive the generator that supplies the voltage necessary to fire the plugs which ignite the fuel. Unlike the APU, however, once the pilot exhausts all of his compressed air, there is no more power for him to use. Once the compressed air was used up, the helicopter might as well be a boulder. It sure as hell wasn't gonna fly.

Colonel Pittman said, "We should talk to General Vaught and say now, that without six flyable helicopters at the refueling site, Desert One, we cannot go forward."

In the early afternoon, Pittman and I discussed with General Vaught the entire helo-insertion plan, starting from the carrier in the Gulf of Oman to a refuel site somewhere in the desert, on to Teheran and a hideout location, ending with the move to Manzariyeh. We reappraised the number of personnel and before we had finished, the total number of personnel needed to fly to Teheran had grown to somewhere in the neighborhood of 120.

Toward the end of this discussion, I told General Vaught that Pittman and I were now convinced that because the airlift requirement had increased to nearly 120 men and their equipment, a minimum of six flyable helos would be required to go on from Desert One. It was a matter of weight. Without six helicopters the load at Desert One could simply not be lifted to Teheran. General Vaught listened carefully to us and accepted our findings and endorsed the recommendation.

To assure us of having six helicopters able to fly from Desert One, the staff planners added two additional choppers as backups to the six already on board *Kitty Hawk*. These two additional helicopters would eventually be onloaded to the carrier *Nimitz* (CVN 68), which was sailing to replace *Kitty Hawk* in the Indian Ocean. *Nimitz* would also receive the six Sea Stallions carried by *Kitty Hawk*. When I asked if there was a chance of adding more backup helos to *Nimitz*, General Vaught, Chuck Pittman, and their planners stated that only eight of the kinds of choppers we were going to use, RH-53Ds, would fit on her hangar deck. It was also pointed out that it would be imprudent, because of salt water corrosion problems, to park them on the carrier's flight deck. Another planner pointed out that Soviet photo interpreters would spot the presence of so many choppers on the flight deck and determine they were there for one reason and no other.

Another item had me edgy. After the embassy had been

stormed, Delta would move with the freed hostages across Roosevelt Avenue, which ran the entire length of the embassy's eastern wall, to await the arrival of the helos in a soccer stadium. It was important that the helo pilots practice flying into a stadium setting. We knew of one at Fort Carson, Colorado, which could be used for this purpose. General Vaught thought if we did it we'd run into a large security problem.

I said, "Well, I think it's a mistake if we don't do it."

"Maybe if we have the time we'll do it, but I just don't see us taking the time to run in and out of a ball park."

"Yes, sir."

On Saturday we began where we had left off on Friday. The hostages would be flown out of Manzariyeh first, followed by Delta and the Ranger unit. The size of the entire force, including released hostages, it was pointed out by one of the air planners, now posed a lift problem for the C-130s. Consequently, these aircraft would be replaced by larger C-141 StarLifters.

A wide range of issues surfaced.

The meteorologists, who had been selected from the Air Force's Air Weather Service, presented their long-range forecast for the region. They pointed out that throughout Iran there were several small weather stations, which were, during the reign of the Shah, fully staffed. Information gathered by them had been shared with the rest of the world. With the chaos that spread across the country following the Shah's departure, these stations, except for ones in the larger cities, had been abandoned. It was therefore going to be very difficult to get an accurate fix on the weather any mission into Iran would face.

Although crucial questions remained—the exact locations of Desert One and the hideout—I left the conference feeling very good. The scheme appeared sound. Its various threads were being slowly and carefully braided together.

★ THIRTY-SEVEN ★

AFTER REFUELING IN the desert, the location where Delta could hide during the daylight hours before they left on the second night for the embassy was selected. The site lay at the edge of the salt wastes around Garmsar and the southern foothills of the Elburz Mountains. Delta Force would lie up in a secluded wadi about four miles northwest of Garmsar and nearly fifty miles southeast of Teheran. In an area of abandoned salt mines, it was near an improved road. The road was important because of the decision reached earlier that six large 2.5-ton covered trucks would pick Delta up at this site and transport it through Teheran to the compound. A separate hideaway for the Sea Stallions had also been located. After they'd dropped Delta near the wadi, they would fly to a more rugged hill area ten to fifteen miles northeast of our hide-site. There they would wait, concealed under camouflage netting, until summoned that night to the soccer stadium by Delta. Toward this end I assigned two radio operators—equipped with gear that had been designed and built by Delta to interface with specific satellites—to go with the helos and establish a communications link back to the assault team hiding in the wadi. With both hideout locations identified, it became a matter of keeping these areas under surveillance to determine whether they posed any potential risks. A line of the Iranian State Railroad, which lay just to the south of the wadi, worried the Delta planners. How many trains ran here? On what schedule? Only

Bob could tell whether the intel section's fears were real or imagined.

No one, however, could remove the heartburn the fuel blivets gave everyone. The parachute riggers had successfully found a way to drop them to the ground. But even though seven or eight successful rehearsals had been run in January, the feeling lingered that the blivets were trouble. The suspicion that they weren't the answer to our refueling question never went away. No one, however, could come up with anything better than the blivets until Chuck Gillman (pseudonym) had his inspiration.

I'd known Chuck in southeast Asia where he had managed air operations in Laos for the CIA. I felt he knew more about flying in support of special operations than anyone in the Agency at that time. At one of the blivet drills—this particular one was at the largest and most secure of Fort Bragg's four drop zones, the one known as Holland DZ—Chuck was standing near me. The drop went well, and as I began to get ready to return to the Stockade, he walked over to me. He wasn't satisfied with what he'd seen. "Suppose you can't find the buggers or they fall in a gulley and you can't move them? I can see they pump too slowly. What needs to be done, Charlie, is to land fuel-bearing planes in the desert. Get some tankers and refuel the helos from them."

These aircraft would be EC-130s, which were capable of carrying 3,000 gallons of fuel in gigantic bladders. The argument against this method of refueling had always come from the Air Force staff planners who, without knowing the exact landing site, were afraid the crust of the desert floor would not support an EC-130. Their objection made sense to everyone. Chuck Gillman had the answer. "Let's fly a STOL [Short Takeoff and Landing], 2-engine aircraft from a neighboring country to a carefully selected spot in the area that the planners are considering for Desert One." In other words, let's get serious about a site, then dispatch a special aircraft with people on board who can confirm that EC-130s can land and take off from there. He continued, "I've flown all over the area and I know it can be done. We'll survey the site, take photographs, and dig some soil samples, anything that will convince the Air Force they should fly and land fuel birds in there. As a matter of fact, let's get an Air Force officer to go. He'll lend more credibility to anything that's done."

We ratholed General Vaught in the conference room at the Stockade. He had with him the CIA's liaison officer to the JCS. It was nearly 2200 hours and everyone had had a long day. Chuck Gillman presented his idea. A Harvard man, he was very articulate. Chuck could sell anything. I was told by friends in the Agency that whenever they had a hard brief to sell, they always sent Chuck Gillman. An hour later General Vaught, too, was convinced that this was a sound concept. He said he'd try to sell it to the Chairman, General Jones.

During the next couple of days General Vaught surfaced the idea at the Pentagon, and from his telephone calls to me it sounded like General Jones would try to get White House approval for a STOL flight.

Delta went west again to rehearse with the helos. Some of the men didn't think the pilots had improved very much and began to have second thoughts about them. I didn't think it was as bad as they did. One day the weather turned foul. Dark purple clouds rolled in covering the sky from horizon to horizon. A great thunderstorm developed and the rain fell like Niagara. Because of the electricity in the air, one of the chopper pilots decided it was unsafe to fly. No Lips said, "We got a whole chopper-load of people here, sir. If we're in Iran and it rains and there's lightning, what are we going to do?" But General Gast continued to reassure me the pilots were getting better. Their CO, of course, knew they had improved, yet I wasn't totally convinced about Colonel Seiffert. I have to live with someone for a long time, share a foxhole with him, before I trust him totally.

A new navigation system had recently been pushed on the helo pilots. Called PINS (Palletized Inertial Navigation System), it was to be an alternative to the Omega system they had been using and were familiar with. Every system required a backup, for the same reason a gunfighter wore two guns. It was prudent, but the technicians who were providing PINS instruction didn't believe the pilots had their hearts and souls in learning it. On the other hand, everyone wanted to have confidence in these leathernecks. If not them, who? If not now, when? The Marines got the benefit of the doubt.

I had one officer at this time, a young man, who I was a little concerned with. He'd never been in combat before but he wasn't ashamed to talk about being scared. We talked for hours. Everyone was scared. Any man who wasn't had to be plumb crazy. If you don't respect fear then there's no way you can handle it. Fear can be damn dangerous, but if you can come to grips with it, wrestle it, understand it, then you've got a chance to work around it. I didn't want to be in a tight spot being shot at and have around me men who were not at least a little scared. I listened a lot to one of my young officers and did some reassuring. When the time came he functioned and he functioned well.

Everyone was leaning forward. Delta was ready to go. They remembered what Moses had said, "If you don't think you've got the edge, say so and you won't go." No worry about that. Delta had the edge.

The men were especially high the day they learned the planners had finally pinpointed the Desert One location. They'd found a remote site in the vast Dasht-e-Kavir Salt Desert, 265 nautical miles southeast of Teheran. It was ninety miles from any habitation, and that, the small weaving center of Yazd. It was now a matter of determining whether the desert floor there would support EC-130 fuel birds. General Vaught's air planners needed the STOL mission to confirm the choice and the White House continued to be pressed about it.

I also needed to confirm certain aspects of our assault plan on the Embassy and became more and more convinced that it was vital to Delta's success to insert one of our own people in Teheran. It was necessary to look over all the arrangements and examine critical areas through Delta's eyes. I respected Bob, but of course he didn't know anything about Delta. I didn't want to risk the lives of about 120 guys to someone I didn't know. I pressed General Vaught on the idea. After a while he warmed up to it.

When the word got out that we were considering infiltrating a Delta operator into Teheran ahead of the actual rescue, many of the men volunteered. After careful consideration, four operators were selected and began specialized training. This training consisted of learning Iranian customs and taboos, memorizing streets and boulevards in Teheran, studying transportation that moved through the capital, learning some Farsi and the Iranian monetary system, and learning to live under a cover story. Delta received a lot of help in this area. The intelligence services provided instructors and personnel who had lived in the city.

The four Delta operators who had been chosen were all from the right cut of cloth. Any one of them could have performed this mission. Buckshot, however, was something special and he became the primary candidate. As the training proceeded, it was apparent no appropriate cover could be found for Buckshot and he was reluctantly pulled out of the program. His Robert Redford looks didn't help matters. He didn't exactly disappear in a crowd. Moreover, I felt he was needed as my second-in-command. At this moment Dick Meadows stepped forward and I thought this was unusual. Dick had been on the Son Tay raid that had the aim of rescuing our POWs from the North Vietnamese—only to learn its intelligence was outdated and the POWs had been removed to another location. The raid, no matter the outcome, had been carefully planned and skillfully executed. I don't know why Dick volunteered to go to Iran, but I suspect he thought, being a civilian, the mission would go off and leave him behind. After much arguing, the intelligence community reluctantly accepted Dick. They gave him the code name Esquire.

There were three others. They too were trained by DOD and went into Iran at the same time as Meadows. Two of these men had Special Forces backgrounds; both spoke fluent German. The last man was in my judgment the bravest. We'd gone through the Defense Department's personnel computer looking for someone with a military background who spoke perfect Farsi. We found the most unexpected hero you could imagine. He was an Air Force sergeant, an E-6, who was leading a mundane military life. His family had been born and raised in Iran and he spoke the language flawlessly. When he heard what we wanted him to do he volunteered immediately. I was extremely impressed with him. Having had no prior experience in this kind of work, he ran a larger risk than the others. He accepted those risks and stepped forward because his country needed him.

The plan was to infiltrate these four DOD agents into Teheran a few days before the rescue mission and, along with Bob, they would eyeball all the sites, check on the driving arrangements, and identify possible problem areas. There was much that needed to be done and not much time to do it in. The trucks had to be moved, the warehouse where they were going to be stored needed watching, routes had to be gone over and memorized, alternate routes had to be found, someone had to man the radio and both targets—the embassy and Foreign Ministry Building—needed to be watched.

Then something happened which was so stupid I couldn't believe it. Bob was brought back to this country and, astonishingly, he was sent to the *Pentagon* to visit with me. I became very angry with his handlers for having taken this risk. It was against all security rules. They should have known better. Bob was asked to look over the hide-site because photos weren't telling the intelligence people if the nearby railroad line would interfere with the plan. They also asked him to check out routes from the hide-site to the embassy gate, density of traffic flow on the possible routes and location of reaction forces, potential checkpoints and street construction in the neighborhood of the compound. I was concerned about the hide-site.

"Have you been there?"

"Yes, I've been there. When I go back I'll return to the area and reexamine it again to verify that it's the right place."

"It's important that we pin it down. If we miss it in the darkness we'll never link up."

I wanted to know everything I could about the site. I wanted to know who lived in the area and what they would think when they heard helicopters flying over their heads.

"They won't hear anything, Colonel, because there's no one there."

"What will happen if we come in from this other direction?"

"There are shepherds living over there. You better keep on course. They are more used to hearing the crowing of the morning cock than they are of helicopters."

An Iranian, who will be known as Al, was young, fit, and very well acquainted with Teheran, having been one of the Shah's bodyguards. He spoke nearly perfect English. Because Delta needed someone with his expertise the intelligence community handed him over to us. He fit in and was well liked by the operators. He made it clear time and time again that he could not afford to be taken prisoner in Iran. I supposed he may have worked for the National Intelligence and Security Operation known as SAVAK. He had a price on his head. It was peculiar that he would want to go back to Iran with an American rescue force. There were specific areas in the plan which Al was not permitted to know. If, in fact, he was captured, it was prudent not to have him know too much. When his feet were put to the fire, would he really accompany Delta on its mission?

Another detail caught my attention. It came under "old business." I received a letter from Stuttgart. It was marked URGENT! Written by some numb-nuts from the U.S. Army Europe transportation office, it informed me that they could no longer afford to store my furniture and if I didn't collect it they were going to auction it off. I called General Vaught.

★ THIRTY-EIGHT ★

IT WAS MID-MARCH.

The rehearsal scheduled for that afternoon was out at the range where the operators had laid out and built an area to the embassy compound's scale. Every distance had been marked out and a section of wall had been built for the men to climb over.

I would have gone out to the rehearsal with the troops except I got tied up on the phone. When I hung up I walked through the Stockade. Maybe someone there who had been left behind needed a lift. Something told me to check S & T, the Selection and Training area.

No one was in sight. The room was empty. But lying on the floor was something that angered me. There, without a soul around, were thirty or forty pounds of high explosives. Fast Eddie had been using the area for his workshop. On the table were mounds of blasting caps. Nearby was a pair of crimpers and a galvanometer. In other words, left out, completely unattended, were all the makings necessary to build a large explosive charge.

I jumped into my pickup and raced out to the range. Red, White, and Blue Elements had ridden out to the range in trucks, gone over the wall, taken down the embassy mock-up, withdrawn to another area representing the soccer stadium, and there, lined up into helicopter loads. Delta had run this exercise a hundred times at least. It had become drudgery. In mid-March, people began to say, "Aw shit, not again!"

At the range I skewed to a halt and began looking for three

people. There were no excuses for what I'd found at the Stockade. I grabbed Buckshot.

"You've left a mess in S & T and I'll not tolerate leaving explosives unattended. You know the rules. Go back now and straighten it up!"

I grabbed Sergeant Major Shumate. He had nothing to do with leaving the explosives, but he was responsible for that area.

But this was nothing to what I did to Fast Eddie.

"You're stupid! Do you know what you did? You don't? You left forty pounds of explosives laying in the middle of the floor in the Stockade—unattended!"

"Yeah, but Boss—"

"I don't give a rat's ass. Now you get yourself up there or you're going out of this unit. A sergeant, no less, and in this unit!"

"Boss, it was just a mistake. I didn't think it would make any difference."

"You run off half-cocked. You don't think things through. Just get your ass up there!"

Buckshot, when he came back to the exercise, was muttering, "Well, this makes the twenty-second time I've been fired." It fell off him like water off a duck's back. But I'd gotten his attention.

Walt Shumate, on the other hand, was really bent out of shape. Before he went over to see me, cunning devil that he is, he stopped by to see Ish.

"What's wrong with the Old Man?"

Once he'd gotten the lay of the land, he walked over to me. He said, "I don't think you were fair to me. I wasn't a party to that and I don't think I deserve what you gave me."

"Sergeant Major." I didn't even call him Walter. "Sergeant Major, I don't want to discuss the matter with you."

Fast Eddie stayed away from me entirely. He really screwed up and now he was a very concerned citizen. He was afraid I'd lost confidence in him and that now I'd change tasks and give his wall responsibility to someone else. To get back in my good graces, he wanted to do something extraordinary, something that would prove why I shouldn't lose respect for him.

In mid-March there was nothing else happening that could be called exciting or dramatic or even mildly interesting. My chewing out subordinates was the only action at hand. It was a down time, a time of lethargy, of mild depression.

Six full-blown rehearsals had been conducted—C-130s, choppers, Rangers, the whole bag—six of them and another had been scheduled for the end of March.

A hundred times the embassy mock-up on our back-lot at the range had been assaulted. Hundreds and hundreds of times the nine-foot wall, which had been built right in the Stockade, had been climbed and dropped over. The days of March were dead days.

Life for Ish had become a lot more livable because 90 percent of the questions that had bedeviled him in November had been answered. We now believed that the hostages were being kept in four buildings: the DCM's residence, the Ambassador's residence, the chancellery, the staff cottages. We knew which way the doors opened, the location of the keys and other unlocking devices. We had a track of the routines the guards kept to, and where they stayed. The workbooks were thick with detail.

No one knew precisely where those ZSU-23-4 Light Armored Chassis were, but in the event they should rumble up to the compound, we were working on something that would neutralize them.

The dumps, which still came in twice a day, were shorter, and didn't contain much new information. Ish, however, continued to work toward the ideal—trying to determine, room by room, where each of the hostages was, and how precisely they were being guarded.

The Red, White, and Blue Elements were out shooting in the morning. They were getting ready to go back to Yuma for their seventh complete rehearsal. The comment most often heard was, "We're finally going to learn how to get on a C-130." No one would laugh.

Buckshot would arrive before me, around 8:00 A.M. He'd

be back in the SCIF (Secure Compartmented Information Facility) reading the night's traffic when I'd come in. He'd ask whether we should respond to a certain request he'd read and in most cases he'd have already drafted something for my approval. Then he'd go down and spend the morning watching the troops.

Boris could wait until the afternoon before he'd go to the range to work on a modification he'd made on the HK21's mount.

In the morning, to help him with his language skills, he'd have read several Russian language newspapers and journals.

Allen, who is a very serious individual, would be in at 7:30 A.M. studying the model. He was a troop sergeant in Blue Element and his time was spent double- and triple-checking the plan, trying to find if he'd missed anything.

Then he'd hold a troop meeting where everyone would discuss his role and tasks. If anyone had a new idea this would be the time when it was discussed.

Allen would then go down to the range where he'd run into me and side by side we'd bust caps until shortly before lunch.

Walter Shumate would call in, "Say, Country, something has come up with my old car. I'm going to take it down to the shop and get it fixed. I'll be in around noon."

Fast Eddie was very, very busy. He'd have come in to see me the day before.

"Boss, tomorrow I want you to come out and see the last shot on the wall. I've got it all designed. Want you to see it."

I'd seen his wall come tumbling down perfectly ten times. This time I would have declined his offer and he'd be really let down. I'd send Buckshot.

At lunch, on this day in March, Buckshot would come back from Fast Eddie's demonstration full of praise.

"Boss, you should have seen it. It went down beautifully."

This would make Fast Eddie very happy.

In the afternoon Walter would come in and work on his locks. He'd sit back in his area fumbling with them, taking them apart, putting them back together again.

I'd go back to him and we'd sit chewing the fat: talk about

Ron Terry getting killed in 'Nam, talk about Operation Masher, about trouble we'd had with the First Cav, about Plei Me and about living out in the jungle.

Allen, after chow, would grab one of the guys from B Squadron and they'd go out and run five miles. When he came back he'd grab some guys from his troop and from another one and they'd go out and play a very competitive game of volleyball.

Buckshot would conduct a meeting that afternoon about the Yuma rehearsal. He would convince me that he needed to go up to the Pentagon to help the planners coordinate the exercise.

Then he'd go out and play in Allen's volleyball game.

After he showered and cleaned up, he'd grab me, "Let's go have a couple of beers with the troops."

Country would already have gone home. So would Sergeant Major Shumate. He'd have left before Country.

Buckshot and I would have an informal session with some of the operators over a couple of Buds.

An operator would grouch about one of the rules he didn't like. "You know, Boss, those special weapons, every time we want to use them we got to get official permission."

I'd gone out and purchased seven or eight exotic handguns, Walther PPKs, HK P7s, Colt Pythons, and I'd learned if you let everyone use them they were going to get torn up.

Buckshot, who would have had two beers by then, would get a laugh. "You guys know you gotta see Daddy to get permission. You know how he is with his new toys. Come on, Boss, we're all grown up. We know how to handle—"

"Bullshit!" I'd say. "I've done some checking back there. I tried you guys out. Those weapons got screwed up. I had to go out and buy some new ones, so I ain't changing that policy." Some eyes would roll.

"We know you feel strong about the shooting house." This would be from another operator. "I know the last time we tried it we blew out all the fluorescents, but this time we've got a new tactic and a smaller charge. We'd like to show it to you in the morning."

"I'll be there. What time do you want to do it?"

Someone in the back would speak up. "Boss, why in hell do we need another rehearsal out at the range tomorrow? Come on, lighten up. We go over that damn wall as fast as we're ever gonna."

"Speed for its own sake," I'd explain for the hundredth time, sounding each time more and more like a professor, "is the worst thing we can do. The object is to work on method. It'll be done faster when it's done more methodically."

If the truth was known, I, too, was tired of climbing up and down that bloody wall.

It would go this way for an hour or so. Usually, at the end, we'd end up talking about the mission. For some questions there were no answers. "When is the President going to decide about the STOL flight?" "When should we darken our hair?" "When are we going to go?"

On the way out of the Stockade. Buckshot and I would walk past a quiet intel shop.

Ish would have left around 6:00. He was back to getting eight hours of sleep a night.

I'd arrive home disgusted with the Administration for not having the guts to use us. Over a drink, if there was anything decent, I'd watch television, if there wasn't I'd read. Anything to prevent myself from thinking about the mission. Sometimes I'd find myself grinding my teeth. "Fuck it. They ain't gonna send us!"

The first of the year had been too early, but February or early March would have been an ideal time to go. The news photographs for that period showed the armed guards spending a lot of time warming themselves around fires they'd laid in 55-gallon drums. It was cold in Teheran. When a guard's cold he is less alert. He has other things on his mind; his bed, his woman, a hot meal. He doesn't want to waste another freezing night, stomping his feet to keep warm, shuffling monotonously up and down the deserted, windswept streets around the embassy. This was good for the planned mission. It was better to go into Iran when the weather conditions favored us rather than them.

For Delta, mid-March was not only monotonous, it was damned frustrating!

★ THIRTY-NINE ★

OUT WEST, ON March 25–27, we did yet another rehearsal. General Vaught traveled with the assault team. Each step of the plan was gone through and conducted in real time. Accurate distances were flown, the truck ride was made, role-playing guards were taken out as they patrolled a mock compound wall, the wall was climbed, dummy buildings were hit and cleared, the chopper rendezvous was made, the Rangers—at a make-believe Manzariyeh—held the airstrip, and C-141s successfully lifted everyone out. Seventh time, and it had gone again as smoothly as the Xs and Os on the blackboard. Delta returned to Fort Bragg.

Suddenly, good news! The STOL aircraft mission had been approved. Well how about that! Things began to look up. Life moved over to the fast lane. Dick Potter was briefed and dispatched to Egypt to set up an advance base in the event the go-ahead was given. He was a hard-charging officer and there was no doubt he'd get things done.

On 31 March the STOL returned from Desert One with all the necessary information. The crew consisted of two pilots—Jim and Bud. Jim, it needs to be said, has but one leg. The pilots were accompanied by an Air Force major. On the ground, they had dug soil and rock samples and taken photographs. For good measure, they had accomplished another task. Before obtaining approval to fly the aircraft into the desert, a lot of work had gone into developing a package of special lights, which could be carried on board the STOL.

When the plane landed, the crew implanted these beacons in the desert floor. The lights were designed to allow a C-130 to turn them on by remote control, while it was still two to three miles out. These landing beacons, which outlined the landing area, were small, and if the Air Force pilots weren't looking for them in the right grid they'd never see them.

The flight has a postscript. After the mission had been flown, I lunched with an intelligence chief who had done much to sell the STOL concept to the White House. Only after the President had agreed to the flight, only then, did this man discover, to his amazement, that one of the pilots had only one leg.

The mission flown by those three brave men was expertly done. While they were on the desert floor, they observed some vehicular traffic; but it did not interfere with them. When they returned they brought the proof necessary to convince the Air Force planners and everyone else concerned that EC-130 tankers could, indeed, land and take off in the desert. Good-bye blivets, hello fuel-birds.

The next step was a variation on a theme.

Colonel Kyle: "It doesn't make sense now, Charlie, for Delta to fly off *Nimitz* in the choppers. Why don't you consider flying from Egypt with the C-130s and meeting the choppers at Desert One?"

This was straightforward and made sense to everyone.

Shortly after reaching this decision, the following conversation with General Vaught took place:

"Charlie, we gotta figure out command at Desert One. Do you want it?"

"I don't really know whether I do or not. I see it only as a transient place."

"Jim Kyle, by rights, oughta have it. Most of the activities at Desert One are air-related—landing and refueling."

"I agree with you, General. I don't have time to fool with this. I gotta get my equipment and men off the 130s and onto the choppers. Once they lift off, I see it then as my operation."

"Good. Then we're in agreement. What do you think about my going to Desert One?"

"General Vaught, I don't think that you can help Delta there. I would prefer you back in Egypt, where you can best influence the action. What if we get into trouble? What if we need something? The second night could be sticky, at Manzariyeh. We might need real help there."

"I'm going to be there."

"That's your decision. But, as for going in and standing around Desert One, I don't see how you'll accomplish anything."

"O.K. We're agreed on Jim Kyle. Colonel Kyle should be in charge of Desert One."

"Absolutely. Delta will take care of security."

I liked and trusted Jim Kyle. I knew Desert One would be in good hands.

The question of General Vaught at Desert One is an interesting one. It was important he position himself where he could best influence and support the whole mission. It was my judgment he should be in Egypt the first and second nights. His going to Manzariyeh was all his doing. If something had gone sour there, I do not know how he would have influenced the action on the ground. If a sharp firefight unexpectedly developed, the lieutenant colonel commanding the Ranger contingent didn't need a two star general and his staff looking over his shoulder. Generals should act and perform like generals, not battalion commanders.

I didn't feel I should have to worry about Desert One. As Moses had said to me, "Charlie, you've got a full plate as it is." And, I did. No matter how many times we rehearsed or discussed our contingency plans—our alternatives—some problems remained. One kept setting off alarm bells in my subconscious. Once we took down the embassy, and as we waited for the choppers to lift us out of the Amjadieh soccer stadium, we could be attacked by an enemy mechanized unit. Against it Delta could not last long. The mission did not allow us to engage armor. How long would it take an Iranian military unit to get organized and react to the raid on the embassy? An armored cavalry unit was stationed in Teheran. Equipped with armored vehicles purchased around the world—British Chieftains, American M48 and M60A1 medium tanks, Russian BTR-60s and ZSU-23-4s—this division had one contingent stationed six miles away, in the northeast suburb of Saltanat Abad, and another one much closer—just blocks from the embassy at the Imperial Iranian Army Ordnance Depot at Abbas-Abad. The Russian ZSU-23-4 is a particularly formidable weapon. Delta would have no chance against this vehicle, which mounts four 23mm cannon on a light armored chassis and utilizes both target-acquisition and tracking radar. The weapon scared us a lot.

The best judgments, based on message intercepts and analysis of the state of the Iranian military, indicated that it would, under ideal conditions, take ninety minutes for any element of this armored cavalry unit to organize and react in strength. The division's leadership had been decimated by the Khomeini government. When this fact was coupled with the unit's known lack of spare parts and maintenance capability, the intel planners determined that it posed little threat to Delta. The National Police, with their Scorpion-type armored cars that carried .50-caliber machine guns or 76mm cannon, were of greater concern. The police appeared to be more loyal to the Ayatollah than the Army, and more militant. The intelligence analysts could never pinpoint where they were positioned or what they were capable of doing. And then there were those Soviet ZSU-23-4s. What if they managed to arrive on the scene while Delta was still in the stadium waiting for the choppers?

Another contingency plan was called for and it was hoped it would not have to be used. Provision was made to have two AC-130E/H gunships on station over the city. One of them would fly over the embassy and prevent any armor from clanking down Roosevelt Avenue. The other would circle Mehrabad International Airport, where there were known to be two Iranian F-4 Phantoms on strip-alert.

There was never any intention just to arbitrarily shell Teheran. It was a matter of neutralizing any threat Delta could not handle. Two backup gunships were called for, in the event the first two ran low on fuel. Having them overhead made the

Delta operators feel more comfortable. Some of us had worked with gunships in 'Nam and knew their 105mm howitzer and 20mm Gatling gun could help us in Teheran. Morale soared. No way was Delta going to be pinned down and not be able to get the hostages out. That particular alarm bell stopped ringing.

One other use for these aircraft was agreed upon. As soon as the hostages and Delta had safely left Teheran, the gunship circling the compound would begin to methodically destroy the embassy's buildings. It would just chew them up till its guns ran dry. There was no sense leaving behind anything the Iranians could use as further propaganda.

The mission awaited White House approval to move ahead.

On Tuesday, April 15th, the RDF (Rapid Deployment Force) conducted a command post exercise on the Fort Bragg reservation, which General Jones planned to visit. The Chairman's office had called and requested I please pick him up in the afternoon and take him to the Stockade, where he wanted to talk to me.

This would not be General Jones's first visit to the Stockade. Right after New Year's, he'd dropped in. He was scheduled at that time to spend an hour with Delta. He left six hours later. General Jones understood communications and he was elated with our package. He was carried away. He fired weapons, watched demonstrations, talked to the operators, even had lunch with them. It was a day everyone enjoyed.

On the Tuesday of his visit to the RDF exercise, I found the location on the reservation where the games were being played. It was within the 101st Airmobile Division's headquarters command post area. I wore civilian clothes that afternoon and drove a leased car. The day was blustery and cool. It had rained hard the day before. The secondary roads were still wet, especially the rough dirt trail that led out to the 101st's command post.

An MP stopped me at the entrance to the area. "Sir, you can't stay here. There's an exercise about to begin." I showed my identification and told him I was there to pick up the Chairman of the Joint Chiefs of Staff. This rattled him. He called his headquarters for instructions. All of a sudden a little bitty short fella with his helmet right down on his nose—he was a senior officer of the 101st, but looked like Beetle Bailey—trotted over to me. He arrived out of breath. "Get that car away from here. There are no civilians allowed out here. You will leave. Now!" I was playing in his ballpark, so I respectfully told him who I was and what I was there to do, then showed him my ID. "I don't care who you are. You are not allowed here. Get out before I have you arrested." When I'd gone to my wallet, he'd seen my Colt .45, which I carried cocked and locked. This made him even more nervous. "Colonel," I said, "I'd like you to track with me. I'm here to pick up the Chairman of the Joint Chiefs of Staff and you're getting ready to ruin your military career." He backed off a little then. "All right. Drive your car off the road and park it in those bushes"; he pointed to a spot 100 yards across the road. I complied with the request and sat in the car and watched General Jones's arrival at the command post.

Before it ever happened, I knew what would happen next. Sure enough, before I even had time to smoke a cigarette, an MP came running out of the tent, jumped into a jeep, and, splashing water every which way, drove up to me. "Sir, would you follow me?" I said, "I'm not authorized to go into that area." "Sir," he said, "you gotta follow me." General Warner, now a four star general, who had replaced General Hennessey as commander of REDCOM (Readiness Command), came out and greeted me. He killed me with kindness. "Charlie, just give me a couple of more minutes and General Jones will be ready to go." "Whatever you say, sir." He's the 900-pound gorilla and he can do as he pleases. There was no way General Warner could have been more considerate.

My friend the colonel, Beetle Bailey, stood about six feet away, his helmet down around his nose, his head tilted back so he could stare holes in me. General Jones, dressed in fatigues and a nylon flight jacket, came out some few moments later. "Charlie, are you ready to go?" "Yes, sir," I responded. Then I walked over to the little colonel and, in my most pleasant voice, said, "You have a nice day." I couldn't help myself. I can't stand colonels who act so high and mighty and are shot in the butt with themselves.

General Jones and I drove off. On this particular Tuesday, way out in the boondocks of Fort Bragg, there was nothing but mud, rutted trails, and rain-filled potholes. General Jones said, "Pull over, Charlie. I want to talk to you about Iran. What do you think?"

He wanted me to look him square in the eye and tell him, "Sir, we've got to do it. We're ready." And I did.

"I think we are, too," he answered back. Then he told me he'd been down to Hurlburt Air Force Base and spoken with the pilots of 8th Special Operations Squadron who would fly the 130s. He sensed everyone there was ready as well.

We talked for nearly ten minutes.

"General Jones, I'll ask you to do one thing. Delta's been told to get ready, then to step down, seven times. Sir, I can't get these troops up but one more time. If we're going to go, this has got to be it."

"I would agree with you. I think we're ready."

"I do, too. In fact, I know we're ready. Now's the time to do it."

"O.K. Good. I'm glad you feel that way. Let's go on to your headquarters. I want you to go over the plan with me one more time."

★ FORTY ★

THE CODE NAME of the mission to free the hostages was Eagle Claw. As described to General Jones, the basic plan was this [see pp. viii–ix for map]: Three troop-carrying MC-130s and three-fuel-bearing EC-130s would depart from the island of Masirah, which is off the coast of Oman, and fly to Iran, where they would land 200 miles southeast of Teheran at a location called Desert One—at 33° 05' N by 55° 48' E. On the ground they would wait for the arrival of eight RH-53D helicopters.

Launching from the carrier *Nimitz* somewhere in the Gulf of Oman, the eight helicopters, flying a different route and in four sections of two each, would arrive approximately thirty minutes after the last 130 had landed.

On arrival, the RH-53Ds would refuel and on-load the assault force of 118 men.

Unless six helicopters—a minimum figure deemed necessary by the air planners to lift the combined weight of the assault team and the equipment—were able to depart and fly to the next location, the mission would be aborted at Desert One.

Once the helicopters had refueled and on-loaded Delta, they would proceed toward Teheran and the 130s would return to Masirah.

Flying two and a half to three hours, the helicopters would land at Delta's hide-site—at 35° 14' N by 52° 15' E—ideally one hour before sunrise.

After Delta had been off-loaded, the RH-53Ds would fly to their hide-site fifteen miles north of Delta, where they would spend the daylight hours hidden in the hills around Garmsar.

At Delta's landing zone, the assault team would be met by two of the DOD (Department of Defense) agents who had been placed in Teheran several days before. They would lead Colonel Beckwith and his men five miles overland to a remote wadi sixty-five miles southeast of Teheran, and there Delta would remain concealed throughout the daylight hours.

After last light, two of the DOD agents would return to the wadi, driving a Datsun pickup truck and a Volkswagen bus. One of these vehicles would transport the six drivers and six translators, who had come with Delta, back toward the outskirts of Teheran to a warehouse where six enclosed Mercedes trucks were stored.

The other vehicle would carry Colonel Beckwith on a reconnaissance of the route to the embassy. Once the route and the vicinity around the compound had been checked, Beckwith would return to the hide-site. The six trucks would already have arrived and be waiting.

Delta, which had for this mission been reorganized into a Red, a White, and a Blue Element, would climb aboard the trucks around 8:30 P.M. They would be driven north along the Damavand Road, where they would encounter a permanent 2-man checkpoint at Eyvanekey and at Sherifabad. If for some reason the trucks were stopped and searched, the guards would be seized and carried with Delta.

The next step had some flexibility built into it. The precise route through Teheran to the embassy and the method the trucks would use to traverse this course, convoy or leapfrog, would be determined at this time and would rest largely on the recommendations put forth by the DOD agents and on what Colonel Beckwith had been able to observe.

A 13-man assault team, tasked to rescue the three hostages being held in the Foreign Ministry Building, would travel in the Volkswagen bus and take a different route to their target.

Between 11:00 P.M. and midnight a select group of operators would drive up to the embassy in the Datsun pickup and with .22-caliber suppressed (with silencers) handguns tak down the two guard posts and the walking guards along Roo sevelt Avenue.

Driving two abreast, the trucks carrying Red, White, an Blue Elements would follow a little distance behind. When th assault team reached a position on Roosevelt Avenue acros from the soccer stadium, they would leave the trucks anc using ladders, swiftly and silently climb over the embassy wa and drop into the compound.

Red Element, comprising forty men, was responsible fo securing the western sector of the compound, freeing any hos tages found in the staff cottages and commissary, and neu tralizing the guards who were in the motor pool and powe plant areas.

Blue Element, also forty men, was responsible for the em bassy's eastern sector and freeing hostages found in the Dep uty Chief of Mission's residence, the Ambassador's residence the Mushroom, and the chancellery.

The smaller 13-man White Element was responsible for se curing Roosevelt Avenue and eventually covering the with drawal of Red and Blue Elements to the Amjadieh Socce Stadium. One machine gun, an M60, was positioned to enfi lade Roosevelt Avenue to the north and another, the HK21, t cover it to the south.

Two AC-130s flying on station over Teheran would preven Iranian reinforcements from reaching the embassy compound Using a predetermined grid system that pinpointed targets an zones in the area of the embassy, Major Buckshot and Ser geant Major Foreman were responsible on the ground for call ing in, if necessary, covering fire from the gunships.

Inside the embassy compound, once Red Element—whic had the farthest to travel and most area to cover—was in po sition, the wall was to be blown.

This large explosion signaled the beginning of the assau on the buildings. Any armed Iranian guards encountere would be killed and the hostages located and freed.

The operation would take approximately forty-five minutes Major Snuffy (pseudonym), who was acting as Delta's ai officer, would already have alerted the RH-53Ds outside of Garmsar and by now they would be orbiting north of the city.

At his signal, the choppers would begin to arrive in the vicinity of the compound.

If, as was expected, the poles placed in the embassy's open acres could be removed, the first helicopter would be called directly into the embassy grounds. There it would load all the freed hostages, who would be accounted for by Delta's medics.

A second chopper could also be brought in.

If the poles could not be removed, the alternate plan was to move the hostages across to the soccer stadium.

Once all the hostages they'd liberated had been lifted out, Red, followed by Blue, would withdraw through the gaping hole in the wall and cross Roosevelt Avenue to the stadium, where, accompanied by White, they would load on the remaining helicopters.

Sometime during the assault on the embassy, the 13-man Special Forces team tasked to assault the Foreign Ministry Building would begin its operation. Their plan was to scale the outside of the building and enter through its third story windows. They would then eliminate any resistance they met and free the three hostages.

Outside the building, in an adjacent parklike area, one of the helicopters would make the pick-up.

While these operations were going on and the targets in Teheran were going down, thirty-five miles to the south, in Manzariyeh, a Ranger contingent would fly in, take, and secure the airfield there. They would hold the field until the helicopters arrived from Teheran.

Once everyone had arrived in Manzariyeh, all of the hostages, drivers, translators, helicopter pilots, crews, DOD agents, Special Forces assault team, and Delta Force would be airlifted out of Iran on C-141 StarLifters.

The Rangers would then dry up Manzariyeh and be flown out themselves.

A contingency plan covered the eventuality that not enough

helicopters would be available to lift the hostages and the assault forces out of Teheran at one time.

In that case, in the soccer stadium across from the compound—if, after removing the hostages, there were not enough RH-53Ds to remove the assault force—Delta would take up a defensive position around the stadium's perimeter.

The remaining helicopters, however many there would be would shuttle back and forth between Manzariyeh—where they would unload the hostages and refuel—and the stadium until every member of the assault team had been removed.

If no helicopter had been able to return, Delta would be prepared to evade and escape.

General Jones listened very intently. While the plan was being described, he had several times nodded his head in agreement and on occasion asked a question.

There was one hell of a load on his shoulders, keeping all the elements of the plan in his head, evaluating all the components, weighing the various pros and cons, and interfacing with Dr. Brown at the Department of Defense and Dr. Brzezinski at the White House.

It was obvious to everyone at the briefing, by the penetrating questions he had asked, that General Jones was on top of everything.

General Vaught, too, was up. Their contagious optimism spread to Delta.

To those standing in the room, I said, "Hey, we gotta do this thiing!"

I still had lingering doubts about whether we'd actually go but at least, there was now a good chance we'd deploy to Egypt and stage.

★ FORTY-ONE ★

ALL DURING FEBRUARY and March, people kept bringing up the rules of engagement. What will they be? What kind of document should we give Beckwith? Hell, I didn't need any damn document. Some staff officers, the ones who worry about their bosses' bowels, spent a lot of time focusing on this aspect. The rule was not to take any lives unless it was warranted. If Delta became involved in a firefight, it had to be able to use whatever force was necessary.

At the White House briefing Wednesday night, April 16th, the subject had come up. General Vaught introduced it very smoothly. The President had said, "As far as I'm concerned, Colonel Beckwith has my approval to use whatever force he needs to save American lives."

President Carter understood where we were coming from. He'd been driven to the end of his patience. Now it was time to act.

I recalled the briefing held that afternoon, before we all went over to the White House, when General Meyer expressed his concern to General Jones about the command and control at the Pentagon of the Iranian operation. He feared it might be overcontrolled. When President Carter brought up the subject, "David, this is a military operation and you're going to run it," he almost used General Meyer's exact words. I don't know whether General Jones or General Meyer talked to the President after their meeting and before his, but I do know the situation was handled perfectly. From Desert One, Jim Kyle and I, back to General Vaught in Egypt, back to General Jones at the JCS, back to the President. It was clean, simple, and direct. A precedent had been set that night in the White House. I hope future American presidents, if faced with a similar situation, will follow.

Following the President's brief, the generals and I left the White House around 10:00 P.M. The streets of Washington were nearly deserted, and the driver made good time. Everyone expressed his satisfaction. The talking was over. Now it needed to get done.

The blue Dodge pulled up in front of the River Entrance of the Pentagon. Generals Vaught and Gast went ahead into the building. General Jones took my arm and we began to walk down the darkened street. The night was balmy. It was cherry blossom time.

"You know, I thought it was very important you go over to the White House this evening. I wanted you to see what took place and to meet the President. I wanted you to be involved." He stopped and looked at me. "You got a tough job, Charlie. God bless, and I'll see you when you get back."

There was an Army King-Air at Davison Army Airfield standing by to fly me back to Bragg. I was greeted by the two warrant officers who flew it. They were glad to be going home that evening. I thought to myself, If you fellas only knew where I've been and where, in the next few days, I'm going. History is gonna be made.

The fifty-minute flight to Bragg seemed like ten minutes. My mind raced from one point to another: when and where to inform the guys . . . last minute checks . . . what to tell Katherine . . . remind everyone to be careful about how they assembled at the Stockade . . . tell them to use a cover story of another rehearsal out west. My mind ricocheted back and forth, covering all the potential problems Delta could have leaving Bragg. There was a lot to accomplish before we left.

Two C-141s were coming to get Delta on Sunday morning, the 20th. At 0730 hours we would on-load at Pope Air Force Base.

I told the troops on Thursday that we were moving forward

o Egypt, but not that the mission was a go. I did, however, nform Buckshot and Country that we were not going on another dry run. The men spent the rest of the week cleaning and checking equipment. There wasn't anything better to do. wrote a letter to my wife telling her how much I loved her and our daughters. It was given to my adjutant, Captain Smith, who was staying behind, and he was told to hand it to Katherine in the event something happened to me.

By early Saturday night, Delta was cocked and locked. Country informed the unit they were to assemble at headquarters at 0230. A little earlier in the evening, one of the noncommissioned officers, Sergeant Holden (pseudonym), had arrived home and discovered a prowler in his home. He lived off the post and alone. He'd grabbed his 9mm Browning and taken the intruder out. Captain Smith called me around midnight to tell me of the incident. He assured me everything was kosher and that Holden would be at the Stockade on time.

With the unit together—they were dressed in casual civilian clothes—I told them, "We have in our midst one of our mates who I'm very sure will pull a trigger, because a few hours ago he did." Sergeant Holden, who was still in an emotional state, didn't think this was too funny. I then told the operators we were going to Iran. I thought the Stockade's roof would come off. Oh, wow! The President's message to them, about where the buck stopped, was also passed along.

Delta then loaded up in trucks and was taken down to Pope Air Force Base to meet the C-141s.

At Pope I was introduced to two Iranian generals whom General Gast had told me to expect. They'd come to the United States when the Ayatollah Khomeini assumed power in Iran. Both were intelligent and well educated and neither was "Joe Shit, the Rag Man." They spoke Farsi and I thought they might be helpful to us in Teheran. One of them knew the Iranian Air Force very well and it was decided he would fly with the helicopters and stay with Seiffert. I hadn't made up my mind about the other one. "What the hell," I thought, "I'll work with him until we get to Desert One, then I can see what happens. If he doesn't work out I'll dump him and he can return to Egypt on one of the 130s." I issued both of them new revolver, what we call a wheel-gun: a.357 Magnum Smit & Wesson. Delta didn't have a large supply of Smiths, but provided them to these generals because I felt it befitted the rank.

The two MAC (Military Air Command) pilots knew nothin of their destination. They'd been given an altitude and a com pass bearing, but nothing else. One of them, after lookin around for a while, walked over to me. "You act as if you'r in charge." "I'm foreman of this here ranch," I said. "Then sir, how much fuel should I put in this bird?" I recommende he put on every drop he could. He hollered to the crew chie "Fill 'er up."

It was night when the transport planes landed at Frankfur West Germany. A fresh MAC crew came on board. The didn't say much, as they had been briefed and knew their fina destination. Delta was also joined in West Germany by a sma 13-man cell that had been carefully selected and trained t take down the Iranian Ministry of Foreign Affairs building. I mid-November it had been discovered there would be two sep arate targets. Intelligence sources learned that three America Embassy officials were being held outside the compound, i the Ministry of Foreign Affairs. Delta was committed to th embassy and didn't have the additional personnel to take dow the Foreign Affairs building. Subsequently, it was determine that a select group would be formed for this task. They cam from a Special Forces unit in this country and were com manded by an old friend who had much experience in specia operations activities. He spoke several languages and the me under him had high regard and respect for him. Delta traine with this cell infrequently but maintained close coordinatio with it. Because of security it was determined that this cel should prepare and train in Europe. A building similar to th one in Teheran was found in West Germany, and at night thi unit rehearsed its assault plan. They worked very hard an were as ready as Delta to accomplish their portion of the mis sion. This unit was under my operational command.

The mission now numbered 132 men: 2 Iranian generals

12 drivers; a 12-man Road Watch Team, including translators, who would secure Desert One; the 13-man special assault team; and Delta's 93 operators and staff.

The Road Watch Team would return to Egypt on one of the C-130s. One hundred and twenty men would continue to the hide-site.

This group didn't include Al. He hadn't made it. At the end his blood turned to water and he had a change of heart. I hope he doesn't play stud poker. He'll never win a pot.

★ FORTY-TWO ★

IN THE MORNING—it was Monday, 21 April—when we landed at Wadi Kena, Egypt; Dick Potter, Delta's deputy commander, was there to meet us. The heat hit us like a wall. It felt like we were walking into a blast furnace. Everyone was beat; we had just flown halfway around the world. Because of all the Gatorade that had been consumed, a long line formed at the latrines.

Dick briefed me on the form; where we would base, sleep, train, and pointed out the location of General Vaught's headquarters.

Lieutenant Colonel Potter is a professional officer who doesn't miss the details. More important, he is the kind of officer who checks to make sure each task is accomplished in good order. If Dick Potter had not gone to Egypt, very little preparation would have been done before Delta's arrival. I'm not sure I ever told Dick how much the Delta operators appreciated what he did for them.

A day or two before we arrived there had been a disagreement over the use of a generator. An Air Force lieutenant colonel responsible for setting up the base had wanted it to run the air conditioning system in the headquarters area, and Potter had wanted it to run refrigerators that were going to store plasma and other medical supplies. The discussion had reached the shouting stage when General Vaught stepped in. Both officers explained their needs to him. "Now listen here," General Vaught said to the Air Force officer, "let me explain the chain of command. There's Jimmy Carter, there's General Jones, there's me, and there's Dick Potter. Now, did you hear your name anywhere?" That was the end of the discussion!

North of the Aswan Dam, not far from the pyramids, the Russians had built an air base at Wadi Kena. The base consists of more than thirteen reinforced concrete hangars and support buildings, which range from one story wood-frame buildings to ramshackle huts. Delta's billets were in one of the large hangars and even at a distance the shoddy workmanship could be detected. A 250-pound bomb would have caved it in. When Potter arrived, he had found the concrete floor partially covered with broiled human feces. Only through his hard work, and that of some others, had the area been cleaned and made germfree.

Outside the base an endless desolate landscape disappeared into the heat of a cloudless sky. And there were the flies. There were clouds of them. They were everywhere, in, on, and about anything that moved or stood still.

Everyone tried to sleep, but whether it was because of the blazing heat of the day or the excitement of the mission, not many Zs were logged on Monday. Dick had acquired several trucks, which permitted us to work further with the drivers. It still needed to be determined whether the assault force would be driven to the embassy by Iranian or Farsi-speaking American drivers. I tried to sleep, but spent more time worrying than anything else. I was still afraid the mission would be canceled. My shirt was black with sweat.

The sun went down, but nothing cooled off. We worked with the drivers. One of the Americans was a Navy captain, Butterfield. He'd been on the faculty of the Naval Academy at Annapolis, and when it was discovered he spoke fluent Farsi he was sent to Fort Bragg. He didn't care what it was he was going to do as long as he got a chance to go. In Teheran, all these men had to do was drive or act as assistant drivers and at the appropriate time get out of their trucks and jump on a helicopter. But none of them had to go to Iran. They were all volunteers.

I'd gone over to see General Vaught. His SATCOM (Satellite Communications) package had been installed, but hi headquarters, two command trailers that had been flown i from Europe, was nothing fancy.

Excitement, expectation, and energy were in abundance You could almost touch it. The pucker factor was also in ev idence. People were feeling the stress.

I asked General Vaught if Delta could test-fire its weapon before they left and arrangements were made to use a make shift range the next night. In the early evening, which seeme as suffocatingly hot as the day, I continued to monitor th progress of the drivers. The four Department of Defense con tacts, who were in Teheran and with whom Delta would lin up at the hideout, would recommend how they thought th trucks should enter the city. This was not going to be a prob lem.

The three Delta Elements—Red, White, Blue—spent th night running over their tasks. The ground was laid out wit white tape indicating the distances between the embassy build ings, and the men practiced their maneuvers. The next tim they did this it would be for real.

All the operators were weighed again with their equipmen to make sure no one exceeded the 270-pound-per-man limit It was necessary that the weight not go over a certain mark o the helicopters would be unable to fly Delta out of Desert One The formula between weight and lift had been carefull worked out.

The confidence level was right.

Everyone tried to get his metabolism turned around fron daytime to nighttime.

All weaponry was stripped, cleaned, and reassembled knives were given new edges.

The men took PT.

While we were still in Egypt an event occurred that migh have had great impact on the mission. One of the U.S. Em bassy's cooks was permitted to leave Iran. Reportedly, on th plane a CIA agent managed to sit next to him. This cook no only knew where the guards were stationed but where all thei prisoners were being held.

In the middle of the night, the last one we were to spend in Egypt, I was awakened and told of our good fortune. The information that was passed reported that all fifty-three hostages would be found in the chancellery.

Making use of this intelligence, and in consultation with Buckshot and the commanders of the Red, White, and Blue Elements, I modified the assault plan.

Blue would now pick up more security responsibilities leaving Red to concentrate its entire effort on cracking the chancellery. Because of the building's size, the ninety rooms that needed to be cleared, and its hardened status, it would be a tough nut to crack. To help Red, I gave it two teams, eight operators, from Blue.

The plan now was for one of Red's teams to force the staff door in the east end, then race down the darkened central corridor and open the main entrance, which faced south, to the rest of Red Element.

Blue would neutralize the guards' quarters at the motor pool and power plant. This critical area would be covered by several well-placed machine guns.

No one felt sorry to leave Egypt. The dirt and flies were left behind as Delta was flown in two C-141s to an island, Masirah—which the men instantly, and predictably, nicknamed Misery—off the coast of Oman. As we had flown over the Red Sea to the Gulf of Aden, the thought that we would not turn back—that we were actually going to go and do the mission—sank in. If there ever was a chance for the operation to be canceled, it would have been while Delta was in Egypt.

Earlier on Thursday, the 24th, before we had left Wadi Kena, everyone had been high-strung. After troop inspection we'd gathered in one of the hangars. Flies were everywhere. Major Snuffy, standing on a small, crudely built platform, read passages from 1 Samuel: "And there came out a champion . . . named Goliath . . . his spear was like a weaver's beam. . . . And David said, 'The Lord who delivered me from the paw of the bear, will deliver me from the hand of this Philistine.' David . . . took out a stone and slung it and struck the Philistine on his forehead and Goliath fell on his face to the ground."

We'd then prayed for guidance and strength. Suddenly, Buck
shot began singing "God Bless America." All the troops joine
in. Their voices swelled in chorus filling the empty hang
with sound that echoed off the concrete walls. "From th
mountains, To the prairies, To the oceans white with foam
Everybody was really up. God, you could feel it, "God ble
America, my home sweet home." General Vaught turned
our psychologist, "Well, Doc, what do you think?" "They'
up higher, sir, than I've ever seen them." Amen.

Delta landed at Masirah about 1400 hours. General Ga
was there to meet us. Some tents had been put up. There we
soft drinks and water and lots of ice. Somebody had gone
a lot of trouble to make Delta comfortable. Some said it wa
unnecessary. People laughed. Most everyone went into the 1
man tents, the canvas walls were rolled up, and got off the
feet. The night was going to be a long one.

Buckshot, Major Snuffy, and I went over on that sunbake
afternoon to the MC-130s and EC-130s to check the schedu
one more time. We bumped into Jim Kyle, the commander
Desert One. There weren't any problems. An Air Force co
onel, one whom Kyle had selected to go along and assist hi
during the landings, refueling, and takeoffs, voiced his conce
about the three troop-carrying 130s being overloaded. Tongu
in cheek, he hoped we'd be able to get off the ground. Th
scared me. "Hells-bells, Colonel. It's a little late to be talkin
like that." Jim Kyle jumped all over him, "You don't kno
what in the hell you're talking about. This has all been worke
out and there isn't going to be any problem getting off th
ground. If you don't know what you're talking about, kee
your mouth shut!"

By 1630, the time selected to board the 130s, Delta For
was dressed for the mission. They wore Levi's, unpolished C
boots, and field jackets that had been dyed black. On the rig
shoulder of each jacket was stitched an American flag, whic
had been covered by tape. When they reached the embass
the tape would be ripped off. On their heads they wore knitte
dark blue Navy watch caps. No one wore any rank. There wa
no need to.

★ FORTY-THREE ★

BY 1800 HOURS on April 24th, the first MC-130 was in the air. It carried Col. Kyle and his Combat Control Team, the Road Watch Team, Major Fitch and the Blue Element, and me. The other five aircraft would follow an hour later.

Over the Gulf of Oman, the plane flew at a couple of thousand feet. As the MC-130 hit the Iranian coast west of Chah Bahar, it dropped to 400 feet. Sitting near the rear cargo hatch, Wade Ishimoto felt a blast of hot air. He knew he was in Iran.

The ground below rolled toward the darkening horizon. To the north, far away, the hills looked like blue smudges and soon grew in size; behind them, farther still, the black mountains rose steeply.

To fly through the seams and into the gaps of the Iranian ground radar tracking system, which under the Khomeini regime had begun to break down, it was necessary to fly a lurching, stomach-tumbling route—hard to port, hard to starboard, up and down, sharp again to port, a sudden dip. It went this way, irregularly but constantly, for several hours.

Some of the Rangers in the Road Watch Team became airsick and remained so the entire flight.

Delta's operators sat shoulder to shoulder, their equipment strung overhead in the webbing or else strapped to the inside of the fuselage. No one spoke much. The cabin interior was lit by small red lights—an aid to night vision once Desert One was reached. There was not much movement. The men re-

mained inside themselves like a unit waiting for a comba
airborne drop.

I thought about the year I'd spent with 22 SAS. I though
of the names and places: John Woodhouse and John Edwards
the Rat, Peter Walter and Gloom, Sergeant Major Ross; Troop
ers Scott and Larsen; Harry Thompson; Crab Stakes and th
Brecon Beacons and Sherwood Forest; Corsica and Malaya
the old Gurkha Camp at Gerik and the hospital at Ipoh. Mayb
these memories came back because I'd been thinking earlie
that day of Johnny Watts. He was the Senior British Arm
Representative to the Government of Oman. If he'd known w
were in Masirah, I felt sure he would have greeted us as w
deplaned—dressed in full battle gear, demanding to be take
along. As a former brigadier in the Special Air Service Reg
iment, he had spent many hours helping me form the idea
that led to Delta. It was appropriate that afternoon to feel clos
to him.

About thirty minutes out, I looked aft and saw there wer
only a couple of guys still awake. The rest were snoozing
getting their rest. I moved from the cabin and climbed a sho
ladder into the dimly lit cockpit. There wasn't much room
The pilot and copilot were hidden from me behind their hug
chairs. Jim Kyle sat with his back to the bulkhead, monitorin
the radio signals back to Wadi Kena and Misery.

It was hard not to be concerned about the trucks and, more
what we'd actually find in the streets of Teheran. Had a nev
roadblock been established? Would all the hostages really b
found in the chancellery? Could those Soviet ZSU-23-4s, wit
their lethal 23mm cannon, reach Delta while it was still in th
stadium? How many helicopters would crank tomorrow night
But my main concern was the route from the hide-site to th
wall. If we got to the wall I believed we were home free.

The MC-130 was more than halfway to Desert One whe
Kyle slapped my shoulder. He grinned. "The helicopters hav
launched. All eight got off." "Wonderful," I said. "That'
great."

How many people have the opportunity to do what I'v
done: find a new command; build it from scratch; and then

after creating a unique, the most beautiful, and the finest unit in the United States Army, take it off to war and fight it! I was all smiles.

At almost 2200 hours, right on schedule, the MC-130 closed on Desert One. Three miles from touchdown, the pilot switched on the remotely controlled lights at the still-distant LZ. The STOL mission had done well. The beacons were faint, but there.

"Here we are!"

The MC-130 flew one circle over the LZ, then landed west to east. A hard-packed, unimproved road had been selected and the landing wasn't as rough as some we'd done in training.

After we'd taxied off the road and come to a halt, the rear ramp was lowered and the small Road Watch Team, whose job it would be to guard the site's flanks, unloaded. These were mostly Rangers, but there were some Delta Force support people among them. They deployed once their motorcycles and quarter-ton jeep had been driven down the ramp.

I walked off with them, turned right, and headed north, toward the road. It was a cool, clear night; the stars were easily seen. There was enough light from the moon to recognize people thirty or forty yards away.

Before the Road Watch Team was actually in blocking position, a big Mercedes bus, its headlights showing the way, drove into our perimeter. I hollered, "Stop that vehicle," and fired once at its tires. A Ranger also fired. It thudded to a stop. Blue Element, under Major Fitch, which had just deplaned, surrounded the bus and ordered its passengers off. There were forty-five people on board, mainly elderly folks and very young kids. Perhaps three or four were adult males. The passengers were at first lined up on both sides of the hard dirt road and then moved off to the south side, where they were carefully searched and closely guarded. A plan had been prepared for this. They would have been back-hauled out on a C-130 later in the evening and returned the same way the following night to Manzariyeh. The mission was later accused of not looking at all the eventualities. This was an unfair assessment. We had planned for such a mishap and when it occurred it was handled routinely.

Speculation had been that most of the Iranian road traffic that could come through Desert One would come from the east. Accordingly, the strongest security contingent was placed down the road in that direction. The second and smaller force was just beginning to position itself to the west of the LZ when from that direction a gasoline tanker truck drove into view. Capt. Wade Ishimoto, one of the security force leaders, was out in front on a Yamaha motorcycle with a Ranger named Rubio. As the truck continued to drive toward the LZ, it was hit by an M72 LAW (Light Antitank Weapon) fired by Rubio. It immediately began to burn furiously. Ishimoto rushed toward the truck on foot, yelling in Farsi a phrase he had memorized, "Biya enja!" which meant, "Come here!" When no one responded, he returned to Rubio and the motorcycle. At that instant, a second and smaller vehicle drove up behind the burning truck. The driver of the tanker leaped out of his cab and ran for the second truck. Once he jumped in, this vehicle made a hard U turn and raced for the darkness. Ishimoto's motorcycle failed three or four times to kick-start. When the engine finally caught, the small truck was out of range and too far ahead for it to be caught. It escaped down another track.

I did not believe the Iranians who had run away could have seen, or identified, the C-130s. If they had, who knows what they would say they saw? Would anyone believe them? All things considered, the possibility that two truck drivers saw the rescue force was no reason to cash in our chips and go home. Of course it was a risk, but it was one I elected to take.

The fire from the petrol truck blazed brightly the entire time Delta was on the ground, the flames reaching 300 feet in the sky. The night was brighter than ever.

Jim Kyle walked over, "What do you think, Charlie?"

"It's all based on how many Iranians we can haul out," I said. "Let's don't get excited until we get eight or ten vehicles in here and have to establish a parking lot."

The C-130 sat facing west near the road, its engines idling. Once Kyle organized the Combat Control Team that was responsible for air traffic operations, once the security force had deployed, and once Blue Element had unloaded, he gave the O.K. to the pilot. Into the brightly lit sky the 130 lifted and was soon out of sight.

For the moment we were alone on the desert floor. I dug my heel into the ground and found the crust to be particularly hard to break through.

The second MC-130, the one carrying Major Coyote's Red Element, landed shortly afterward. Buckshot trotted down the ramp and saw the flaming tanker. He was laughing, hitting on all cylinders.

"Welcome to World War III," I said.

This MC-130 was immediately unloaded. It carried, amongst other equipment, the mountains of camouflage netting, which were to be used to cover the helos the next day. This done, the aircraft repositioned itself outside the LZ; the third troop-carrying 130 landed and was followed in short order by the three tanker EC-130s. The last four aircraft taxied down the road and lined up north to south, a full two football fields apart, to await the arrival of the helos. The second C-130, the one which carried the Red Element, then taxied back out onto the rough strip and took off for the return flight to Masirah.

Jim Kyle and the Air Force did a great job. Delta's arrival had been handled very smoothly, just like in the rehearsals. All that needed to be done now was wait for the Sea Stallions.

Thirty minutes behind the arrival of the fuel-birds, the choppers were scheduled to come in.

Thirty minutes.

Delta began to break into three smaller groups, and with their equipment they pre-positioned themselves for loading onto the helicopters. There was a good deal of movement on the ground as the men went about their business moving and shifting equipment. Based on footprints alone, I can imagine why the Iranians later claimed there had been a force of 800 on the ground.

Since this was the last pit stop before sunrise, everyone took the opportunity to relieve the pressure on his kidneys.

The helicopters were due in fifteen minutes.

While we waited, I happened to see one of the Iranian generals. I did a double take. His holster was empty. "Where is your weapon?" I asked. "It fell out," he said, "when I got off the aircraft." Two operators were sent back to the plane to see if they could find his Smith & Wesson revolver. After a thorough search they reported they couldn't find it. I knew what had happened. Once on the ground, seeing the bus and the burning oil truck, he had panicked and thrown his weapon away. He was scared. I told him we didn't have generals in the American Army who threw their sidearms away. I let him have it and put him down as hard as I could. It made no difference he was a general if he wasn't much of a soldier. Right then I made up my mind that he was going back with the Iranians who had been on the bus. He was going to be baggage.

During this time, the satellite radio was also set up and Delta's primary radio operator, Mr. Victor (pseudonym), a warrant officer, had made contact with the two agents who were at the hide-site. I was told, "All the groceries are on the shelf." It meant everything outside of Teheran was in order. They were waiting for us. There were no problems.

The tanker truck blazed on.

There was a good deal of noise from the idling engines of the four parked C-130s.

Fifteen minutes passed. No sign of the helos.

I walked among the men as they sat in small groups. The night had gotten a little cooler. Some, with their jacket collars turned up, were munching C rations.

Everyone was checking his watch. The choppers were five minutes late.

Fast Eddie, I noticed, was in a group that contained members of White Element. He is a big man and with the packs of explosives he was carrying he looked in the desert larger than life. He was beaming. Next night, about this same time, at the wall, he'd be even happier.

Boris, also a member of White, was sitting close by. His machine gun was wrapped and lay next to him. Twenty-four hours from now, he and his HK21 would be guarding the southern approaches to Roosevelt Avenue.

I looked into the night. I couldn't see or hear the choppers. They were ten minutes late.

Walter ambled over to me. "Well, Boss," he said in pure West Virginia twang, "I guess this'll be our last one. We're both getting old. We do this one, do it right, we'll be finished."

I knew that if anything went wrong at the embassy, Walt Shumate was the kind of man who would try to fix it, make it right. Plans are only so good; and when unforeseen events occur, people with experience are a great help at those times. In 'Nam I'd seen Walter in some tough spots. I was glad he was with me.

The helicopters were twenty minutes behind schedule. In rehearsals, we'd been working with tolerances of only ten minutes.

The troops did some grumbling. They were becoming tense, edgy. Somebody would look at his watch. The guy next to him would say, "Shit, what's new? Just like in training. Same old problem."

I was now very concerned. Just looking at the time, we could see that the operation was going sour. Buckshot was worried with good reason: we would not have enough flight time to get to the hide-site before daylight. He asked Snuffy to do a map recon and pick some alternate sites en route—just in case we had to put down somewhere. Pacing, he said, "I wish to hell they'd get here. Come on. Let's go!"

I walked off to be by myself and to collect my thoughts. The stars above were very distinct. This load I was carrying was getting heavier. What would General Bob and General Shy do? Follow the plan and do what's right. I had learned a long time ago from Boppy Edwards a small truism: to make a simple plan, inform everyone involved with it, don't change it, and kick it in the ass. At this point I made up my mind! No matter when the choppers arrived—and no matter when we arrived at the hide-site—we would go ahead.

It was obvious now that Delta would land at the hideout after first light, not before. But that was only half of it. There was the matter of the four DOD agents who were waiting for us outside of Teheran—two at the hide-site, two in the warehouse. How would they react when we didn't show up on time? How long would they wait? We had good communication with the hide-site. They were informed that the helos were late. But even so, they could wait only so long. There was nothing anyone could do. First light in Teheran was going to be 5:30 A.M.

"Damn, damn, damn. Where are they?"

Thirty minutes went by. Then five more.

Jim Kyle was in contact with General Vaught during this entire time. Finally, a message relayed via Wadi Kena arrived, "The choppers are ten minutes away!" Buckshot smiled at me.

You could hear it before you could see it, that peculiar whop whop sound the rotors make. I went out to meet it as soon as it touched down. I expected to see Colonel Seiffert, the Marines' CO. The pilot wore his helmet and goggles. I walked around the chopper with him, because the first thing he wanted to do was relieve himself. Only after he took off his helmet did I realize I was speaking to Maj. James Schaefer. This officer had made an impression on Delta, especially the men who knew helicopters. He was one of the original pilots. Delta felt Jim Schaefer really had his act together. While he took his piss, I said, "Are we glad to see you! How you doing?" He looked at me. He said, "It's been a hell of a trip." Then he spoke further, words to the effect that if we had any sense we would move the helos out into the desert and load everyone on the C-130s and go home. I slapped him on the back to assure him. I didn't understand how tough a time he'd really had; and he didn't elaborate on his statement. He was all business. Then, he went back up into the RH-53D's cockpit and moved his helo (designated Number 3) behind the northernmost fuel-bird and began refueling.

Shortly after Schaefer arrived, maybe ten minutes later, the second helo came in. Oddly, it came in from a different direction. The third arrived from still another direction. So, too, did the fourth. The fifth and sixth came in together and also from another direction. No two came through the same hole in the sky. Spread out, an hour to an hour and a half late, and coming from different directions.

The seventh and eighth helos never arrived at all. Obviously, something had happened. There was now no room for any error. Already we'd lost our two backup choppers.

When the second chopper had landed, I walked over to it. The pilot, Captain Paul (pseudonym), stood out in front. He was as well liked as Schaefer, a hell of a good man. The Delta operators liked to fly with both of them. Now, on the ground, he began to walk away from his chopper. He spoke a lot, he was talking fast, and he was saying some pretty strong things. Buckshot, Major Snuffy, and Major Fitch were with me, listening.

"I don't know who's really running things at my level, but I'll tell you this much, that some very careful consideration ought to be given to calling off this operation. You have no idea what I've been through. The damnedest sandstorm I've ever seen hit us. It was tough! I gotta tell you, I'm not sure we're going to make it. I'm really not sure we can make it."

I thought back to Schaefer. He hadn't said much, but he too seemed in bad shape. This shocked me. I comprehended what I heard, but the possible consequences of what I heard were drastic. Here were two very strong officers whom we'd observed and knew, who now were pretty well shattered.

Major Snuffy, the man who had read Samuel in the hangar at Wadi Kena, said, "Holy mackerel, you know, this guy—Gol' darn, it doesn't look good."

But we felt there was nothing to be done about it. Now, with six helos on the ground, Kyle was very busy handling the refueling traffic. Schaefer's (#3) and Paul's (#4) helicopters were positioned behind the fuel-bird farthest north of the road. Seiffert (#1) helicopter and another one (#8) were behind the EC-130 nearest the road, and the other two (#2 and #7) were refueling from the 130 south of the road.

Delta began, as the choppers arrived one by one, to line up behind them in helicopter loads. Everyone knew the drill; take your equipment, get in line, wait for orders to board.

Ninety minutes late, Ed Seiffert, the skipper of the helo unit, had been the last to land. I went up to him at once. He was late. I was frustrated. I was thinking, "We'll land at the hideout no earlier than dawn, maybe later, in full daylight. Delta needs to on-load and we need to get the hell out of Desert One. The longer the refueling takes the more daylight I'm going to be confronted with at the other end. I want to load and go."

I jumped aboard Seiffert's helo as soon as he had repositioned it for refueling. Seiffert and his pilot were talking to the other helos when I sat down on the jump seat near them. Seiffert was on my right. The rotor blades overhead made a racket. I hollered, "Glad you're here. Request permission to load, Skipper. We need to get on with it." He was too busy checking with his pilots to pay me any mind. Time continued to tick away. I waited as long as I could before shouting in his ear, "Hey, remember me! What do you think? When can I load?" He continued to ignore me. I was getting very anxious, not to say pissed. I'd been sitting now four or five minutes. To get his attention I rapped his helmet with my palm. I got it.

He took off his helmet, leaned over in his seat and shouted so I could hear him. "I can't guarantee we'll get you to the next site before first light."

"I don't care."

"There's no guarantee, Colonel, we'll get you there during darkness."

"I know that."

"O.K. You've got permission to load."

Finally! I jumped off and grabbed hold of the Delta officers, "Let's get cracking and load."

Twelve helo rotors whirred and sixteen C-130 engines roared. The sound was nearly deafening. To communicate it was necessary to put your face right up to the other person's and yell—or use hand and arm signals.

The helos, as they changed the pitch of their blades while they repositioned behind the fuel-birds, created whirlpools of wind. Through blowing sand and dust, Delta started to move forward.

The first unit, in two files, lugging its equipment, began to climb aboard their assigned helo. It was Seiffert's. I ran to the second helo, maybe twenty-five yards away. Over half of that unit was already on board. Two other choppers, the ones south of the road, were another 200 yards away.

The noise was numbing.

I walked very fast. As I crossed over the road, through the swirling dust I saw that the Delta units assigned to these choppers were already in the process of boarding.

About the time I arrived, one of the pilots climbed out of his cockpit and walked over to me. He said, "The skipper told me to tell you we only have five flyable helicopters! That's what the skipper told me to tell you."

"Jesus Christ Almighty!" Did these pilots want to go, really want to go?

I immediately began looking for Jim Kyle. He wasn't far away. "Hell, Jim, we only got five flyable helicopters. Go talk to Seiffert. I've already got his permission to load. You understand this bloody air lingo. Go talk to him. Let's get cracking. I'm losing valuable time."

Jim and I took off. Kyle was all business as he climbed aboard Seiffert's helicopter. I waited outside in the noise and wind trying to control my impatience. I suspected Ed Seiffert was in no mood to talk to me.

Eight to ten minutes went by. The operation was now over ninety minutes behind schedule, yet I was hoping against hope that Kyle would come off and say, "Climb on board. Good luck, you're on your way. I'll see ya, and God bless." Instead, he said, "Charlie, there's only five flyable helicopters. Let's go to the radio. Helicopter Number Two has hydraulic problems and Seiffert feels it's unsafe to go with it."

I was totally pissed. "This is a hell of a state of affairs. Those goddamn pilots know we can't go forward with five helicopters. Jim, I can't go forward with five. We gotta go back."

Kyle and I talked for a few minutes and reviewed the plan. "How in the hell am I going to lighten the loads? These helicopters can only carry so much weight. To get to the hide-site I need to lighten their loads. This means I gotta leave behind eighteen to twenty men. Everyone's doing two jobs as it is, some of them three."

At the radio, Kyle called General Vaught and explained the situation. General Vaught came back, "Ask Eagle"—my call sign—"to consider going on with five." This made me even angrier. I flashed back to the meeting, the one of January 4th, when Pittman and I had recommended we not go on with fewer than six. General Vaught had accepted that recommendation. No more questions remained. It was final! I can't even remember, now that I have the time to wrestle with this, anyone saying during the JCS brief, that if we went to five helos we'd abort. But General Vaught knew this. So did General Gast and Colonel Kyle and Colonel Pittman. At the Stockade in early January, it was inserted into the plan. The pilots knew we couldn't go with fewer than six. Everyone in Delta knew.

"Ask Eagle to consider going with five." I lost respect right then for General Vaught. Damn, I thought, how in the hell can the boss ask me that! He should know it will be a disaster if we go forward with five. There isn't any way. I'd have to leave behind twenty men. In a tight mission no one is expendable *before you begin!* Which twenty would I leave?

With five helicopters, Delta, minus twenty men, lands at the hide-site in daylight and then the helos fly to their location in the mountains, but hell, we all knew the eccentricities of choppers. There was a good chance that two of them would not crank tomorrow. That would leave three helos to pick up fifty-three hostages, Delta, the DOD agents, and the assault team and their three hostages freed from the Foreign Ministry Building. What if one of them got hit with small arms fire as it comes in? That would leave two. Two for 178 people. It was just too close.

But! But! If I go with five, which men do I leave behind? I can pull the drivers. But they're the only ones who speak Farsi. Beckwith, you're crazy. This is ludicrous. It doesn't make sense. Stay with the plan.

Kyle asked me again, "What do you think?" "Ain't no way, Jim. No way! You tell me which one of those 130s you want me to load up. Delta's going home."

"Don't worry about that, Charlie. Scatter them out and load on any of the aircraft."

Whether Jim agreed or disagreed with me I never knew. He didn't say. He's that kind of an officer. My message was passed on to General Vaught. Kyle then called Ed Seiffert over to us. The other helo pilots stood around us in a circle. "What's your recommendation," Kyle asked, "about these helicopters?" I said, "I hope to hell we don't leave them here." There was a short discussion. Seiffert said, "We need to turn them around and take them back to the carrier." This was agreed on.

Before Major Schaefer could return to *Nimitz*, he needed to top off his tanks. He'd been the first to refuel and had sat on the ground the longest, his engines idling, while he waited for the rest of the squadron to arrive. Receiving permission, Schaefer, who had repositioned his chopper to begin loading Delta, ran off to move back up behind the fuelbird.

"Let's break it down. Get everyone off the choppers. We're going home as soon as we can clean this place up." Delta began loading onto the C-130s. Major Fitch's element, the forty guys of the Blue Element, began loading on the EC-130 farthest north of the road—the one which was going to refuel Schaefer.

All the aircraft would leave on Colonel Kyle's orders. Nothing would leave on mine.

I went from one C-130 to another, working out in my mind the number of men who had to be put on board each one. I also wanted to make sure none of the C-130 pilots took off on their own. "Hey, don't leave here on your own initiative. We gotta get Delta on board."

I grabbed one pilot by the arm and shouted over the noise of his engines, "For God's sake, don't leave." He leaned toward me, "Ain't nobody going to leave here, Colonel, until we got everybody." I wanted to hug him! I hadn't had time to sit or to cry. There was too much to do just drying up Desert One.

I turned around and began to walk quickly toward the head of the line. It was nearly 2:40 A.M. Some of the C-130 pilots had started to gun their engines. Dust was blowing all around. Between wind gusts, I saw one of the choppers lift off and bank to the left. It slid slightly backward. Then, BAL-LLOOEE! It wasn't a bomb, not a CRACK! It was a THUMP! A gasoline explosion. A blue fireball ballooned into the night. Obviously, the chopper I'd just seen lift off—it had been Major Schaefer's—had struck the northernmost EC-130, the one on which Blue Element had just boarded.

I broke into a run, but got no farther than the road. The heat was too intense to get closer. The helicopter closest to the conflagration was about to cook off itself. Its .50-caliber ammunition would go off any minute. The flames were reaching 300 to 400 feet in the sky. It turned as bright as day. Because of the intense heat, I was afraid the aircraft closest to the inferno might also catch fire and explode.

Kyle! I looked around and saw him busy on the radio. He didn't need me in his knickers.

I thought of the Blue Element and Major Fitch. In the flames I saw where the chopper had hit the aircraft's port side. Redeye missiles were going off now, pinwheeling through the night like it was the Fourth of July. It looked like there were people moving through the fireball. The first few men from Blue Element whom I came upon couldn't tell me for sure that everyone had gotten off.

In the distance, the tanker truck continued to burn. The bus stood where it had been stopped. Nearby, next to the road, the passengers remained hunkered together. Silhouetted against the flames, the five helicopters sat on the desert crust.

Major Fitch ran up to Buckshot and reported everyone from Blue Element had escaped, but that one of his operators, in going back to pull out an aircraft crew member, had badly burned his arms. Buckshot told me Fitch, considering what he'd been through, seemed rather calm.

Kyle was still on the radio when I walked over to him. "How about it?"

He said, "I gotta get security in. Soon as I get them, we're going to get out. What do you think about these choppers now?"

"It's a hot sonovabitch out there," I said. "The second one could go any minute."

"What about the others?"

"They need to be destroyed."

One of us said, and to this day I don't remember who, "Let's get an air strike in on them." Jim got General Vaught on the radio and recommended he be given authority to bring in the air strike.

There was a lot of movement on the ground. I wanted everyone out of the desert as soon as possible.

I walked back to the last 130 in line. Buckshot had just jumped off and was going down to help get the Road Watch Team back.

Some of the planes had begun to taxi to their takeoff positions.

Off to the side I watched the Marine pilots running as hard as they could for our aircraft. Once on board, the ramp was drawn up and slammed closed.

I climbed up into the cockpit and our aircraft began to move. It taxied in a half circle. We were then third in line to take off. The two in front lifted off.

The fuel truck had nearly burned itself out, but the chopper and 130 were still burning violently.

It was almost 3:00 A.M.

After being on the ground for four hours and fifty-six minutes, Delta was leaving Desert One.

Down the unimproved road we rolled. The big 130 began to pick up speed. Suddenly, we hit an embankment. I remember having seen it on the ground; it must have been three feet high. We were moving fast by then and the nose of that C-130 jerked almost straight up. Then it dropped hard. "We've just bought the farm!" If there's such a thing as luck . . . The plane bounced on the ground. The pilot gave it more power and somehow managed to get it back into the air. Next thing I knew, we were gaining altitude.

Had we been able to keep to the plan at Desert One, the six fully loaded helicopters would now be nearing the hide-site.

As it was, we hit the Gulf of Oman sometime after first light. I looked down and saw a small dhow sailing on the slate-blue sea.

★ FORTY-FOUR ★

IT WAS GOING to be another crystal clear, hot day. You could see the Oman coast across the channel, floating above the heat. At least three times on Misery I was asked by General Gast to account for all the ground element personnel. No one from this group was missing. However, five airmen and three Marines were unaccounted for and presumed dead. Major Schaefer had been lucky. He was still alive, but badly burned. I watched while he was loaded onto a Medevac C-141. He and the other badly burned survivors of the crash were met in Egypt by a C-9 that carried a special burn unit.

All the way back to Masirah, I had felt lifeless. Oh, shit. I felt let down. And I cried. That's when I really sat down and said, Jesus Christ, you know, what a fucking mess. We've just embarrassed our great country. I was at a low ebb. I didn't want to talk. I didn't want to do nothing. And shot through all these emotions was the fact that I was highly pissed.

When we landed, the Marine helicopter pilots and crews went over a little way and stood in a group. Some of them wore that thousand-mile stare. A lot of people in Delta were angry, upset.

I said, "Don't say anything to those pilots. Leave them alone. Don't do or say anything!" I also thought of the DOD agents in Teheran. Kyle had been using the radio and there was lots of traffic to handle. Getting off the ground took priority. There was no time to contact the hide-site and tell them we wouldn't be coming. They were on their own now. (I learned later the hide-site had been contacted by the commu nication center at Wadi Kena and informed of the decision no to go forward.)

Everyone but the wounded, who left separately, loaded ont a C-141 StarLifter and was flown out of Misery as quickly a possible.

It was over. It had been a failure. I sat dazed. After all tha time and work and sweat, to come away empty. I began t realize what that failure would mean. Our country would b embarrassed. We'd lost eight good and brave men. And now what would become of the hostages? God Almighty, after al the effort, here we sat, going back to Egypt—all because c those bloody helos.

General Vaught met us as we touched down in Egypt. In little private room in his command trailer, he asked me wha I thought. He had retained his composure but he was ver tired. I walked him right through all of it. I repeated why si helos were essential to our success and I had the feeling h accepted my explanation. Whether he did or not I didn't giv a shit, because that was the way it was. I didn't think I ha to justify anything. The plan was followed to the letter, an we did precisely what I knew was right. It was right on Jan uary 4th; and it was right on the morning of April 25th. I ha no second thoughts about the decision to abort at that time. have none now.

All the troops had arrived in Egypt. They returned to th same hangar where, a lifetime ago, but not more than thirt hours before, they'd sung "God Bless America" and had hear the story of the boy David and the giant Goliath. There the had left their personal belongings and now were retrievin them. It was there that I vented some of my frustration. I getting out of the burning C-130, Blue Element had left with out their equipment, which had been stored in the aircraf Some of the men had taken their weapons, but most hadn't. ripped into them. It was unfair, I realize, yet I told them, "Yo guys, as you came off, should have reached up and grabbe something. Goddamn, a lot of money burned up in there." Th men didn't appreciate this. "We were lucky to get off with ou asses," I said, "Well some of you picked up your weapons. Why in the hell didn't all of you?" I was wrong. You know, by then I was angrily frustrated and had to let it spill out.

One of the officers who was going to be a driver paid no attention to me, and I really snapped into his ass. "If we ever do this damn thing again, I'll make sure people like you don't come along!"

In the desert I had never called anyone a coward. In Egypt it was a different matter. One of the Delta guys asked, "Are we going to go back again?" I replied, "I sure as hell hope so, but we're not going to go back with those people," and I gestured toward the group of drivers. The thirteen men who were to have taken down the Foreign Ministry Building felt I was talking about them. I apologized for the misunderstanding and told them I had been referring to the other crowd—the drivers. I don't remember using the word "coward," but I gotta tell you, I was emotional. At this time, I may have also called the helo pilots cowards. Some people say I did. I really didn't care. I carried a great deal of stress from the time we left Egypt for Iran until we returned. That's what I got paid to do. And I'm not a perfect person.

One thing I was sure of. My mind had been made up. I was not going to be a party to a second attempt if General Vaught was the Task Force Commander. What he had asked me in the desert was to me unforgivable.

The story of what had happened to the two Sea Stallions that never reached Desert One soon came to light. The first to abort was chopper Number Six. Just two hours into the mission, this helicopter received an indication that one of its main rotor blades was about to malfunction. It landed at once. Another helicopter (Number Eight) landed with it. When it was determined that Number Six could not proceed farther, its crew climbed aboard the other chopper, which then proceeded to Desert One.

Helicopter Number Five, the one in which Colonel Pittman was flying, turned back to the carrier four-fifths of the way to Desert One, when, after flying through several cyclonic sandstorms, it began experiencing instrument problems.

In Egypt we found the air strike had not been sent in to destroy the five Sea Stallions that had been left behind. General Vaught had gone up the chain to General Jones with the request. I understand the White House decided against it for fear the strike would endanger the lives of the bus passengers. Delta had brought along incendiary explosive devices that were going to be placed properly on the helos at the hide-site and be used if any one of them failed to crank the next night. The crew chief could have been briefed. All he would have had to do was pull the pin and there would have been no flyable helicopters left for the Iranians to find. But at Desert One the charges were still with Fast Eddie, and when everyone scattered to load on the C-130s, I didn't know where he was. Time ran out. Unfortunately, I did not have in my hands an M16 loaded with tracers. If I had, I would have set those damned machines afire.

On the StarLifter, which was returning Delta to the United States, I asked one of Blue Element's troop sergeants, Allen, to have a talk with me. He'd been furious for what I'd said to the men about leaving their gear behind in the burning aircraft. We found a little privacy in the back of the cockpit. "I want to apologize to you and to the men. Please pass this word to everyone. I realize now how lucky you were to just get out alive. I should have thought before I spoke. It's a lick on me."

★ FORTY-FIVE ★

GENERAL VAUGHT AND I hadn't slept for a long time. We didn't sleep any on the flight back across Europe to Washington. In the plane, we discussed over and over what had happened and what we thought would happen. I learned then that the choppers, when they had been put on *Nimitz*, were not accompanied by any of our own maintenance people. It was like having your neighbor knock on the door and ask you to take care of his dog while he's gone, but then not giving you any dog food. The carrier provided their own maintenance to the Sea Stallions. These mechanics and their officers had no idea what the choppers were going to be used for. Who knows how they were handled? I know that two of them never got to Desert One. In Vietnam, the people in the high-risk, special ops business who relied on choppers learned they had to put their own mechanics to work on the helos. A helicopter needs tender loving care. In special ops when a chopper doesn't crank, it's usually a matter of life and death. In the regular Army or Navy it isn't. That's a big difference.

I learned that the pilot who had been killed on the 130 was Richard Bakke. At Hurlburt, during the Air Force's training phase, Bakke had seemed to be the pilot who always led the way in dirt landings and takeoffs, and low-level flying. Getting in and out of Iran was one fine piece of airmanship. Those Air Force pilots did a hell of a job, and there was none of them better than Rick Bakke.

We landed at Langley Air Force Base in Virginia and were

greeted by General Otis. He was professional and, of course, very sympathetic. General Vaught went off with him to the Pentagon. I suspected General Vaught wouldn't get to sleep for several more hours.

As Blue Element was transloading from the StarLifter to a C-130 for the return to Camp Smokey, the aircraft crew chief, who hadn't a clue who these men were, delivered a verbose, professional emergency-proceedings briefing, which covered how to exit a 130 if it should catch on fire. When he was through, the guys, many of them with singed hair and still smelling of smoke, gave him a standing ovation.

Delta and I flew back to Camp Smokey early Sunday morning and, once the men were settled, I, too, found my cot and fell asleep at once.

At 1100 hours, Sunday morning, April 27, I got a phone call from the JCS, on secure, stating the President would arrive our location that afternoon and that more details would follow.

General Vaught and General Jones arrived around noon and they had lunch with us. The Marine pilots, the drivers, and their Farsi-speaking translators were also there.

Although it hadn't rained, the day was cool and cloudy. Because Camp Smokey was nearly socked in, the presidential helicopter came in very low.

President Carter was accompanied by Dr. Brzezinski, Dr. Brown, and two secret service agents.

When the President came over to me, I apologized for the mission's failure. Walking over to the hangar where the men had assembled, he put his arm around me.

General Vaught climbed up on a platform and gave a short Knute Rockne speech. The troops were lined up in military formation, but wore civilian clothes. When he was finished, General Vaught introduced President Carter.

He spoke softly and sincerely.

No matter what happened, he appreciated what these men had done for their country. Then he expressed his concern for the hostages, who, you could see, still commanded his full attention. We needed to continue, he stated, to help him find a way to get them released.

After this short message, he told me he wanted to meet and speak to each person individually. The President then walked through the formation, shaking each man's hand. He spoke to most for a minute and to some, longer.

Dr. Brzezinski followed behind the President, also shaking hands and murmuring greetings. Although he wore a sport coat, he also wore a pair of what looked like ski boots. Boris had spotted them, and when Dr. Brzezinski appeared before him, he said, in perfect Polish, "I like your shoes, sir." This surprised Dr. Brzezinski. He and Boris then carried on, in Polish, a conversation that must have lasted several minutes.

Before he returned to his helicopter, the President told me in his gentle voice, "I have been remiss in not knowing more about Delta Force. I am very impressed with what I've learned about them and what I've seen today. I didn't know we still had people like this, people who would sacrifice everything for their country. Colonel Beckwith, I am very proud of these men."

★ FORTY-SIX ★

THE NEXT MORNING was gray and cool. A morning that again promised rain. General Vaught was calling to tell me he had heard rumors that I intended to come to Washington on Tuesday to denounce the raid to the press. This was completely untrue. Hell, all I'd done after the President left was get a little rest and work on the After-Action Report. I told the general I'd spoken to no one and had no intention to do so. Why in blazes would I want to go up there and criticize the mission? It didn't make any sense.

The clouds lifted later in the day and the sky brightened. Later still, in the early evening, it must now have been around 1900, the secure telephone rang. Buckshot answered it. He came into my office. "Boss, the Secretary of Defense wants to talk to you." I thought he was trying to play games with me to buck up my spirits. "Aw, don't bullshit me." "No, Boss, it really is."

After three or four minutes of this I picked up the phone and found it wasn't Dr. Brown, but that, indeed, someone from his office was calling. I was to come to Washington the next day and go before the press. I replied. "I'm not going up there and do any press conference. I'm just not going to do it."

"We're not going to discuss it," he said. "There'll be an aircraft at your location to pick you up in the morning. When you arrive, you are to report immediately to the Office of the Chairman of the Joint Chiefs of Staff."

In my living quarters, I tried to sort all this out. I felt that if they were pushing me before the press they were looking for a fall guy, a victim. No one knew too much about Delta. Yes, there'd been a few odd articles that had leaked out but, by and large, our existence was a pretty well-kept secret. The average person in this country didn't know about Delta and maybe that's the way it should be left. I didn't sleep well that night.

I flew to Washington the next day and reported to General Jones. He told me I would be going before the national press that afternoon around 1400 hours. I begged him to change his mind, "Sir, you can't do this to me." He didn't get angry and he didn't sympathize with me. He never raised his voice, "It has been decided you will do this and you will." I finally asked his permission to go and see the Chief of Staff of the Army, General Meyer. I knew Moses would fix it.

I literally ran down the halls of the Pentagon to the Special Ops office of the JCS. These were the same halls where three years before I had walked looking for information and assistance I needed to organize Delta Force. Now I was again looking for help, but of a different type. I quickly explained to General Vaught what I'd been ordered to do. He became very angry and together we went over to see General Meyer. We asked permission to see the General and were immediately shown into his office. After he listened for a few minutes, General Meyer said, "You are not going before the press. I will get back to you around 1300 hours, but you are not going to talk to he press, Charlie." He knew nothing about this. It made no sense to him either.

Later, while I waited in General Vaught's office, I calmed down. "Hell, the Army's not going to let these political guys do this to me." There then appeared on the scene some Army public affairs officer. General Vaught said, "I know this officer, Charlie. Let him talk to you and tell you how to handle the press, just in case . . ."

This officer, a nice lieutenant colonel, sat with me for an hour outlining all the techniques I needed to get through a press conference. It went in one ear and out the other. His system was not Charlie Beckwith's. I'd talked to the press in

Vietnam several times, so that part wasn't bothering me. What kicked the wind out of me was losing my cover and having to answer questions about sensitive classified matters.

A little after 1300 hours, neither the Chief of Staff of the Army nor one of his representatives had gotten back to Charlie Beckwith. Instead a civilian from the Department of Defense Public Affairs Office, a Mr. Ross, stopped in to tell me I was expected at General Jones's office at 1330 hours. I wasn't angry any longer, just scared. "Somebody's trying to set me up."

General Jones told me, "Charlie, you can talk out there about anything that happened up to Desert One. But, don't talk about anything beyond that affair."

I said, "I'm prepared, if necessary, to lie about any CIA or other intelligence participation in the mission. It's no one's business. In my view, it could affect the national security."

Dr. Brown, who was listening in the background, spoke right up and really bit into my ass. "We don't lie about anything up here. If you get a question you believe is sensitive and will in your view affect this country's security, all you will say is, 'I can't answer that question and I suggest you ask my superiors about it.' " This impressed me. I felt I was dealing with honest brokers.

I was taken upstairs to a press briefing room. While I was being introduced I remembered what Buzz Miley had told me long ago: "After you're asked a question, before you open your mouth, think about it for forty-five seconds." I answered every question I could to the best of my ability. The reporters took me chronologically, more or less, through the events at Desert One. I believe I was questioned for thirty or forty minutes.

Q: Did you have some colorful words for those choppers for being late? Like—

A: Yes, sir. I did say to the helicopter commander, "We're late; we are going to make up some time. I want to load my packs and get cracking."

Q: Did you give them all hell for being late?

A: I usually give a lot of people hell, sir. My soldiers are on time and I expect all the other people to try and get on time, sir. I try to be punctual.

But you have to appreciate the ordeal these people had gone through. At that point, I myself didn't appreciate it. I had no idea—it wasn't until yesterday, in fact, that I realized—the ordeal the helicopter pilots had experienced.

Q: Colonel, at this point, I know the book said that you had to go; and you being the good soldier, you said abort. But didn't you feel at that time that you could have gone—as a soldier you could have gone on with five?

A: All due respect, sir, you don't know where you're coming from.

Q: O.K., please explain.

A: I have been there before. I was not about to be a party to half-assed loading on a bunch of aircraft and going up and murdering a bunch of the finest soldiers in the world. I ain't going to do that. I have been in the army twenty-seven years. I don't have to do that. I get paid for shouldering responsibility, and being a leader. I wanted to get the job done, but under those circumstances, it was a no-win situation.

Q: Could you tell us what went through your mind though? You had some sort of emotion at that point, didn't you?

A: The only things I had on my mind was we failed and I have got to get soldiers out of here.

Q: What did your soldiers say?

A: We didn't stop and talk, sir. We didn't have time, everybody was on the double, unloading helicopters, grabbing everything we could find and taking people up to start loading the 130s. Some of the people couldn't load on the 130s because refueling was going on with the helicopters. So we had to wait outside. At the same time the watch was ticking. I am getting worried about being caught somewhere in the desert of Iran at first light. I don't like that.

Q: Colonel, you mean the discipline was such that none of your men allowed themselves to express emotion—

A: Not at that time; they were too busy. When we got back

it was a different story. A lot of people were very unhappy. We were very disappointed.

Q: Sir, I wonder if you could give us your thoughts on, or your feelings about, having to leave the bodies and was there any effort at all to recover any of the bodies?

A: I had three years in Vietnam and I don't like to leave a body. But anyone who wastes additional human life, which is the most precious thing on the face of the earth, to go and get a body out, then I don't think that's very prudent when it's impossible.

Q: Why did the mission fail?

A: Sir, I don't know.

Q: Was it bad luck or—

A: That's all I can say, I don't know.

Q: Are you sort of reliving the whole thing at night?

A: Yes, ma'am. Hell, who wants to be part of something we worked so hard to do—only to have it end as it did?

Q: Colonel, you said you had never rehearsed aborting the mission?

A: With a 130 on fire and all that—no, we'd not done that, sir.

Q: Colonel, there are rumors that you are going to retire or resign in protest or something of that sort?

A: That's pure bullshit, sir.

Q: Have you testified before any committees today?

A: No, I haven't.

Q: You have not been on the Hill? Are you going today to the Hill?

A: Not to my knowledge. I'd like to go see my family.

Q: Have you not seen them yet?

A: No.

Immediately afterward I was taken downstairs to the Secretary of Defense's office, where I was turned over to a brigadier general who was wearing civilian clothes. We chatted for a short time. He said, "Do you know where we're off to now? No? Well, we're going over to the White House."

I said to myself, Now what? I was tired of explaining. I

vanted to be left alone. In the car on the way over, I thought hey were still looking for a patsy. They would have to come ıp with a very good scheme now, because the press conference ıad gone well.

Dr. Brown met me and accompanied me into the Oval Office. Dr. Brzezinski was with the President. There was a short ›ause. President Carter looked at me. "I have just read the vire service report about what you said to the press and I want o thank you for that. Colonel Beckwith, unfortunately, there vere some people who felt you and I were at an impasse over he wisdom of conducting this mission. I did not want to put 'ou in front of the press, but I really had no other alternative. appreciate what you did and now, welcome to the kitchen." told him I'd been blown out of the water. I was finished. He aid, "I'm sure, Colonel, you will be able to handle it." We hook hands and Dr. Brown and I turned and left.

Dr. Brzezinski caught up to us. "Colonel, I have something ›n my conscience. May I speak to you for a moment?" He ed the way to the Rose Garden. It reminded me of a little 'rench cafe. There were these little metal chairs with fancy iligree backs. "Colonel, I was with the President the whole ime he was monitoring the mission. When he received word here were five flyable helicopters and you recommended the nission be aborted, I almost asked the President to order you o continue. If I had, I feel, he would have done so. What vould have been the consequences if you'd been told to go orward?"

The answer was simple. First, I gave him the reasons behind ny recommendation, then I answered his question. "I wouldn't e here today to tell you about it. It would have been a disster."

Dr. Brzezinski said. "That's good enough for me."

It's the answer to a hypothetical question I asked myself vhile I was being driven over to the Army airfield at Fort Belvoir. It was an honest one. If General Vaught had ordered ne to leave Desert One for the hide-site with five helicopters, would have experienced audio transmission problems. "I can't read you, sir. Over. Say again. You're not coming in Over! Over!"

I joined the troops that evening. Slowly we began to get back into gear. At first everyone was somewhat short-tempered. There wasn't much conversation. The support people who'd been left behind at Fort Bragg were very sympathetic. Of course, they wanted to know what had happened. They didn't need to know. We wished they weren't there. Delta needed to be left alone.

★ FORTY-SEVEN ★

SOMEWHERE BETWEEN SENATOR Goldwater's compassionate and laudatory remarks and Senator Warner's persistent hammering of General Vaught, Senator Nunn asked me the question.

It was during a meeting of the Senate Armed Services Committee which, along with General Vaught, General Gast, Colonel Kyle, Lieutenant Colonel Seiffert, and other key personnel who had made up the JTF staff, I was asked to attend.

The senators conducted their business around a large, dark rectangular table. A passel of powerful legislators, among them Senators Stennis, Thurmond, Jackson, Goldwater, Nunn, and Hart, were there that day to ask the question—why?

When it became Senator Nunn's time, he turned toward me. "My first question will be directed at Colonel Beckwith. I'm not asking him because he is from my native state, but rather because he was the ground commander and because he happens to be on my right.

"You know that the people in this country are very concerned about what happened in Iran. We are not doing very well. The Son Tay raid was a dry hole. During the *Mayaguez* incident, fifteen of our people were killed. We are tired of rescue missions which fail. We need something to give us a lift. America needs a win.

"My question is in two parts. Colonel, what did you learn

from this mission and what can we do to preclude this kir of thing happening in the future?"

"Senator," I replied, "what did I learn from this operatio I learned that Murphy is alive and well. He's in every drawe under every rock and on top of every hill. Sir, we purely ha bad luck.

"I've known the answer to your second question since I wa a captain. What do we need to do in the future? Sir, let m answer you this way. . . . If Coach Bear Bryant at the Unive sity of Alabama put his quarterback in Virginia, his backfie in North Carolina, his offensive line in Georgia, and his de fense in Texas, and then got Delta Airlines to pick them u and fly them to Birmingham on game day, he wouldn't hav his winning record. Coach Bryant's teams, the best he ca recruit, practice together, live together, eat together, and pla together. He has a team.

"In Iran we had an ad hoc affair. We went out, found bi and pieces, people and equipment, brought them together oc casionally and then asked them to perform a highly comple mission. The parts all performed, but they didn't necessaril perform as a team. Nor did they have the same motivation.

"My recommendation is to put together an organizatio which contains everything it will ever need, an organizatio which would include Delta, the Rangers, Navy SEALS, A Force pilots, its own staff, its own support people, its ow aircraft and helicopters. Make this organization a permane military unit. Give it a place to call home. Allocate sufficie funds to run it. And give it sufficient time to recruit, asses and train its people. Otherwise, we are not serious about com bating terrorism."

Senator Nunn said, "Fine." Then he asked General Gast question and the hearings moved on.

That evening I returned to Bragg and continued to pick u the pieces of my life. A routine superimposed itself on Delt Wounds closed and healed and the world began to turn mor slowly. I became interested in things I hadn't thought abo for several months—my younger daughter's grades, how th car was running, whether Katherine needed a new coat, wh ind of football team the Georgia Bulldogs would have that all.

Some of the humorous incidents that occurred at Desert One egan to make the rounds. For example, after the bus had been topped and its passengers had been searched and gathered ogether, one of the guards left to watch them was a Ranger vho was a black man. An Iranian who spoke broken English sked him who we were. Our soldier had replied. "We're Afican commandos." The guys thought that was pretty funny.

Another of the operators received a real surprise. When he ad debarked from the C-130, he went to what he thought was is assembly position. In the dark he walked to a group of eople huddled by the road and asked, "Is this helo load numer six?" When no one answered, he looked real hard and saw e was talking to the Iranian bus passengers.

But his surprise was nothing compared to that of the Blue Element operator who had dozed off on the C-130 just before he helicopter crashed into it. At the explosion, he had awakned and joined the line of guys exiting the plane through one f the hatches. There was smoke and fire. The engines were till running and the aircraft was shaking violently as the chopper continued to cut into it. The operator evidently thought hat while he was dozing the 130 had taken off and was now irborne. When it was his turn to leave he automatically asumed a freefall parachute position and jumped. He landed pread-eagled on the ground. Afterward his mates asked, aving jumped, what he was going to do next without a parachute? "I don't know," he answered. "I was just taking one hing at a time."

Most of the nightmares take place in the embassy compound.

The first one I had took place at Desert One. Delta loaded onto the helicopters and took off and no one ever heard from hem again.

They're usually crazy things and they never repeat themelves.

Another dream has to do with the wall. We've climbed over

it and Fast Eddie has detonated his explosives. Glass is sha
tering everywhere. Katherine said I woke up shouting.

These dreams triggered nightmares I used to have after Vie
nam. The old ones returned. Plei Me. I've dreamed Plei M
many a time. I've seen John Pioletti throwing up as he's loa
ing the body bags into the helicopter—dreamed that at lea
fifteen times.

I've also seen Captain Pusser's body as it looked when
was brought through the wire after it had lain in the sun f
several days—swollen, brown, unrecognizable. I think I wa
reminded of it by the photographs I saw in the newspaper
a crew member who had burned to death on the C-130.

After a heavy conversation, maybe with Buckshot, a
we've talked for three or four hours about Desert One, the
that night I'll have a nightmare or a dream.

I've awakened as the hostages are being removed from
building I've never seen before and as one of the helicopte
is crashing in the stadium.

In some dreams I awaken before Delta ever gets to Ma
zariyeh. In none have I ever dreamed whether the missio
would have been successful or not.

In the weeks following my return from Iran, I spent man
solitary hours examining and reexamining the lessons we ha
learned from the effort put forth to rescue the hostages. If w
could find in the mission basic principles on which future mi
sions could be based, then everything that had happened mig
not be wasted. It was possible, if we were smart, to come o
of Desert One stronger than when we went in. I had appeare
before the Congress on three separate occasions and ca
away hopeful that both the legislative and executive branche
of government were willing to act on what had been learne
The question was just how far they—and for that matter th
Defense Department and the Joint Chiefs of Staff—would b
willing to go.

Would a system be devised that fairly and accurately re
cruited, assessed, and trained the necessary personnel to mak
up a permanent joint organization tailored to perform the task

Delta had recently undertaken? Or would the JCS get hung up on a force that for public relations and other reasons consisted of all the services?

Had our government truly learned the importance of strong intelligence agencies and the need for stay-behind agents? Could it be expected that we'd raise the priority of information collected by the Department of State and the CIA regarding terrorists and their activities?

The command and control mechanism that the mission used had proved to be viable and responsive. During the time at Desert One, it had been able to act rapidly. Future administrations could use it as a model.

Have the bureaucrats in DOD and other governmental agencies by now learned to accept help from our free world allies? Would we again reject vitally needed assistance from the British and West Germans—as we had during the Iranian crisis? I wondered.

Basing rights around the world for Delta had been a problem since day one. Maybe now State or DOD will have staging sites in hand. Next time speed might be critical. There may not be time for diplomatic negotiations.

Early on in the planning of the mission I was embarrassed to learn that Delta could not coordinate with our State Department those contact points we had taken a lot of time and effort to establish. Because of State's notorious reputation for not being able to keep a secret, DOD ordered Delta not to talk to State. Somehow this problem with the State Department must be overcome. In the future, every appropriate agency in our government must be used.

I recall staff officers in the JCS, on the JTF, and in one instance on my own staff, who became obsessed with the rescue plans. It's very easy to be swept up in something and then to lose sight of everything else. This is a mistake. Clear thinking and sound decisions are the result of balance and perspective.

Delta was ready to undertake the mission in mid-January when the weather favored us. Political considerations delayed it until mid April. National resolve is weakened by many forces. The longer the crisis is allowed to run, the more suc forces come into play. The longer a government waits to re spond to a terrorist incident, the harder is the rescue by mili tary means.

It's important to be able to predict a terrorist incident befor it occurs. People in government, I remember, laughed whe the subject of predictive intelligence first surfaced. If the ter rorists can be cut off at the pass, it might not be necessary t circle the wagons.

Since the decision to respond to terrorist acts is a politica one, it is critical the President of the United States have first hand knowledge of the existing military capabilities for deal ing with terrorism. President Carter's first visit to Delt occurred the Sunday following the return from Desert One.

The lack of psychological operations applied skillfull against the Iranian government removed a valuable weapo from our arsenal. The purpose of psychological operations i to maneuver and manipulate the enemy in the most subtl ways. We didn't use them in Iran and we didn't use them wel in Vietnam—yet our adversaries are very successful in usin them against us.

I lost many hours of sleep on the most imponderable of al the lessons I had learned—how to harness up Murphy. With out luck playing its role, Murphy will surely surface.

Finally, I wondered if the system would draw upon the ex perience I had gained and use me again.

I hadn't seen General Meyer from the time I'd gone to hin in the Pentagon about appearing before the press until he vis ited Delta at Fort Bragg in mid-May.

I went out to Simmons Army Airfield to pick him up, an on the way back he said to me. "Oh, by the way, Charlie, yo know the work you did for me about forming a joint militar organization to combat terrorism, I'd like to see it again."

I couldn't remember anything formal like a written brie but it was something we'd talked a lot about.

At the Stockade, he met and talked to the troops and thei wives. He was particularly generous in his praise for th women. He appreciated the support they'd given to their men and to Delta and to their country. The women understood.

After General Meyer mingled with the families for a while, he and I went into my office and spoke of the future.

He was going to move me out of Delta. I'd had the command longer than was usual. He also felt I might be more valuable to the Army in the United States and not with Special Operations Task Force Europe. Katherine, I felt, would be particularly pleased with this news. We talked some more about a new joint unit and I was very pleased to know he wanted me to help form some of the basic principles that would lay at its foundation.

In the staff car driving back to Simmons, General Meyer said, "Charlie, I'd like you in Washington tomorrow at noon. I want to see then what this new joint organization should look like."

After our ad hoc effort into Iran, I'd done a lot of soul-searching and was convinced that a permanent joint task force was vital if our government was going to continue to be serious about combating terrorism.

As I returned to the Stockade, I recalled the recent discussion I had had with General Sam Wilson when we designed on the blackboard in my office a tier-type organization, which would fall under the Joint Chiefs of Staff. Our proposed organization consisted of Army, Navy, and Air Force elements that would train and act together in the event of another crisis.

The rest of that day and through the night Buckshot, Logan Fitch, Country, and I worked on the proposal, completed the necessary charts, and collected the supporting documentation.

General Meyer looked over the proposal the next noon. He made one structural change then took the chart, which showed the entire proposed organization for a Joint Special Operations Command, and left the room.

I don't know where he went, but ten minutes later, when he returned, he was smiling. "Now, go back to Bragg, Charlie. Start putting some meat on the bones."

★ EPILOGUE ★

by C. A. Mobley

"No Comment"

Delta Force doesn't exist.[1]

It is not based out of Fort Bragg. It never ferreted out an destroyed secret SCUD missile sites in Iraq, nor did it hel plan security for the Atlanta Olympics. General Noriega wa never a Delta Force target, and regular Army forces rescue Kurt Muse from his Panamanian jail cell. Delta Force heli copters never orbit over American cities while operators prac tice their trades on abandoned buildings.

At least not officially. The Department of Defense will nc comment on Delta Force, but will admit that within the De partment of Defense there are special mission units that ar trained, equipped, and targeted to respond to a number of sce narios, including acts of terrorism and events involving weap ons of mass destruction. That's their story and they're stickin to it.

But if Delta Force *did* officially exist, you'd recognize it a the organization Colonel Beckwith created. Just look for th most potent stand-alone special forces unit, one made up o superb soldiers honed to a killing edge by grueling trainin and esprit de corps equipped with the latest in high-capacit weapons, frequency-hopping communications, and lethal tech nology. You won't see them coming, because Delta Force op erates with dedicated stealth air assets skilled at inserting an extracting teams without attracting attention. You won't knov where they are. Surprise is a primary tactical advantage, and Delta Force operations remain shrouded in secrecy to avoid disclosing operational capabilities to the wrong people. But whenever you see a hostage extraction that seems to take place overnight with no planning and no publicity, you'll know Delta Force has been there.

Like most military units, Delta Force is evolving. Building a military force is like stocking a toolbox.[2] Sometimes you need a sledgehammer, the sheer raw power of divisions supported by mechanized infantry, mortars, and tanks. For other missions, only an ice pick will do.

If he were here today, Colonel Beckwith would probably be planning the *next* Delta Force. It would be an ice-pick force, one that borrowed heavily not only from existing special forces but from civilian organizations as well. Colonel Beckwith would insist that it remain as shrouded in secrecy as his present-day Delta Force is, although he'd certainly understand and use the deterrence potential of publicity to attempt to prevent violence (and as a tool to ensure funding). He would make use of every new technological toy that he could get his hands on, and he would take his team on a wider range of missions. One chain of command would encompass not only field operators but intelligence, logistics, air support, and transportation as well. Delta Force analysts would coordinate and evaluate products from outside Army, military, and civilian agencies.

But why would the next Delta Force look like that?

Military organizations tend to be reactive, and they take mistakes seriously. The price of a lesson learned is counted in bodies rather than dollars. Analyzing an organization's past provides valuable clues about where it's headed.

Although everything about its composition, chain of command, and operations is classified, Delta Force probably executed the missions listed below. Let's look at those, see how they went, then speculate on how Delta Force has incorporated those lessons into its structure.

First, a caveat. Information is classified for good reasons and divulging it unnecessarily will get people killed. For that reason, I am relying solely on open-source unclassified material and information already published in the press. Bear in mind that the operations you're most likely to hear about are the ones where something went wrong, and there are probably many other operations that we'll never hear about. With that in mind, let's look at Delta Force's past in order to project what the next generation Delta Force might look like.

Operations

Missions: Hostage rescue is the meat and potatoes, Delta Force's *raison d'être,* beginning with the unit's first major operation, rescuing American hostages in Iran in 1980 and continuing on to the present day. The unit is particularly adept at extracting hostages from aircraft, and probably maintains close ties with major structural and component manufacturers both in the United States and overseas in order to keep its databases current. Strong working relationships with both area experts and translators drawn from all parts of the U.S. government are probably in place, although Delta Force's preference would be to use its own unit assets whenever possible. Under current budget restrictions, however, Delta Force probably makes it a point to train regularly with analysts and linguistics experts associated with predictable trouble spots, perhaps even providing them with quasi-military training enabling any civilian to at least nominally pass inspection as a member of the military. Publicized missions indicate that international politics is one of the major problems Delta Force faces. According to publicized accounts, the Algerian government refused to allow the forward-deployed Delta Force to participate in TWA flight 847 rescue operations, as did the Italian government in the rescue of Gen. James Dozier. Given Delta Force's expertise in airline hostage scenarios, it is probable that the unit has developed additional cover stories, public affairs relationships and media affiliations that allow it to operate under cover of other governments' forces. Most certainly Delta continues its liaison with the British SAS and the other overseas contacts hat Colonel Beckwith developed, and those relationships have xpanded to include operations in other parts of the world. The less mention you see of Delta Force, the more likely the nit has been there.

Additionally, there are indications that Delta Force trains xtensively with the two other American hostage-rescue teams, he FBI's Hostage Rescue Team, or HRT, and Seal Team Six, nd the reasons should be obvious. Federal regulations prevent nilitary units from operating inside the United States in law nforcement situations, but do allow some forms of coordiation and support. In a domestic hostage situation, the FBI's IRT would be the lead agency. Delta Force might be tasked o draw up the plan of attack itself, provide insight into the errorists' motivations, or serve as technical observers. For intance, if a mortar were needed to punch through a cement vall, Delta Force might provide the equipment, aim it, and how the FBI weapons agent how to push the button that acually fires the weapon. For offshore (perhaps an oil platform utside the twelve-mile limit) or marine hostage rescues, Delta 'orce would operate closely with Seal Team Six. The SS *chille Lauro* cruise-liner mission probably cemented the reationship between the elite Navy Seal community and Delta 'orce. The cruise liner seized by terrorists had a large Amercan contingent onboard, and both Seal Team Six and Delta 'orce were forward deployed and poised to act. Before pernission could be obtained from the Italian government, the errorists negotiated safe passage with the Egyptian governnent. During their trip to Egypt onboard an Egyptian Boeing 37, U.S. fighters forced the aircraft to land in Sigonella, Italy. talian *carabinieri* interfered with Delta Force's operations and he terrorists escaped. Given Delta Force's determination never o repeat a mistake, the unit probably insists on absolute oprational authority for missions conducted with foreign lawnforcement authorities.

In addition to developing coordinating relationships with ther hostage-rescue agencies and units, Delta Force clearly elieves that an ounce of prevention is worth a pound of cure. According to one source, "Since the early 1980's, only one in

three acts of terrorism has been identified in time to affect th
outcome."[3] The unit has built upon its core competency
hostage rescue to include preventive measures as well. Saf
guarding senior officials and counterterrorism operations[4] no
constitute regular missions for the elite unit. Delta Force als
teaches other nations its unique brand of ice-pick-to-the-bra
terrorist prevention. Surveillance of terrorist camps in cou
tries such as Libya and training the rogue nation's neighbo
on effective deployment of Stinger missiles kept Libya i
check during Operation Manta in the early 1980s.

Preventing trouble may not be as glamorous as killing te
rorists and saving tourists, but Delta Force undoubtedly is wil
ing to forego adrenaline rushes in order to stop trouble befo
it starts. The unit measures success in live hostages, not dea
terrorists.

Transportation: Perhaps no lesson is as deeply engrave
in Delta Force's corporate memory as the failure of Dese
One. After recruiting and training the special breed of hel
copter pilots needed to support his fledgling force, fighting f
the assets to make Desert One succeed, Colonel Beckwith
overwhelming frustration and anger over the mission ech
throughout the first edition of *Delta Force*. Routine plannin
now places heavy emphasis on the environmental factors e
pected onscene. Contingency planning covers the entire rang
of possible climates, ranging from broiling heat and sand t
arctic scenarios, with tropical-storm and typhoon condition
thrown into the middle. If anything's going to stop Delta Forc
in the future, it won't be the weather.

Delta Force's transportation requirements fall into two basi
categories: getting there and onscene. Special command an
control arrangements allow the unit priority access to the long
range transport aircraft that now come under the command
the unified Transportation Command. For onscene operation
the Air Force Special Operations Command has dedicate
Pave Low helicopters, MH-60G Pave Hawk armed escort hel
icopters, AC-130H Spectre gunship for precision air cove
MC130E and H specially modified Combat Talon cargo plane

to transport paratroopers and refuel helicopters. While the 160th Special Operations Aviation Regiment (SOAR) continues to provide helicopter services to Delta Force, Delta Force now reportedly has its own squadron. In addition to the standard special-operations helicopters—and perhaps someday the V-22 Osprey—Delta Force has helicopters painted in civilian colors with false tail numbers, enabling it to join the gaggle of news helicopters that invariably deploy to spots of interest. There may also be aircraft camouflaged as civilian law-enforcement units since one of Delta Force's hottest priorities is expanding its capabilities in urban terrorism environments. Few standard-issue military pilots outside Delta Force's inner circle practice in the tight quarters of narrow passageways between towering office buildings. Handling the wind currents howling down man-made canyons and identifying hot landing zones in civilian environments requires exceptional judgment and experience.

Weapons: Delta Force has always concentrated on its shooters and today's force is no exception. The close-range weapon of choice is no longer the .45, but a variety of 9-millimeter pistols and the Heckler & Koch MP-5 machine gun. In 1987, Delta Force reportedly moved into a new facility at Fort Bragg in an area formerly known as Range 19. The new facility houses at least six weapons ranges: demolition, pop-up target, and sniper facilities among them, along with a variety of mock-up buildings and aircraft. The force's expertise in explosives and techniques for forced entry has grown exponentially since Colonel Beckwith's day.[5] Global positioning systems and over-the-horizon targeting packages can substantially increase both the range and accuracy of longer-range weapons.

Intelligence and Coordination: The first go/no-go checkpoint for a potential Delta Force operation is whether the hostages have been located. There's nothing more frustrating for Delta Force than to be forward deployed and poised to act but at a standstill because intelligence sources cannot locate th hostages.

Delta Force has always had particular intelligence needs tha couldn't be satisfied by ordinary intelligence efforts. Hard ex perience with faulty intelligence has resulted in the creatio of an internal intelligence organization that understands th particular needs of Delta Force. The analysts provide tailore products, including advance infiltration into the target area fc last-minute updates.

The second go/no-go prerequisite must be permission fron the host nation for Delta Force to act, and Delta Force prob ably has some exceptionally clear-cut requirements for for ward deploying. Given the option, the unit is unlikely t tolerate another SS *Achille Lauro* operation. Based on th number of times Delta Force has forward deployed and no been allowed to operate, the issue of coordination clearly call for a harder look.

Personnel: One of the first battles Colonel Beckwith fough in Desert One was over the number of personnel required t successfully execute the mission. While Delta Force retain the small-team concept, the command itself has grown from a force of approximately 100 to more than 800 personnel. Delt Force personnel comb Army records twice a year to look fo potential candidates. Some sources indicate that Delta draw on other services as well for candidates, but this is most prob ably done through standard interservice transfer procedures fo particularly motivated candidates.

Delta Force experimented briefly with recruiting female op erators, abandoned the program, and has reportedly since be gun recruiting women for its special squadron in order to allov the actual shooters to travel as "married couples." The female are said to be trained in espionage and covert operations tc provide cover for advance infiltrations.[6]

Another hard lesson from Desert One was the lack of reli able communications. Delta Force probably has increased th number of computer and communications specialists, not only for intelligence work but to monitor and maintain advanced secure communications networks.

The Future

While past operations provide valuable clues to understanding Delta Force's institutional culture and future, military organizations don't grow in a vacuum. National security strategies, current threat analysis, planning models, and funding considerations also fuel the tactical and doctrinal changes in any military organization.

When Delta Force was first organized, the Army chief of staff emphasized that Colonel Beckwith would need to identify a gap in the spectrum of capabilities then resident in existing special forces, show a gap in U.S. capabilities, and then prove that establishing Delta Force was the best way to remedy the deficiency. Today, the military-wide mandate for joint operations adds an additional layer of complexity to the "find the void" approach to force planning and structure. Single-service funding considerations are giving way to a more unified national approach to both special forces, military operations, and national strategy in general. Contrast Colonel Beckwith's concern over JCS's determination to have every military service have a piece of the Iranian hostage rescue with the operation in Peru following the takeover of the Japanese ambassador's residence, and with Delta's cooperation with SAS and GSG-9 in Desert Shield/Desert Storm.

Today, most operations are purple, the military term for joint, taken from the color of the joint operations qualification badge, and Delta's no exception. There's more cross-training, more coordination between the various SOF groups than ever before. International special warfare games pit teams from countries against each other, and Delta Force is alleged to be a frequent winner in the competitions.

Even the chain of command mirrors this cultural shift. Delta Force—not that it exists, mind you, but if it did—reports to the Joint Special Operations Command (JSOC) operationally.

It is funded through joint special operations budgets, and most probably has equipment that is at least nominally compatible with that of other U.S. and allied special forces. Dedicated frequency-agile radio circuits, miniaturized satellite receivers and hardened communications headsets probably allow each Delta Force operator complete coordination with every military and civilian agency in the area.

At the same time, as money pots shrink, all units start looking for broader missions. In this funding climate, it would be reasonable to see Delta Force undertaking a number of more traditional special-forces missions and to operate even more closely with allied forces.

Joint operations are a good thing. They're cost effective and a force multiplier. Yet despite the advantages, there are some drawbacks.

Heresy: Jointness isn't the universal answer

Colonel Beckwith's tour of duty with the British SAS gave him particular insight into joint and allied operations, and put Delta Force in the forefront of joint operations. His original Delta Force had a strong British flavor (as do many American forces, particularly the Navy). The structure of the operating forces, the exercises, even the qualification tests were drawn directly from his experiences serving with the British SAS.

But his experience proved that not every element could be transferred from the British SAS to his new organization. Recall what happened when Delta Force was deployed for what the operators believed was a real hostage rescue. When they learned that the entire evolution was a test of whether or not the team would actually shoot, they were outraged. One journalist claims that Delta Force persuaded the colonel it was a mistake. The British, they argued, might have to test to see if their operators would shoot, but the American forces needed to be tested to see if they wouldn't. The difference in British and American military cultures mandated an entirely different approach to the problem. Colonel Beckwith agreed, and the xercises in the future were designed to test Delta Force's ring discipline.

Similarly, one right answer to a problem is not necessarily ie right answer for every service, and this becomes particu-ırly evident during new aircraft acquisition programs. Delta eeds lift, stealth, maneuverability, and hardened armor. Other ervices may need long unrefueled cruising ranges and no ar-ıor. Because procurement programs are required to investi-ate—and give some preference to—joint applications, the nd result can be an aircraft that is mediocre in a wide variety f missions.

The other downside to complete jointness is losing the key ıgredient that makes units such as Delta Force so effective: nit integrity. Each service has its own distinct culture, a way f doing business that tends to establish uniformity in unfore-een situations. The culture derives not only from the parent rganization, but from the specific mission and the equipment nd training within a unit as well.[7] In small group operations, nit integrity is a critical factor. It's an old truism that a soldier oesn't risk his life for his country—he risks it for the buddy n the foxhole next to him.

Cross-training and cross-pollination work well and develop omfort zones in working with joint and allied forces. Cross-reeding is a bit trickier. Within the United States, all the ervices are committed to maneuver warfare rather than over-vhelming force as an approach to current operational art. Of ourse, special forces lead the pack—they've always under-tood maneuver warfare, the concept of applying just the right mount of force to the opposing forces to tip the battle. It's a ame of skill, fueled by solid intelligence and the ability to hink outside the box, and the ground forces remain ahead of he pack in practicing it. For some services, skimpy budgets ave been the impetus as much as sound operational thought, ut maneuver warfare has been a good idea since the days of un-tzu and earlier.

But not everyone speaks the same language yet. There's an ld story about a National Guard unit assisting local law en-orcement during urban riots. One police officer ran toward the target building and yelled, "Cover me!" The Nation Guard, trained by the Army, immediately laid down a wit ering barrage of fire, not what the policeman had had in mir at all. Similarly, Navy officers assigned fire-support missio with the Marine Corps quickly learn that "destroy" mea "create a smoking crater where that weapon is," and that pe haps what the officer really meant was "suppress."

But regardless of the remaining inconsistencies in languag at least most services now have an electronic common tongu

"Get me the duty webmaster."

Today, Colonel Beckwith would probably have had a sma detachment of communications specialists riding along to s up a satellite communications channel to access a dedicate web. One of his troops might have been the designated wel master for the operation, responsible for accessing the late intelligence from a classified mission web site and E-ma (both classified and unclassified) and tapping into the aircra carrier's tactical link to receive a direct feed on the missin helos' positions. He might have even been videoconferencin with the airwing commander to receive continuous updates o the mission progress.

Modern warfare has become networkcentric. Frequency agile cryptological equipment and joint-compatible data ne enable every fighter to share the same data picture. There a advantages to this: operations that require a high degree c coordination and approval have shorter waits before the high authority can be briefed and give the go signal. Indeed, th task force commander might be receiving direct video fee from opticals and acoustic sensors mounted within each ind vidual team member's helmet. Were Desert One mounted tc day, Colonel Beckwith would have known why helicopte were late and when he could have expected to see them (a least in theory. Mister Murphy still plays in the real world.)

The primary disadvantages of networkcentric warfare a readily apparent. First, the sheer amount of data can be ove whelming. It's essentially useless until it's correlated and turned into information.

Second, with increasing access to first-hand data on the battlefield, there's the eternal temptation to micromanage the war. Vietnam demonstrated the difficulty of having the commander in chief personally reviewing targeting lists. How much more damaging would it be to have a president directing individual fields of fire as the battle progresses?

Colonel Beckwith would have had the answer—he certainly had it during his last operation. When asked what his response would have been if he had been ordered to proceed with Desert One with only five helicopters, he came up with the answer that every field operator would immediately understand: feigning communication difficulties.

In the end, military operations—and particularly precision extractions and hostage rescue—comes down to a guy on the ground with a gun and an on-scene commander.

I could tell you, but I'd have to kill you.

The face of war changes—yet stays much the same. Perhaps one of the most insidious demons in military planning and force structures is the compulsion to fight the last war all over again.

So what will the next war look like? What forces will be needed to counter that threat?

The proliferation of tribal warfare since the end of the Cold War has prevented many of the supposed peace dividends from ever materializing. Disbanded, disillusioned military men from a number of nations form groups of warriors that are an altogether different foe than an organized military force.[8]

The enemy is harder to identify. The causes of war run deep in some cultures and carpet bombing isn't likely to solve any of them. It's increasingly difficult to distinguish bleeding combatants from dead civilians. Within the United States, terrorism is on the increase. Civilian organizations struggle to catch up

in the wake of the Atlanta Olympics, the World Trade Cente
Oklahoma City, and the Unabomber.

The culture of the enemy is not the only factor to conside
In the aftermath of Vietnam, the American public is increas
ingly intolerant of casualties, both overseas and within th
United States.

Whither goest—more heresy

There are at least some indications that the Army—and pa
ticularly Delta Force—regards preparing for urban operation
as an integral part of its mission. RAND, a civilian organi
zation often used as an Army think tank, has published at leas
one unclassified precis of the difficulties that the Army ca
expect to encounter in urban warfare, noting a number o
weaknesses in the Army's current capabilities. Telling the dif
ference between civilians and targets is crucial, as is devel
oping the technology of forced entry into urban structure
RAND notes that a number of sophisticated devices such a
hand-held lasers are in the Army inventory, but reserved fo
special units (Delta being a likely candidate). Additionally,
number of weapons that are currently being phased out of th
inventory could prove of critical importance in urban warfare
Light antitank weapons are excellent for punching through ce
ment walls, as are bazookas.[9]

Cities pose special problems for assault forces. Maneuverin
helicopters through cordons of skyscrapers, and avoidin
power lines and snipers stationed on adjacent buildings are a
continuing challenges. Collateral damage is another significan
problem. How many fire departments are prepared to deal wit
a Class Delta (metallic) fire involving burning helicopter air
frames and military weapons cooking off? What about casu
alties? Civilian or military hospitals? How to maintai
operational security when wounded men and civilian casualtie
begin to flood local medical facilities?

In an ideal scenario, Delta Force would be working closel
with local government to both gather intelligence, distinguis

between friend and foe, and arrange for damage control and extraction of casualties. Delta Force, along with other special forces, appears to be anticipating this problem by working a number of realistic scenarios in American cities. In some cases, those exercises have proved less than satisfactory, particularly from the viewpoint of the local population.[10] One report notes that the U.S. Army Special Operations Command "has conducted at least 21 such [military] exercises in 21 U.S. cities, including Atlanta, Chicago, Dallas, Detroit, Houston, Los Angeles, New Orleans, Miami, Pittsburgh, and Seattle." The report continues: "In city after city, the exercises have drawn fire from frightened residents who are not told beforehand that the roaring helicopters flying in circles several hundred feet overhead late at night—blacked out except for one that keeps on its tiny red taillight for safety—are trying to get as close as possible to the buildings they appear about to crash into."[11]

To be effective, training for urban warfare needs to be realistic, and the need for interagency is not limited to dealing with local police departments. Federal agencies need closer coordination as well,[12] particularly the State Department. Too often Delta Force is in place and ready to move—and left sweltering in hangars or in barracks while the necessary political arrangements are made.

At some point, faced with today's wars and the mandate for joint operations, Colonel Beckwith would be considering the issue of *posse comitatus*.

Posse comitatus

Posse comitatus simply means using federal military forces for law enforcement inside the United States.[13] As with many of our basic constitutional rights, *posse comitatus* was a reaction to a known evil rather than a statement of universal natural law. Before the Revolutionary War, British troops slaughtered civilians with impunity in the colonies. British military tribunals often summarily acquitted them.

The first laws against using our own military inside the United States was enacted in 1878. Today's law prohibits using the military in domestic law enforcement unless specifically authorized by Congress or the Constitution and does not allow for military intervention based solely on actions by the secretary of defense or an executive order from the president.

The prohibition on *posse comitatus* is not absolute. The law allows military and civilian cooperation, and every year Congress etches out further exceptions. For instance, training and education between the military and domestic law enforcement is exempt from the prohibition on *posse comitatus*. This law allows the military to teach local law-enforcement agencies how to purchase surplus military equipment, provides for division of expenses, and grants a broad degree of cooperation as long as the military doesn't try to enforce the law.[14] In counterdrug operations, military units can feed information and intelligence to domestic law-enforcement operations as long as the military remains uninvolved in the arrest and prosecution.

The proliferation of nuclear weapons—indeed, all weapons of mass destruction—has given rise to an even more chilling exception to *posse comitatus*. When weapons of mass destruction are involved, and the attorney general and the secretary of defense agree that an emergency situation exists, the military may operate freely in the United States.[15] Thus not only does the legal underpinning for operations inside the United States exist, but some reports indicate that detailed contingency plans for operations exist.[16] In the end, as Secretary of Defense William S. Cohen said, Americans may have to choose between civil liberties and more intrusive means of protection.[17]

These measures are all steps in the right direction, but are clearly no substitute for what is needed: a comprehensive plan marrying military capabilities to local and other federal agency capabilities with intelligence consolidated at every level and expertise available immediately to deal with terrorism. In the days of jointness, shouldn't teams that deploy inside the U.S. in response to hostage situations include every unit that trains for it? Where does jointness end and *posse comitatus* begin? As the lines blur between civilian and soldier, peace and war, terrorism and war, it would seem increasingly probable that the role of the U.S. military within the United States should be reconsidered.

Would Colonel Beckwith have favored such integration?

Perhaps. Certainly he was highly critical of the FBI's operation to subdue the Branch Davidians.[18] Operating with a lack of real intelligence, the failure to provide for evacuation of casualties, and the lack of a definable end state were all weaknesses that he identified, and planning deficiencies that he would not have tolerated in a Delta Force operation.

Certainly, there is danger in removing some of the restraints that prevent military operations inside the United States. Conspiracy groups and the paranoid are already seeing mysterious black helicopters at every turn, citing warnings about America becoming an Orwellian 1984 culture.

But given the proliferation of threats, is there really any choice?

Conclusion

The longer an organization is established, the more it will tend to institutionalize. Traditions and history solidify into standard practice, and opportunities for more effective use of a force may be overlooked.

Every organization needs renegades, leaders, and innovators capable of thinking outside the box. Looking back over the evolution of special forces in the American military, Col. "Chargin' Charlie" Beckwith was exactly the sort of man needed to put together Delta Force, one capable of thinking outside the box, broadened by his experience with the British SAS, yet with the political savvy to understand and use his own monolithic Army establishment to bring Delta Force into existence. In light of what's happened since *Delta Force* was first published, he was a prophet.

There's a need for Delta Force in today's military, and an

even more urgent requirement for the *next* Delta Force. Wit operational tempos at an all-time high, maneuver warfare an the specialized skills of units like Delta Force are the mos effective way to combat warfare bleeding into all phases o life.

If there were a Delta Force, mind you.

RESOURCES

Phone Numbers

Fort Bragg PAO 910-396-5600
Fort Bragg Special Forces PAO 910-432-7585/8650
DOD PAO 703-697-5131
Army PAO 703-697-7589
SOCCOM PAO 813-828-4600

Web Sites

www.specialoperations.com
www.rand.org

E-mail

Parameters@awc.carlisle.army.mil.

NOTES

[1]Oddly enough, it does recruit. USARMYPERSCOM's we page contains the following notice: "The U.S. Army's 1st Spe cial Forces Operational Detachment—Delta (1stSFOD-D plans and conducts a broad range of special operations acros the operational continuum. Delta is organized for the conduc of missions requiring rapid response with surgical application of a wide variety of unique skills, while maintaining the lowes possible profile of U.S. involvement."

[2]Not only do you need a range of forces to bring to bear, bu the composition and structure of those forces must continuall

evolve. War, by its very nature, is chaotic. One of the biggest dangers that military planners face is an almost blinding compulsion, supported and fueled by political structures, to fight the last war.

There are several approaches to planning for military forces. The first is simply to build every possible force to combat every possible threat. The second is to attempt to project what threats the nation will face in the coming years and plan the force structure to combat those. Finally, the planner can rank possible threats by degree of harm to the nation—with one end of the scale encompassing weapons of mass destruction targeted at the United States and the other end low-intensity conflicts in countries that have no political interest for the United States—and juxtapose that list with the probability of that particular event occurring.

[3]Wright, R., *Los Angeles Times,* July 29, 1996. "Despite Gains, Halting Terrorist Elusive." The author was quoting Jeff Beatty, former FBI, CIA, and Delta Force specialist on counterterrorism, citing figures in a Department of Justice publication.

[4]Waller, D. *The Commandos.* (New York: Dell Publishing, 1994) p. 247.

[5]*Ibid.*, 233–35.

[6]*Ibid.*, 249.

[7]Builder, C., *The Masks of War.* (Baltimore: The Johns Hopkins University Press, 1989).

[8]Peters, R. "The New Warrior Class" (1994). *Parameters,* Summer 1994, p. 16. A brilliant and profoundly disturbing article on the proliferation of warrior classes in the world.

[9]RAND Arroyo Center, Army Research Division, *Combat in Cities.* *http://www.rand.org/organization/ard/research.sums/cities.html*

[10]Priest, D. *Los Angeles Times,* April 27, 1997, p. A-22. "Secret Anti-Terrorist Exercises Terrorize Citizens."

[11]*Ibid.*

[12]Some sources have claimed that Delta Force has been involved in a number of hostage situations within the U.S., including the Branch Davidian assault and counterterrorism planning for the Atlanta Olympics. A. Pine. *Los Angeles Times,* August 27, 1993, p. A-10. "Delta Force Reportedly to Hunt Aidid" (summarizing previous Delta Force operations as background for Delta presence in Somalia.).

[13]18 U.S. Code section 1385. "Whosoever, except in cases and under circumstances expressly authorized by the Constitution or Act of Congress, willfully uses any part of the Army or the Air Force as a posse comitatus or otherwise to execute the laws shall be fined not more than $10,000 or imprisoned not more than two years, or both." 18 U.S. Code § 1385. Use of Army and Air Force as posse comitatus; 10 U.S. Code § 375. Restriction on direct participation by military personnel.

The Secretary of Defense shall prescribe such regulations as may be necessary to ensure that any activity (including the provision of any equipment or facility or the assignment or detail of any personnel) under this chapter does not include or permit direct participation by a member of the Army, Navy, Air Force, or Marine Corps in a search, seizure, arrest, or other similar activity unless participation in such activity by such member is otherwise authorized by law.

[14]10 U.S. Code § 380. Enhancement of cooperation with civilian law enforcement officials.

a. The Secretary of Defense, in cooperation with the Attorney General, shall conduct an annual briefing of law enforcement personnel of each State (including law enforcement personnel of the political subdivisions of each State) regarding information, training, technical support, and equipment and facilities available to civilian law enforcement personnel from the Department of Defense.

b. Each briefing conducted under subsection (a) shall include the following:
    1. An explanation of the procedures for civilian law enforcement officials.
        A. to obtain information, equipment, training, expert advice, and other personnel support under this chapter; and
        B. to obtain surplus military equipment.
    2. A description of the types of information, equipment and facilities, and training and advice available to civilian law enforcement officials from the Department of Defense.
    3. A current, comprehensive list of military equipment which is suitable for law enforcement officials from the Department of Defense or available as surplus property from the Administrator of General Services.
c. The Attorney General and the Administrator of General Services shall:
    1. establish or designate an appropriate office or offices to maintain the list described in subsection (b)(3) and to furnish information to civilian law enforcement officials on the availability of surplus military equipment; and
    2. make available to civilian law enforcement personnel nationwide, tollfree telephone communication with such office or offices.

[15]18 U.S. Code section 831(e)(1) *http://terminalfrost.cimplement.com/document/posse.html;* The Attorney General may also request assistance from the Secretary of Defense. . . . Notwithstanding section 1385 of this title the Secretary of De-

fense may . . . provide such assistance to the Attorney General if—(A) an emergency situation exists (as jointly determined by the Attorney General and the Secretary of Defense in their discretion); and (B) the provision of such assistance will not adversely affect the military preparedness of the United States (as determined by the Secretary of Defense in such Secretary's discretion).

[16]Macko, S. Emergency News Network Daily Report, August 27, 1996: "The Threat of Chemical and Biological Attack." *www.emergency.com/chembio3.htm*

[17]*The Times of the Ark-La-Tex,* September 15, 1997. *www.inetvs.com/gpni/970917b.html*

[18]Sahagun, L. *Los Angeles Times,* March 4, 1993, p. A-16. "Experts Criticize Tactics Used by Federal Officials in Assault."

INDEX

Members of the military are indexed with the highest ranks associated with their names in this book, but specific grades within ranks are not indicated.

See also Glossary of Special Military Terms and Acronyms (page xi).